SCRIPTURE & CONTEMPLAT
CONFERENC

12-14 July 20

Centre for Applied Carmelite Spirituality,
Carmelite Priory, Boars Hill, Oxford OX1 5HB, UK

A conference on Carmel and Biblical Spirituality, informing and enriching the spiritual life. Talks both academic and pastoral by top speakers and an experience of contemplative prayer.

KEYNOTE SPEAKERS

Dr Susan Muto
(Epiphany Association, Pittsburgh, USA)

Dr Margaret Barker
(International speaker and biblical scholar)

Fr Matt Blake OCD
(Carmelite Community of Gerrards Cross, UK)

Sr Jo Robson OCD
(Carmelite Community of Ware, UK)

Dr Roderick Campbell Guion OCDS
(Carmelite Institute of Britain and Ireland)

Fiona O'Reilly
(Catholic Voices, UK)

REGISTRATION DEADLINE: 31 MAY 2019

CONTACT US: events@cacarmelitesp.co.uk
+44 1865 735133 or 730183   www.cacarmelitesp.co.uk

1

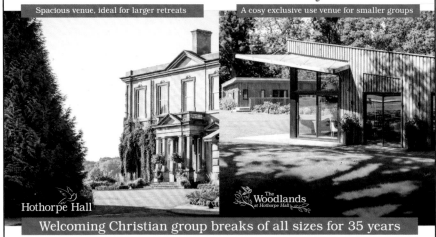

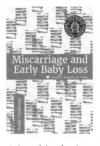
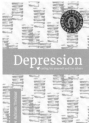

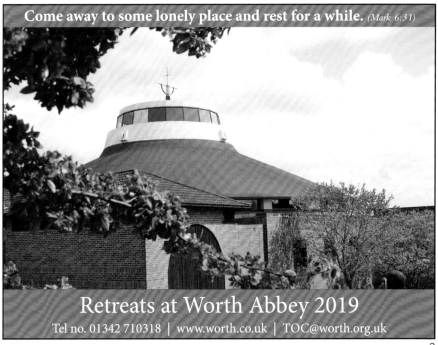

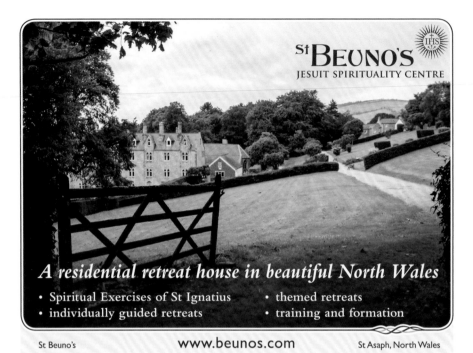

Contents

ISBN 978-0-9927207-5-9

Retreats is published annually. No. 198

Editorial production group:
Jill Keegan
Alison MacTier (Managing Editor)
Alan Mossman (Production)
Jill Brace (Listings Editor)

Cover design: Judy Linard

Cover Image:
copyright © veroxdale/Bigstock.com

Reprographics by The Alpha Xperience,
148 Kings Road, Newbury,
Berkshire RG14 5RG.

Printed in England by Bishops Printers,
Portsmouth and distributed by
Redemptorist Publications.

Correspondence relating to *Retreats* should
be sent to the Retreat Association office.

**The Retreat Association
PO Box 1130
Princes Risborough
Buckinghamshire
HP22 9RP**

tel: **01494 569056**
fax: **0871 715 1917**
website: **www.retreats.org.uk**
email: **info@retreats.org.uk**

Registered charity no. 1150792.
Company limited by guarantee 08385106.
Registered in England and Wales.

the
Retreat Association

The Retreat Association is a national Christian organisation set up to help people find ways of exploring and deepening their journey with God through spirituality and prayer. We offer support in the following ways:

FINDING A RETREAT
We offer advice to people on finding a retreat and promote the value of a retreat.

SPIRITUAL DIRECTION
We maintain a network of regional contacts who can help find a suitable guide for those looking for a spiritual director or companion.

TRAINING
We provide a list of courses for those who are interested in training in **spiritual direction** and who would like to increase their skills, knowledge and confidence. Please contact the office for more information (details opposite).

RETREAT ASSOCIATION ICON
The Icon of the Samaritan woman at the well was created as a gift to the Retreat Association in 2018 by iconographer John Coleman. Our hope and vision is that this beautiful image will encourage others to take time out in prayer and quiet reflection. We would like as many people as possible to have this opportunity and, thanks to the generosity of retreat centres, churches and cathedrals, the Icon will continue to be on display at a number of venues in 2019. Please see page 78 for more information.

RETREAT ASSOCIATION ICON EVENTS
During the time that the Icon is on display at these venues, many will be organising specific events such as quiet days. Keep an eye on our website or contact us for more information.

THINKING ABOUT GOING ON RETREAT FOR THE FIRST TIME?

INTERESTED IN SHARING YOUR FAITH JOURNEY WITH A COMPANION?

Please go to our website **www.retreats.org.uk** for more information about **retreats** and **spiritual direction**.

RESOURCES

We have a wide variety of **information leaflets** for both individuals and for those taking their first steps towards deepening their prayer life.
These are available on our website **www.retreats.org.uk/leaflets.php** or by contacting the Retreat Association office.

RETREAT ASSOCIATION LOCAL EVENTS

Why not find out more about the Retreat Association at local events? These include:

- **Stop! In the name of God events.** Through this event (this year on 12–14 July) we encourage people to stop and spend time in silence, stillness and prayer for a day or weekend (see page 68). Details of how to plan or attend an event are available from our website or by contacting the office.

MEMBERSHIP

If you are interested in becoming more involved in the work of the Retreat Association, why not consider becoming a member of one of our member groups? (See contact details opposite.)

The benefits include the following:

- Advance notice of **conferences, events** and **retreats** organised by each group with some opportunities for reductions on booking fees.
- Free subscription to *Retreats*.
- Free listing of Retreat Centres in *Retreats*.
- **Retreat Association Newsletter** and member group newsletter where applicable.

THE **RETREAT** ASSOCIATION

The Retreat Association office
tel: **01494 569056**
email: **info@retreats.org.uk**
website: **www.retreats.org.uk**

MEMBER GROUPS

Association for Promoting Retreats (APR) (mainly Anglican) Contact: Demelza Henderson (Administrator), 2 Brookfield Cottages, The Strand, Lympstone, Exmouth EX8 5ES promoting.retreats@gmail.com

Baptist Union Retreat Group (BURG) Contact: Gill Roberts, 31 Long Grove, Seer Green, Beaconsfield, Bucks HP9 2YN gill-roberts@live.co.uk

Catholic Spirituality Network (CSN) Contact: Margaret Palladino, CSN Membership Secretary St George's Cathedral, Cathedral Clergy House, Westminster Bridge Road, London SE1 7HY catholicspiritualitynetwork@gmail.com

Reflect (Methodist Spirituality) Contact: Mrs Sue Chastney, 4 Benslow Rise, Hitchin SG4 9QX schastney@ntlworld.com

Affiliates of the Retreat Association Contact: Membership Secretary at the Retreat Association office

---

DISCLAIMER
No responsibility can be taken by the Retreat Association for any retreat house, book or product listed or advertised in *Retreats*. The views expressed in the articles may not necessarily reflect the views of the Retreat Association.

Editorial

Welcome to the 2019 edition of *Retreats*. We hope you will find it a helpful and encouraging resource for the year.

Our theme for this year is 'Welcome' and we are enormously grateful for the generosity of the writers of our 12 articles who have brought their own unique insights and experiences to share with us.

Malcolm Guite introduces our theme by reflecting on what welcome reveals about the heart of God as shown to us through creation. He goes on to reflect on three of his poems as a way of exploring this further – first the story of Abraham and Sarah in Genesis as the source of all welcome, then the invitation to be part of God's family through the Lord's Prayer, and finally the good news about God's unfailing welcome to us and the challenge it brings to our relationships with others.

This call to welcome the other, in response to God's welcome to us, is central to many of our articles: Kate Monkhouse reflects on how the 'loving gaze' of God enables us to offer the same inclusivity and hospitality to others, specifically in the context of a retreat. David Standley, through his work with the L'Arche Community, explores what it means to welcome the other inclusively – a relationship in which we are always learning and being challenged but in which

we are growing ever deeper. Chris Swift describes the care of 'body, mind and spirit' offered by Methodist Homes, where residents flourish in an environment of encouragement and understanding.

Welcome is of course a central theme to those who live and work in retreat centres and some have been inspired to set up their own. Clare Shearman offers retreats in her garden hermitage in Cornwall, where welcome is found in the abundance and richness of God's creation. Angie Tunstall and her husband have opened their hearts to enable those working in a city environment to discover retreat in an urban home on the edge of Manchester.

Don Quilty reflects on the long tradition of hospitality within monastic life and places of pilgrimage which continues in retreat houses today. Sister Maureen explores the ministry of welcome offered by the Franciscan tradition and what this means for religious community life in our contemporary world. Magdalen Lawler and Tom McGuinness describe a Jesuit Retreat Centre in Malta, where the welcome offered to guests is an integral part of the restful and deepening retreats that they have been leading together. Amanda Kimberley reflects on the hospitality of a retreat centre where God's love is demonstrated in 'spiritual and practical' ways.

What is striking across these articles is the power of welcome, its capacity to make change and to work for good that goes far beyond the original encounter. Debbie O'Brien reflects on the activities of a night shelter where welcoming the stranger is at the heart of building relationships between host and guest – both are on a reciprocal journey of giving and receiving and may expect to be changed by the experience. Brother Paolo describes the welcome that has been offered to thousands of people by the Taizé community since the 1940s, bringing Christians together from across the world in a spirit of friendship and reconciliation.

We hope that you will find much to draw inspiration from within these articles and you may also be interested in further reading ideas on pages 51–57. When choosing your own retreat you may find the notes on pages 58–59 helpful, as well as the regional maps on pages 60–63.

It is always a privilege to work on a new edition of the *Retreats* handbook – and this edition has been no exception. It brings together a wide range of people whose lives, in different ways, reflect the breadth and depth of what it means to be a part of God's welcoming creation. We hope that the coming year will bring you opportunities to explore this theme further – wherever you may be on your journey.

With every blessing

Alison MacTier
Executive Director, Retreat Association

Welcome: A poetic reflection

Malcolm Guite reflects on what welcome reveals about the heart of God.

The act of welcoming, the experience of being welcomed, the call both to receive and to pass on a welcome, are central to Christian faith and theology, because the hospitality at the heart of both is also in the heart of God. In the creation God welcomes all creatures into the world through sharing with them the very possibility of existing at all, which is always rooted in God as the ground of all being. In the story of our salvation the spreading wide of Christ's arms on the cross, which had been intended as hatred and torture, is transfigured by his love into a sign of open welcome. As we say in the liturgy, 'He opened wide his arms for us on the cross'[1].

I would like to explore this theme of welcome by bringing together three poems from my last collection, in which I found myself drawing on the word 'welcome' and opening out a little of what it means.

The first is a poem I composed as part of a series called 'In The Wilderness' and it responds to the story, in Genesis 18, of how Abraham and Sarah welcomed three strangers in the wilderness, and in so doing welcomed God and found the promise of God – that in their seed the nations would be blessed – beginning to come true. It is the story of course which gave rise to the famous Rublev Icon of the Holy Trinity:

Abraham and Sarah at Mamre

They practise hospitality; their hearts
Have opened like a secret source, free
*   flowing*
Only as they take another's part.
Stopped in themselves, and in their own
*   unknowing,*
But unlocked by these strangers in their
*   need,*
They breathe again, and courtesy, set free,

'And like the rooted oak whose shade makes room for this refreshing genesis...'

Begets the unexpected; generosity
Begetting generation, as the seed
Of promise springs and laughs in Sarah's
*   womb.*

Made whole by their own hospitality,
And like the rooted oak whose shade
*   makes room*
For this refreshing genesis at Mamre,
One couple, bringing comfort to their
*   guests,*
Becomes our wellspring in the wilderness.[2]

In this poem I played with the links, in sound and semantics, between the three words *Genesis, Generation,* and *Generosity,* for I believe that it is in the generosity of God that our own generosity has its 'genesis', its source and beginning, and that we in turn receive and pass on a tradition of generosity down the generations. But to do so is to rise to a challenge. Our instinct to be generous is being challenged and gainsayed by the siren voices of populist politics. Our faith, rooted in Abraham, calls for resistance!

The second of my three poems, on the first phrase of the Lord's Prayer, goes to the root of our own experience of God's generosity. It is voiced for a disciple who believes that knowing God as Father is something that has been specially reserved only for the 'only begotten son' and is astonished at the invitation extended to all of us; that we too can call God 'Father', that Jesus, far from excluding us, is welcoming us into his family!

Our Father

I heard him call you his beloved son
And saw his Spirit lighten like a dove,
I thought his words must be for you alone,
Knowing myself unworthy of his love.
You pray in close communion with your
*   Father,*
So close you say the two of you are one,
I feel myself to be receding further,
Fallen away and outcast and alone.

11

And so I come and ask you how to pray,
Seeking a distant supplicant's petition,
Only to find you give your words away,
As though I stood with you in your position,
As though your Father were my Father too,
As though I found his 'welcome home' in
you.[3]

This good news of welcome and belonging, which is embedded by Jesus into the prayer he gives us, is also affirmed again at the end of John's Gospel when, after the resurrection, Jesus tells Mary Magdalene to go ' ... *to my brothers and tell them, "I am ascending to my Father and your Father, to my God and your God."'* (John 20:17)[4]

That welcome, which we have all received, and which no power on earth can take away or unsay, then has its natural outworking, if we will let it, in the way we treat others. This is made especially clear in the famous moment in Mark's gospel when Jesus welcomes the child:

'He took a little child whom he placed among them. Taking the child in his arms, he said to them, "Whoever welcomes one of these little children in my name welcomes me; and whoever welcomes me does not welcome me but the one who sent me."' (Mark 9:36–37)[5]

When I was working on this sequence of poems in *Parable and Paradox*, it so happens that I came to this verse on the tragic day when we all saw the pictures of the little toddler, the Syrian refugee, whose body had been washed up on the shore, and my sense of shock and horror at the gap between God's welcome and our own capacity to welcome the stranger was almost unbearable. And yet I also knew that that child, persecuted by one of the Herods of our day, was at last receiving, even through the grave and gate of death, a welcome into the everlasting arms, even as the holy innocents did when they were killed by the Herod of their day. I was also struck, when I read and reread that passage in Mark, by the way each 'welcome' mentioned by Jesus seemed to enfold and enclose another one, Christ is in the child, and God is in Christ. The God who made the heavens and the earth and welcomed us into them, makes himself small enough to be welcomed by us in his turn, if only we would open our eyes and see him:

Whoever Welcomes

Welcome, *the word is always on your lips,*
Each welcome warms another one inside,
An interleaving of relationships,
An open door where arms are open wide.
First welcome to the child and through the
• *child*
A welcome to the Saviour of the world,
And through the Saviour's welcome all are
called
Home to the Father's heart. Each call is
curled
And nested in another, as you were
Nested and nestled in your mother's womb,
As Mary carried One who carried her,
And we are wrapped in you, deep in the
tomb,
Where you turn our rejection into welcome,
And death itself becomes our welcome
home.[6]

'... the very possibility of existing at all ... is always rooted in God...'

Perhaps the best way to begin or renew a vocation and ministry of welcome is to receive again, and even more deeply into our hearts, the welcome that God in Christ is always extending to us.

1 ASB Rite A Prayer 3 © The Central Board of Finance of the Church of England, 1980.

2, 3, 6 Malcolm Guite, *Parable and Paradox: Sonnets on the sayings of Jesus and other poems* (Canterbury Press, 2016). Copyright Canterbury Press, reproduced by permission of the author and publisher.

4 & 5 The Holy Bible, New International Version®, NIV® Copyright © 1973, 1978, 1984, 2011 by Biblica, Inc.™ Used by permission. All rights reserved worldwide.

Rev Dr Malcolm Guite is a poet, priest, Chaplain of Girton College, Cambridge and teaches at the Faculty of Divinity at the University of Cambridge. He lectures widely in England and North America on Theology and Literature, has published poetry, theology and literary criticism and has worked as a librettist. His books include: Love, Remember *(Canterbury Press, 2017);* Mariner, *a spiritual biography of Samuel Taylor Coleridge (Hodder & Stoughton, 2016); and* Parable and Paradox *(Canterbury Press, 2016). Malcolm has a particular interest in the imagination as a truth-bearing faculty and continues to reflect deeply on how poetry can stimulate and re-awaken our prayer life. Malcolm is also part of the rock band Mystery Train, regularly performing gigs at Grantchester, Cambridge and other places around Cambridgeshire. www.malcolmguite.com*

13

Would someone like me be welcome here?

Kate Monkhouse considers attitudes and actions that can facilitate equal access to prayer.

I love going on retreat and feel at home in religious communities. It breaks my heart when I hear people ask: 'Would we be welcome there?' or 'Would someone like me be allowed to visit?' or equally, when I know going on retreat is a challenge for many because of affordability or culture. I understand because I have felt many barriers to worship in church, so I am doubly passionate about retreat houses and monastic communities as spaces to encounter God.

As a facilitator, my job is to make it 'easy' ('*facile*' in French) for people to participate: in community dialogues or in personal prayer. With training in spiritual accompaniment and experience of leading worship over many years, I try to bring participatory peace-building skills to the reflective days I run. I want to make it easier for people to bring their whole selves on retreat and to know that their voices and lives are welcome as they are encouraged to flourish spiritually.

I believe that our starting point for welcoming others is a truly felt knowledge that we are welcome in God. We all need a lived experience that God is delighted to see us when we come to prayer. With that full assurance of God's own hospitality and loving gaze when we arrive in anticipation, we can more freely receive others. Welcome is for me a foundational Christian discipline, in everyday spiritual conversation and in accompanying those who are so often denied an open door.

At the last Retreat Association Conference, I enjoyed exploring with others some of the issues that affect our guests in participating. These can be challenging for all of us, as both retreatants and as retreat leaders. They take time and careful thought. They often require consultation

'God is delighted to see us when we come to prayer.'

and sometimes additional costs. They usually mean opening ourselves up to creative approaches, so we too learn to go deeper along with those we are hosting. Here are some suggestions for how we can best encourage inclusivity within the context of a retreat:

1. Looking around our community or the group of people we will be working with, who is being 'talked about' or 'spoken for' rather than being involved directly in the planning? Discussing practical things such as access needs, dietary requirements as well as forms of wording that will be meaningful and respectful. Reviewing also the profile of speakers and balance of themes on our publicity.

2. Using our experts! We all have people who have led companies, survived as refugees, managed crises, recovered from illness, protested injustice. They may not be experienced preachers, theologians or spiritual directors, but they will often be better placed to speak of grace and redemption in circumstances they have come through, so it's great to involve them and get their ideas.

3. Deepening our understanding of how the ways in which our dignity has been violated shape how we place ourselves in groups or hold our identity. This might be with regard to gender, age, ethnicity, class, sexuality, culture and so on. When we as facilitators can honour dignity by recognising and

'We can explore different resources to give everyone an access point.'

acknowledging these, it can enable people to feel safer and engage more comfortably.

4. Refreshing our knowledge of faith seasons or love languages, as well as learning styles. Remember that within a group there will be people who understand God in different ways: through explanations, feelings, (in)tangible mysteries, being in nature, visuals, objects, in community. It is important there are diverse opportunities in any programme for engagement to help participation.

5. Looking again at how much we privilege the written word above other forms of engagement. Remembering literacy and language. We can explore different resources to give everyone an access point into the message or discussion: large print or simple language Bible, inclusive and foreign language translations, using BSL or Makaton signs, images or symbol flash cards, involving senses and gestures that embrace.

6. Generating new rituals if the old ones have lost their meaning. Getting creative with actions that everyone can take part in as they are able. It can be as simple as a participant bringing a vase of flowers up to the front, lighting a candle, or drawing on a card and placing it on an altar. It could be inviting everyone to bless food parcels or tie a ribbon onto a protest placard – something that has meaning for them.

7. Exploring how we use the space in the room we occupy. So much of church is led from the front and symbolises hierarchy or authority. Either using that format and subverting it so that the voices that are often silenced speak from a place of power. Alternatively, we can reconstruct the space with a different layout of furniture or movements within our sessions, so they indicate all voices are valued and have equity.

These are just some initial prompts for reflection. Each of us, of course, will have our own practice and processes to enrich inclusion. But if in doubt, remind yourself of the uncomfortable times when you were new or were not made welcome somewhere that mattered to you. Prayerfully consider how you can use these experiences to reduce the barriers for those who might be hesitating to come to your place.

When, despite our best efforts, we fall short in offering inclusive hospitality, I have learned that God will turn up and minister to those we have failed to honour. Even when, through our ignorance, we lock doors and close windows, the Holy Spirit will sneak in to sit next to those who are seeking peace. And Jesus, despite our clumsiness, with his loving regard for each person, will show up to touch their heart. In all humility, as hosts of others on sacred ground, let's just not make it quite so hard for God to gain access.

To explore some of these themes further, go to:

www.jrsuk.net – for spiritual accompaniment of asylum seekers

www.livability.org.uk – for churches and disabled people, including on mental health

www.two23.net – for welcoming worship for LGBT+ people, their families and friends

www.othonaessex.org.uk – for affordable retreats, holidays and working weekends

---

Kate Monkhouse has more than 20 years' experience of working in community and multi-faith organisations on trust-building and social inclusion. After dedicating her time to public policy advocacy and political literacy with often marginalised communities, she started to explore conflict transformation and peace-building. Kate now runs occasional retreats on the theme of spirituality and social change. She can often be found at the Royal Foundation of St Katharine and lives at St Saviour's Priory in the East End of London. Kate is currently the Executive Co-ordinator of Creators of Peace, an international network of women across 50 countries. She also is an RSA Fellow and helps run Two23, a network of Christians connected by LGBT+ issues. www.katemonkhouse.com

---

Companions on the road together

David Standley explores what it means to walk alongside those with learning disabilities.

Welcome is at the heart of the spirituality of L'Arche. This is much deeper than a warm embrace or rousing applause. It is welcoming one another as we are, with all our gifts and faults, abilities and disabilities, believing and demonstrating each one of us is precious and beloved, capable, creative, graced, and 'beautiful'. Not always easy. We can all be selfish and fearful, hurt and aggressive. We carry our wounded stories. All of us. This is our spirituality.

I regularly walk with T in the park-like local cemetery in West Norwood. We hardly speak (I sometimes sing, I am not sure it is appreciated…). The silent tombstones with their grieving and hopeful inscriptions watch us as we pass. We share a long friendship.

For some of us God is a loving Father, Jesus is our brother. For some the Church and the sacraments are places of celebration and healing. Others follow a different faith tradition. Still others are not sure of their beliefs or unbeliefs, but we are all on a journey.

Thérèse Vanier founded L'Arche UK in 1974, and L'Arche London in 1977 – jubilant celebrations in 2017, culminating in a festive liturgy in Westminster Cathedral. The spirituality of L'Arche is in the daily living. Each community declares its spiritual identity. L'Arche London says, *'We are an ecumenical Christian community, open and welcoming to people of all faiths and none.'* Thérèse wanted us to ride well with all the churches, belonging locally for those who wish. And parishes discover that the presence of L'Arche can be the leaven in the lump, when people with learning disabilities are truly welcomed.

Welcome in L'Arche has several faces.

1. **The Meal Table** is a special place of welcome, on a daily basis: consistent for residents, hospitality for guests. The recent move to more independent living has been

Photo © L'Arche community. Reproduced by permission.

Eucharist at David's Golden Jubilee of ordination celebration in the London L'Arche community.

for some a personal liberation, but also challenges the community living experience. We try to devise new ways of 'being together'. One such is the weekly 'Communi-Tea', where news is shared, future events flagged up, new arrivals saluted, people leaving thanked and farewelled, with brief interactive prayer and music. Welcome is more than a wave: it is a long-term project, consistently renewed.

2. **The Eucharistic Table** offers a profound welcome, in the spirit of Jesus. Apart from Sundays when people attend local churches as they choose, the Eucharist is celebrated in the community every two weeks, alternately Anglican and Roman Catholic. Those who attend usually will come regardless of which rite it happens to be: they value the Eucharist at a deeper level than the historic divisions. We try to respect the discipline of each Church around receiving Communion. Thérèse Vanier never wanted an exception for L'Arche, on the grounds that people could

not understand the theological arguments – that would be condescending. So, according to which liturgy is being celebrated, we receive the sacrament, or a blessing. There are wavy lines, and no open hand is refused. This is painful, sometimes resented. Yet the brokenness at the Eucharist does mirror the brokenness in all our lives. I am sure that the personal friendship between me and the local Anglican Vicar, David Stephenson, is noticed and reassuring. We each celebrate the Eucharist in the community in turn, and are sometimes present on one another's. We have jointly contributed to community liturgies and retreats.

3. There has been a rich tradition of **Retreat in Daily Life**. For one week in the year, experienced spiritual directors are invited to meet daily with individual participants on the well-known Ignatian model. Some participants will have a learning disability. For them words and reflection are less important; painting, pictures, music,

atmosphere, touch, interactivity, repetition, one-to-one time together . speak more loudly. In advance, directors are helped to imagine less wordy ways of communication, resources are available. Supervision is offered. We all discover different ways of experiencing God's presence. People with learning difficulties can be our teachers.

4. In L'Arche we have a long tradition of **Accompaniment**. The 'Accompanier' is someone who knows L'Arche quite well (for example active volunteer, former assistant, long-term friend), but not within the management structure. S(he) listens to whatever the assistant chooses to share about the daily experience: stress, foreign culture, language, separation from family, misunderstandings, negativity, delight or disappointment about 'L'Arche as a Christian community. It is not counselling, nor spiritual direction. It offers a chance for assistants to hear themselves voicing their experience and their questions. For some it is a journey of self-discovery. There are opportunities for encouragement, reassurance, and discerning where they may find other resources helpful. A listening ear of welcome.

5. **Silence**. Birthday parties are important in L'Arche. They are telling someone, 'We are glad you exist, we are glad to share your life, we are glad you are you.' But welcome doesn't have to be noisy. Opportunities constantly arise for being together in silence. Too often we fill the silence with TV, music or activity. We can also make opportunities for silence. We are

discovering that shared silent prayer is more valued than we thought. We have times of group meditation, often led by an experienced person. We never know what is happening for people. We don't need to know. But there is a palpable bond in being together in silence, perhaps with a gospel story, a phrase from the psalms, some words of Jesus. A meeting – so different from the often too wordy meetings we are engrossed in every day, sometimes all day. A deep welcome.

So, welcome is a long-term project. Welcoming God, letting ourselves be welcomed by God, takes time, a lifetime. It is meant to become deeper and wider. There are times when we can feel we are losing sight of the way. But God's own welcome is deeper and wider than we can imagine. We shall find that out when we arrive.

Father David Standley is a retired Roman Catholic priest. For 40 of these years he has also been a member of L'Arche. L'Arche is a federation of worldwide communities, founded by Jean Vanier in 1964, where people with different abilities and learning disabilities share their lives, resident and non-resident, for their mutual enrichment. He describes a life in which priesthood and L'Arche have become intertwined. He explains, 'My input in L'Arche is as a priest and a friend; in return my priesthood has been shaped and coloured by my life in L'Arche.'

Creating community

Debbie O'Brien reflects on what it means to give and receive hospitality in a winter shelter.

Penny was a guest in our shelter: shell-shocked at finding herself homeless, wary and a bit anxious understandably. By the end of her first evening she was relaxed and giggling over a lively game of table tennis with another guest. Her key worker at the day centre told us that, when Penny ate dinner that night, she could not believe there was avocado in the salad prepared to go with the main meal. She was blown away by the care and attention: that we would think she, and all our guests, are worth this. At the core of the shelter is the church's vision: *'to welcome the stranger and expect to be changed by our Eucharistic commitment to hospitality'*. 'Welcome' is an Anglo-Saxon word meaning 'being pleased to see someone'.

For the past seven years the Westminster Night Shelter Scheme has welcomed 15 guests one night a week for an evening meal, overnight accommodation and breakfast. At a practical level welcome means that we do the best we can with our space – which is a basement used in the daytime as meeting rooms. We have in place health and safety and risk assessment policies, protocols, guidelines for shifts, volunteer application forms and agreements. We set up an area to be relaxing with games, newspapers, empty spaces and art. We provide hot drinks, snacks, creative home-cooked meals, beds, sleeping bags and silence. If there were a shelter Ofsted, we'd probably be OK. And this matters. Safe, professional, accountable.

Penny had a story about avocado that told her she was worth something. The volunteer who cut up the avocado had a story about salad ingredients. Was Penny right to be 'blown away'? What is the story she is telling about herself in the shelter where something as simple as the way in which a salad is prepared becomes so meaningful? Underlying the provision of tea, hot meals and a bed in a winter shelter are deeper stories about welcome and hospitality, the host and guest, the volunteer and the other, that are unspoken.

'Underlying ... are deeper stories about welcome...'

How we speak of the experience of homelessness, of being volunteers – the story we tell and are told – shapes what we mean by welcome.

Each guest spends their day as a client at a day centre, seeing their key worker – then crosses the threshold of the shelter and becomes a guest. The choice that brings a volunteer and guest to the shelter is not an equal one. If welcome is being pleased to see someone but that person is here because they are experiencing homelessness, how do we not feel, even if we don't say it, that there is a 'them and us'? Beneath a volunteer's anxiety about how to speak to a guest may be a story of fear because that person is different, living without a roof – a story of privilege and inequality. We ask ourselves whether it is realistic to be equal. We really believe it matters to grapple with this, to offer generous hospitality – with, and not done to.

There are two spaces in the shelter where we see a different story at work. One that has more openness, less strain and worry, more naturalness and equality, is the meal table. Set up like a café with check tablecloths, candles, individual serving bowls, where everyone sits down together – the conversations and laughter could be anywhere in the world. Silence is respected for those who sit quietly. People pass dishes, serve each other, get up to clear away, to bring the next course. Favourite foods are talked about, recipes from home and other cultures. Across the table, next to a neighbour around food, we make community and acceptance.

The other is the impromptu setting up of an art table, some years ago, that begins to change the story of welcome in the shelter. It is a space without expectations, inviting anyone to use as they want, a reciprocal space shared by guest and volunteer. Everyone has hesitations, or some story of 'not good at art'. Inadvertently we discover something important about welcome – characterised by being equal, offering something to each other but especially a space where a guest helps and encourages a volunteer. Guest becomes host – a reaching beneath hesitant and awkward conversation, beyond words to the experience of being human together. A drawing of a house leads to a story: whose garden is this, where is this house? In a garden what do you like to grow, what's behind that window? Who lives here?

Art leads us to a different place because being there is a choice, a freedom in exploring materials, in sharing our story through expressing individual creativity. It is a place of welcome and acceptance. At both tables something is given and received by those present. At our meal table, the gift of food is shared and eaten. The art table is

'Art leads us to … sharing our story through expressing individual creativity.'

the other way round: we don't know what the gift will be, and end up sharing what has been created.

In our most recent volunteer feedback session we wanted to break open the language we use about being homeless and think what this means: we talked about loss of home, community, family, a place to keep things, about identity and belonging, all the networks that create home and being at home. We asked ourselves about our story of being homeless and began to see that we also had a story about a place of homelessness inside ourselves – somewhere we don't belong, something or someone lost – that there is a stranger within ourselves we need to welcome. From this kind of grappling, a different and slightly scary place opens which is generous to guest and volunteer and where we see each other as equal. It transforms what welcoming the stranger means in our shelter, and the way we see each 'other'. We meet each other in difference.

We don't run the shelter the same way each winter, because we see ourselves as on a journey. We are journeying in the shelter with the guests who come along and together we are giving and receiving welcome. We expect to be changed because we are making relationships with each person who comes, where together we create a space where everyone can welcome, and listen to, the stories we bring, those that are being shared. The avocado in the salad is a lovely story of a volunteer who enjoys creativity in the kitchen, colour, taste and nourishing food for herself and expresses that through giving something special to others. Penny is welcomed and valued by an act of love and passes that on in a crazy, joyful game of table tennis!

Debbie O'Brien has been a coordinator in the Westminster Night Shelter in Central London for seven years and is part of a group of coordinators who grew the scheme from three venues running for three months to 14 venues running for eight months. She has a longstanding involvement with people who are vulnerable, living at the edges and has an interest especially in hospitality, what welcoming the other means, as well as how we speak about and work with those who are going through homelessness.

Following pilgrim paths

Don Quilty reflects on the ancient tradition of welcome offered by retreat centres today.

A pilgrimage or a retreat is often an internal process as well as a physical one. They are both ways of taking a spiritual journey away from the distractions we find ourselves living with and stepping into a sacred space with God.

Today, the Holy Island of Lindisfarne is one of England's most popular pilgrimage and retreat destinations. Among the many visitors coming to the island are pilgrims walking St Cuthbert's Way from Melrose to Holy Island – trudging across the sands on the final trek towards the island, following the poles which mark the safe path. Many arrive to stay with us at Marygate House at the completion of the journey and they often relate how unexpectedly and profoundly they have been affected spiritually on their walk. Since 1970 many others have come on retreat here too. But Holy Island has been a pilgrimage centre for a much longer time: there is a long tradition of people coming here to deepen their relationship with God – to step into a sacred space with God.

We know very little about the day-to-day life in the monastery on Lindisfarne founded in the seventh century by St Aidan at the invitation of King Oswald. We know Aidan chose Lindisfarne to plant his monastery to be far enough away from the king's court in Bamburgh to avoid the distraction of the court, whilst still being close enough to the king to support him and receive his protection. We know that Aidan's monastery was popular: many men came to swell its numbers, including the young Cuthbert who, like many others, discovered 'sacred space' here. Aidan too welcomed students to the school, people who later went on to mission much of the north of England. It is from those early times that pilgrims started to come here, to encounter God for themselves.

We can be sure that in the twelfth century in the Benedictine monastery on Lindisfarne there were many pilgrims. Hospitality was an integral part of their medieval monastic life. In receiving guests, the monks were

'... there is a long tradition of people coming here to deepen their relationship with God...'

following Christ's example and adhering to the Rule of St Benedict, as well as taking on an important role within local society and providing a valuable service for everybody, especially the sick and dying. Donations were welcome, but not necessary. It is from the outreach and welcome of medieval monks, the generous care and love they gave to pilgrims and others, that we derive our understanding of the words 'hospitality' and 'hospital'.

Sadly, today's world can be an inhospitable place where we can sometimes feel disrespected, trodden upon, unappreciated and ignored. When visiting a new place, or community, we can feel 'out of place' and 'unwanted'. This is despite all civilised societies across the globe priding themselves on being welcoming to the stranger and the traveller. Welcome is one of those things we all like to believe we do well and are good at – but sadly sometimes we could do better. Thankfully sometimes the reverse is true – we arrive at a new place and we feel at home and loved. This is the kind of welcome Christians should extend to all other pilgrims on life's journey. We are called to strive to go beyond a commercial sense of hospitality to one of love and charity – because in welcoming the stranger we welcome Christ himself, as he welcomes us.

The team here at Marygate House, in common with other retreat houses, aims to keep this maxim in our minds as we prepare for, welcome and serve retreatants. I have been asked why I work in a retreat house. My response is simple. I do this because I

Lindisfarne Castle on Holy Island.

am called to serve – I am called to serve here. It is no more than a response to God's call to extend the hand of friendship, to be generous, without the expectation of something in return, like the monks of old who resided on this island. The 'welcome' you can receive here at Marygate is also on offer at countless monasteries and convents all around the world today. Thank God monastic hospitality is alive and well – despite being counter-cultural and often lost in a sea of commercialism.

Marygate offers a 'Ministry of Welcome', whereby we provide a safe, welcoming Christian environment for people who visit Holy Island to stay for religious, cultural or educational reasons. Marygate provides a still space for people to listen and to talk to each other and to God. It is a place to encounter creation and holiness, in nature and through everyday life, and its location is perfect for this. We welcome groups of up to 18 people as well as individuals when space allows. We also welcome volunteers – people who come for a few weeks, months or a year. They have the opportunity to serve, often whilst discerning God's call. Marygate is independent, it has no formal links with any church or other organisation and is completely reliant on donations, having no other source of funding. We are grateful that, since it opened in 1970, it has survived on monastic hospitality. It has been likened to a bumble bee, which some scientists have said ought not to be able to fly, but which clearly does! I think we survive through the grace of God and the generosity of our retreatants and guests.

St Cuthbert's Island off Holy Island.

We can live busy lives, bombarded by constant noise and busyness. We can have no time to think, to pray or to be. A retreat can give us the opportunity to step back from our normal environment to redress this. Scripture records Christ going to a quiet place to pray – and we can do the same. Marygate, alongside other retreat houses, provides excellent opportunities to do this: to retreat for a short time. Some, like Marygate, are perfect for first-time retreatants. Wherever you decide to go, I hope you will be made most welcome.

Don Quilty and his wife Sam are wardens of Marygate House on Holy Island www.marygatehouse.org.uk. Don's background is as an administrator having worked in ecclesiastical, charity and higher education sectors. He has previously worked at Launde Abbey in Leicestershire and the Claret Centre in Cambridgeshire. He studied towards holy orders with the Claretian Missionaries at Ushaw College Co Durham, CTU in Chicago and later Westminster College. Don has an interest in Ignatian Spirituality and likes photography and learning to play the guitar. Sam is presently a Church of England ordinand. Don and Sam have two adult children who live far from Holy Island in bustling cities.

Dancing with dragonflies

Clare Shearman explores first-hand what it means to be welcomed by creation.

What began as a five-year plan to move from Australia to the UK to be closer to my parents in Plymouth has resulted in something much larger. Artie and I landed in Cornwall in June 2015. Individually we were led by a sense that the barns we had purchased as part of a farm redevelopment could be the perfect spot for people in need of some time out from busy lives, particularly for people in ministry and for those caring for others. We are a small retreat, occupying six acres of an old farm. We live alongside neighbours who are supportive of what we do. The three retreat spaces are all self-contained and range from a luxurious barn with sea views to a hermitage which is reached via our labyrinth, through some woods to the pond at the bottom of the fields.

I began writing this article about welcoming people to our home of retreat with a working title, 'Welcome to Treargel'. I outlined a little of how we came to be here and what we have been told our welcome looks like to people coming to stay with us – the lovely website, the easy booking system, good directions, the cosy accommodation, the luxury of a home from home and so on.

I attempted to finish the article a few times without much enthusiasm. In fact, by the end of each attempt, I had a sneaky suspicion that perhaps I wasn't that good at welcoming people here at all! The truth was that I had been running on empty for a few weeks and I was in need of a retreat myself.

I saw a window of opportunity and decided to take myself off and spend a night down in our hermitage.

On the way, I walked the labyrinth to see if I was able to discern what I needed to let go of or focus on during my time of retreat. I pulled off some dead wood from a tree that brushed my face on the way into the centre of the walk and, when I got to the centre, I found my 'gift', a piece of dead wood lying in the middle of the centre stone.

The hermitage at Treargel: 'What we have here … is the welcome of God's creation.'

It was dusk by the time I got down to the hermitage and I decided to go straight to bed. I woke early with daylight and looked out of the window.

It suddenly hit me that what we have here at Treargel is the welcome of God's creation. As I looked out of the window of my cosy hut, I felt like a very welcome guest of creation. Everyone got on with doing what they do. Whether I was there or not being pretty incidental, I was made to feel most welcome in their space.

I can report from further exploration, as I sat outside on the deck, that the atmosphere in God's creation was warm – the ceiling of my room was the sky with the sun playfully shining through the canopy of trees, the clouds posing majestically as they slowly drifted across the horizon. I took a fold-up chair to sit in patches of ground where the sun came through to warm my body – the central heating worked quite well!

The walls of trees were painted in multiple shades of green at the time and they

The pond at Treargel where '...no two days will ever be the same'.

whispered too as they flickered in the breeze. The carpet of earth was a little busy – lots of leaves, dropped acorns, twigs, moss, stones, peat and multiple guests on the move. Between the carpet and the walls the space was full of sparkling silver thread weaved majestically by the spiders who shared this glorious space. This retreat was full to overflowing with a very friendly yet unobtrusive community.

The sound system worked exceptionally well. Spoiler alert ... there was no volume control and creation was not quiet! The sound of running water initiated frequent trips to the bio-loo and the birds, sheep, cows, insects, deer, squirrels *et al* kept me awake with their ceaseless discussion, but it is a noise that filled my heart.

The entertainment provided was second to none. Two ducks and six ducklings floated across the pond in front of me, scarpering back to safety if I made a move. I played hide and seek with a couple of juvenile blackbirds who thought I couldn't see them if they played statues on a branch. From the corner of my eye I saw a splash of blue and then, from my hiding place, I caught the moment when the kingfisher flew from a branch and dived to get its breakfast from the pond. Better than a box set of my favourite TV series for sure.

I took the small boat out onto the pond and floated for an hour in the sun – that is when the dancing began. The pond was full of dragonflies and they welcomed me into their space. As I floated they put on their floor and air show just for me – amazing.

I chose the self-catered option and took some hot water and fruit with me but my kind hosts also provided a huge welcome pack of ripe, sweet and juicy blackberries which were delicious.

So welcome, you are most welcome, and will receive a great welcome from God's creation every day of the year here at Treargel's hermitage. We completely guarantee that no two days will ever be the same. The walls and the carpet change by the second, the ceiling moves, the lighting comes on in the morning and goes off at night. NB the power goes off early in winter!

My reflection on the dead wood I received from the labyrinth at the beginning of my retreat was that there was much I needed to clear away to enable me to see the dead wood left standing. The final gift of my retreat was to read the passage from Luke, *'Jesus said: "She is not dead but asleep." They laughed at him, knowing that she was dead. But he took her by the hand and said, "My child, get up!" Her spirit returned, and at once she stood up.'* (Luke 8:52–55) [1]

I have been most warmly welcomed and revived by God's creation in this place – I can recommend it.

Clare Shearman opened Treargel Retreats with her husband Artie in November 2016. She is a Spiritual Director. She runs guided retreats and quiet days at Treargel and also hosts a weekly meditation group on behalf of WCCM (World Christian Community of Meditation). Clare and Artie are members at Riverside United Church in Looe. They are close friends and neighbours of the Chemin Neuf Community at Sclerder Abbey where they can sometimes be found welcoming guests with the Community at quiet days, family days and through volunteering in the kitchen.

Building a community of reconciliation

Brother Paolo describes the welcome Taizé offers to thousands of young people.

Taizé is an international and inter-denominational monastery in eastern France (Burgundy) founded in 1940. For over 50 years the community has welcomed young adults (15–29 years old) from a wide variety of backgrounds for week-long sessions of community building and discussion – 80,000 young people from all over the world take part in these each year, including many who would not describe themselves as 'religious'.

Most of the brothers of the community have been living in Taizé for quite a number of years. It has become our home and, when we see the young adults who have come from all over the world, we feel we want to welcome them as guests. As in any family, we are touched that some people travel very great distances just in order to visit us. And we hope that, as guests, they are going to want to take part in our life for the short time that they stay.

I like Taizé in the summer, when there are a few thousand young people here for the week. Of course, we have got used to seeing a lot of people around, and feel at home in it. It takes a bit of getting used to when you arrive: you're probably not used to seeing so many people around you – at meal times or in the church. (Luckily the dormitories are smaller, you usually stay with not more than four or five others; you can also bring your own tent, if you prefer.)

There's one very special place in Taizé and that is the church. It's in the centre of all the other buildings and it's where we gather together to pray. I say it's special – don't get the idea it's anything wonderful to look at, at least from the outside it isn't. What's special about the church for me is that, when we are in it, all of us, both visitors and community alike, become like guests – in a place where God welcomes us. It reminds me of Jesus, who, even when he was a child, always referred to the place of prayer in Jerusalem as 'my Father's house'.

If you're planning to come to Taizé, I think

The brothers leading worship in the Taizé church.

the most important thing to know before you come is that we will ask you to join in with quite a lot of things. First with the rhythm of our own day: meals together, and gathering in the church morning, midday and evening for prayer. It's an opportunity to live a kind of 'slice' of community life.

Then, there are the activities we arrange especially for our guests, which I suppose can properly be called 'meetings'. Some are in larger groups and are led by one of the brothers of the community, we call them 'Bible introductions', perhaps because the brother leading the meeting introduces us to one or more short Bible passages, providing some ideas of his own and suggesting some lines for us to go on thinking about what they mean for us. Other meetings are in smaller groups that usually include people from various countries. Getting to be friends with a few others who come from different countries and cultures can take a bit of time, as well as trust and the will to persevere. It's always worth it.

I suppose I must mention that we also ask you to do a share of the practical tasks during our time together. I know some families don't let their guests do any washing-up and so on, but really we just couldn't manage that way. (If we had to do all the washing-up when there are a few thousand young people here, it would take away all the joy of having so many guests!) When I see a couple of dozen young people gathered around the big washing-up troughs laughing and splashing, it really does look as if they're having fun. Indeed, I've known lots of people go to join the washing-up team even on days when they're not on the rota. And there are many other ways of doing something for the whole community: vacuum-cleaning the carpet in the church (we sit on the floor, so this is important), giving out food at meal-times, cleaning toilets, giving out song-sheets when people come for prayer. As in a normal family, there's nobody at Taizé paid to do all these things, so we manage together. In fact the practicalities of life are simple, and the effort required for these and other shared tasks isn't very great.

How did all this start?

In 1940 Brother Roger, the founder of the Taizé Community, was 25. He left

'Young people from all over the world' come to spend a week at Taizé.

Photo: Cédric Nisi © Ateliers et Presses de Taizé, 71250 Taizé, France

Switzerland, the country of his birth, and settled in France, recently defeated in war. As he wrote later, *'The more a believer wishes to live out the absolute call of God, the more essential it is to do so in the heart of human distress.'* [1]

At the end of the Second World War he was joined by other men wishing to live a community life. While the first brothers were Protestant, from the mid-1960s onwards Catholics were able to join too. Today there are brothers from some 30 different countries and from all the continents.

The community accepts no gifts or donations for itself. The brothers do not even accept family inheritances. They support themselves solely by their own work.

Starting in the 1950s, some of the brothers began living outside of Taizé, among the underprivileged, to be witnesses of peace alongside those who are suffering. Today, small groups of brothers live in Latin America, Asia and Africa. They are attempting to share the conditions in which the people around them live.

By its very existence, the community is a sign of reconciliation among divided Christians and among separated peoples. It wishes to be a 'parable of communion', a place where people seek to be reconciled every day. If reconciliation between Christians is at the heart of Taizé's vocation, this is not seen as an end in itself, but so that Christians become a leaven of reconciliation between people, of trust among nations, and of peace on earth. Our welcome, which also extends beyond youth to those of any age, is an integral part of that vocation.

1 Brother Roger of Taizé, *The Sources of Taizé* (Gai Publications inc, 2000).

Brother Paolo was born in Gloucester. He arrived in Taizé in 1976 and, interrupting his university studies, stayed as a volunteer there before joining the community a couple of years later. His work is varied: making pottery, leading weekly Bible-study groups, meeting with visitors from the UK, helping organise various international meetings which Taizé holds across the world. See www.taize.fr for further information on the international youth meetings in Taizé.

Welcome awaits you

Magdalen Lawler and Tom McGuinness describe a retreat they offer in Malta.

As part of our Ignatian retreat ministry we have collaborated over many years offering retreats that weave together Scripture, art, poetry, and music. Recently, for two successive years, we have responded to the invitation to give a retreat of this kind at Mount St Joseph, a Jesuit Retreat Centre in Malta during May, and we look forward to returning there once again in 2019.

Malta is an island long associated with Christianity and St Paul. It is also a cultural crossroads with a history that goes back to pre-Christian times. Mount St Joseph, just outside the town of Mosta, is a spacious Centre occupying a relatively high position with striking views of the surrounding countryside and the sea. The Community at the Retreat Centre wanted to offer a retreat for English-speaking people that would be enjoyable, quiet, restful and deepening. They were enthusiastic about our suggestion of five days based on the now well-loved work of the priest-artist, Sieger Köder, whose 'painted homilies' have enabled many people to enter more deeply into the meaning of scriptural stories and

scenes. Indeed, images of the Stations of the Cross painted by Sieger Köder line the entire corridor that leads to the main Chapel at Mount St Joseph.

With its historical associations, and located near the medieval city of Mdina, we were sure that such a venue would appeal to English-speaking retreatants in search of both the sun and silent reflection. The Centre is spacious and cool indoors and surrounded by gardens with groves of almonds, olives and citrus fruit. In early May new flowers abound, offering a sea of colour among a landscape that also reminded us that Malta is rated as one of the most arid nations in the world, along with most of the Middle Eastern countries. There are no natural rivers and water is desalinated for general use, like taking showers, but Mount St Joseph has its own purification facilities for drinking water. In 2017 our theme of Living Water, reflecting on the Woman at the Well in St John's Gospel, also took on new meaning as we tried to weave in a greater understanding of shared resources in our modern world.

Looking towards the sea from the terrace of Mount St Joseph.

The two chapels in the Retreat Centre are very beautiful and lend themselves to quiet prayer and simple liturgies. The building itself is of historical and architectural value and is protected under Maltese law. It is designed in the shape of a wide V: the spacious reception area is the connecting point while the guest room wings form the arms of the V. The design is intended to symbolise open arms welcoming guests inside.

At the suggestion of the Mount St Joseph community, the retreats began with an optional day and a half pilgrim-tour to sites connected with St Paul, and also incorporated other cultural visits. We saw the Hagar Qim Neolithic temples dating from 3000 BC, catacombs from the Roman colonisation of Malta, St John's Cathedral with its Caravaggio masterpiece, and the formidable bastions of Valletta's magnificent harbour. We were accompanied on the pilgrim-tour by Stephen Scerri, manager of Mount St Joseph, and by a very informative local Maltese guide. This year, Stephen incorporated a welcoming visit to his own contemporary Roman Catholic church, blessed with large modern fresco Icons telling the story of Christ. He prepared some beautiful reflections for us at each place we visited to help us enter into a deeper understanding. He spoke of the longing of the ancient people, probably from other parts of the Mediterranean, who built the Hagar Qim temples. He pointed out the impressive structure of the medieval aqueduct, bringing water to the city and especially its hospitals. We prayed that we might bring the water of compassion to all whom we meet. During a visit to the interior garden of a peaceful Carmelite Priory in the bustling walled city of Mdina, Stephen encouraged us to become more aware of the enclosed interior garden of our own soul.

Mount St Joseph Retreat Centre.

One cannot be in Malta without thinking of St Paul. Everyone was aware how near we were to St Paul's Bay, visible from most of the garden and terraces. It was from there that Paul swam ashore after the shipwreck. The Acts of the Apostles recalls the shipwreck and the generous welcome extended by the inhabitants of Malta, who are described as *'unusually kind'* in Chapter 28 of Acts. Our subsequent retreat reflection on 'The Storm at Sea' came alive for the retreatants who had visually experienced the Pauline association with storm and shipwreck. For a number of us, one of the most touching moments was Stephen's reflection at St Paul's Bay – so near to the actual site of Paul's shipwreck. The Scripture account touched us in a powerful way: so much so that we asked Stephen to repeat it during the later retreat presentation.

After the pilgrimage we began the silent retreat. Each morning there was a presentation using Scripture reflections with images, poetry and song. In the late afternoon there was an optional sharing group, so all who wished could come together to share what had particularly struck them from the day's images and prayer. We celebrated the Eucharist each day in the early evening before supper. During the morning and afternoon we offered individual interviews for those who wished. An atmosphere of silence was generously held and respected throughout the retreat and especially in the retreat house. At our final evening together many of the group commented on how close they had all come to each other by sharing this silent atmosphere.

During our morning sessions we looked at images that spoke to us of the hospitality and welcome of God. These included

Crucifix and stained glass in the main chapel.

Fountain and Madonna in the garden walkways.

Rembrandt's famous painting of *The Return of the Prodigal Son* and Sieger Köder's imaginative painting of *The meal with sinners* depicting 'motley guests' gathered around the table. We also spent time contemplating Icons of Christ and the Trinity, experiencing the way in which they may be windows inviting us into the mystery of the eternal.

A number of adventurous retreatants used the frequent buses to continue in pilgrim mode, on occasion, by heading to St Paul's Bay and the sea again – or to Mdina with its wonderful medieval atmosphere of narrow, cool streets and a sense of quiet, even amid crowds. Far from being a distraction from the retreat days, these mini-pilgrims shared how they had 'taken the retreat with them' and found God in such times and places.

In May 2018 we called the retreat 'Love Bade Me Welcome', after the poem by George Herbert, which speaks of the boundless welcome, forgiveness and love of God in the person of Jesus. We look forward to our return visit in May 2019, when we can once again experience the welcoming atmosphere and shared peace of Mount St Joseph Retreat Centre.

Tom McGuinness SJ is currently based in Dublin helping to lead a formation programme for European Jesuits. He has had an interest in writing and recording reflection songs for prayer, many of which are used during retreats led by himself and Magdalen Lawler SND, a Notre Dame sister living in London. Magdalen has a special interest in women's spirituality and in spirituality and the visual arts. Magdalen and Tom have worked together over many years to offer retreats, weaving together Scripture, art, poetry and song.
Mount St Joseph is offering this English-speaking retreat and pilgrim tour again from 17–25 May 2019. For information about the retreat see www.mtsjoseph.org or http://bit.ly/MaltaRetreat2019

Offering the gift of peace

Sister Maureen explores the ministry of welcome in a Franciscan community.

Sisters in the Community of St Francis (CSF) have lived in Metheringham, about ten miles south of Lincoln, since 2010. The 'big skies' in the relatively flat landscape and the mellow stone colour of much of the village, as well as the 'Hello' from everyone you pass in the street as you walk around, encourage visitors to relax and to let the stresses of life subside for a while. Judith Ann and myself are the resident sisters there, and are pleased to welcome people for the day or for a longer stay. In recent years we have learned to adapt and change the ways in which we offer that welcome in order to best meet the needs of our visitors.

San Damiano opened as a result of the need for the Community to move from the large retreat house that we ran at Compton Durville, in Somerset, that had become too much for us. Although it had been the Community's home for nearly 50 years, it was time to let it go. We wanted to continue to have a rural presence so, after exploring a number of possibilities, we settled on the

redundant vicarage in Metheringham. Although it is a fairly large house, we have room for only one person to stay at a time, and there is room for day guests and day groups, so we have learned to welcome people in a different way from the style of our larger retreat house. We ask people who come for the day to bring their own lunch. For a little while, this was a difficult mental transition – it didn't *feel* very welcoming, especially not being able to provide a meal even for small groups, but identifying the practicalities of the situation helped us to recognise that the primary need for guests was a welcoming space with plenty of tea and coffee available to them throughout the day.

We named the house 'San Damiano', after the place near Assisi where St Clare and her sisters lived the contemplative life. It is situated towards the edge of the village, and down a drive; the old churchyard is to one side of us and fields to another. Trees, the remnant of an old forest, give a sense of

San Damiano house.

Sister Maureen walking the labyrinth.

seclusion and contribute to the peacefulness of the place. 'It's so peaceful' or 'It's so quiet' are the two most common responses from our guests. As we welcome people here, we hope that the peace and quiet, along with the rhythm of prayer, including an open invitation to join us at the Eucharist, will provide nourishment for their souls, and that rest and relaxation will provide physical refreshment also. In the quiet, even the 'not religious' may also find that God has made God's self welcome to them in a new way.

St Francis of Assisi wrote in his 'Testament' (verse 23), 'The Lord revealed a greeting to me that we should say, "May the Lord give you peace"'.[1] The peacefulness of the place contributes to the Lord's gift of peace. However, sometimes being alone and quiet simply gives opportunity for thoughts to run riot in one's head, and there is no internal peace. It is good, then, to be able to talk out the 'riot' – as this very act of putting the thoughts into some sort of structure starts

to quiet them down, and the other person reflecting back can give a fresh perspective. What seemed overwhelming can then be seen in manageable segments and peace can start to enter in. So a listening ear from one of the sisters and the more regular ministry of spiritual direction, to help people deepen their relationship with God, are important ministries as an extension of the prayer and the place.

So in welcoming people into our home, we welcome them into our lives. We aim to live simply; *The Principles* of our order state: '*The buildings (of the Community/Society) and the style and manner of life which it permits will be the simplest that are consistent with good health and efficient work.*'[2] We share our table with resident guests, and we try to meet people's dietary needs. So far as we are able, we do our own cooking and housework. The wildlife in the garden – birds, squirrels and sometimes hedgehogs, deer and rabbits – provide entertainment and wonder.

Conscious of our impact on the environment, we are looking more and more towards an ecologically friendly lifestyle. In Metheringham, our house is now warm all year round because we have installed a wood-pellet biomass boiler in place of the oil-fired system, and thermostatic radiators control the temperature in each room. Sometimes there is tension about what we would like to do or buy, with the increase in cost that it entails. Such dilemmas, I am sure, are repeated in many homes, as we reflect on our history of disregarding the needs of the planet and endeavour in the future to reduce waste. We also want to provide a place to visit which is affordable for everyone, and we can welcome a limited number of people who cannot afford the donation we request for their stay, because of the generous donations of others.

St Francis of Assisi started up a new type of religious order, one where the members were not secluded from the world, but very much involved in it and responding to its needs. One of the needs of our time, that some of our Anglican Franciscan houses seek to meet as one of their main ministries, is that of providing a quiet space to pray, reflect and/or rest. It is a privilege to be able to offer that ministry of welcome, in the name of Christ, and to see the change in people as they use that time for renewal of body, mind and spirit.

1 *Saint Francis of Assisi: The Early Documents, Volume 1* ed Regis J Armstrong OFM. Cap, JA Wayne Hellmann OFM Conv, & William J Short OFM. (New City Press, 1999).

2 The First Order of the Society of St Francis, *The Principles*, in *The Daily Office SSF*, (The European Province of the Society of St Francis, 2010).

Sister Maureen has been a member of the Community of St Francis since 1981, and has lived in houses in Somerset, Stepney, Auckland (New Zealand), Newcastle-under-Lyme, Birmingham and now in Metheringham. Having trained as a nurse before entering the community, she used those skills in various ways during her community life, including employment in a local hospital in Birmingham. Her main ministry now, alongside hospitality, is that of spiritual direction, guiding people in retreat, and assisting with the training of spiritual directors in the Diocese of Lincoln. www.franciscans.org.uk Facebook page: The Community and Society of St Francis (European Province)

Called to live in service

Chris Swift describes the work of the MHA celebrating 75 years of hospitality.

Since Methodist Homes (MHA) was founded in 1943, it has maintained a keen interest in ageing and spirituality. Our founder, Walter Hall, was a Methodist minister who was determined to support both the material and spiritual needs of those in later life. He saw the fear of those in his district who were *'one piece of bad luck from the workhouse'* and lobbied leading Methodists to support the call to create high quality retirement living which offered dignity and security.

Today MHA operates 90 care homes, over 70 retirement living schemes and more than 50 'Live at Home' schemes, across England, Scotland and Wales. As we mark our 75th anniversary, the scale of operation has grown enormously, yet the core values and concerns that led to our foundation remain unchanged. This is more than rhetoric. Every residential scheme has the services of a dedicated chaplain, employed by MHA, to ensure that we don't lose sight of the commitment to provide

care in 'body, mind and spirit'. MHA is also the leading employer of music therapists in the UK, ensuring that those living with dementia benefit from the very best care that we can provide.

Deciding to come to live in a care home is seldom easy. Often it is a choice made by circumstances rather than the outcome of a growing awareness of changing capabilities. A new crisis in health, or the loss of a loved one, can tip the balance between continuing to live at home and the need for on-site care with round-the-clock support.

Once settled in an MHA facility, those who may have felt the impact of the 'changes and chances of this fleeting world' can begin to flourish. Time and again we welcome those reluctant to enter residential care who, over the course of a few months, find renewed strength and the rewards that new friendships can bring at any age. Our homes are places where people *live* and where we

'Spiritual care requires us to meet others and show ... that we recognise their experience.'

seek every opportunity to encourage those who might be struggling to feel at home.

Providing spiritual and pastoral care in this context is very different from the way contact is made in the NHS. While most patients today have very short stays in hospital, the average stay in an MHA facility stretches well beyond two years. This means that the chaplains can get to know residents over a much longer period, with a greater chance of meeting relatives and friends. This level of relationship is crucial to MHA's commitment to spiritual care, where the beliefs of residents can be shared with chaplains who become well known and trusted figures in our homes. When this is working successfully, residents tell me that their chaplain is at the hub and heart of the home.

Having spent the majority of my ministry in chaplaincies of one sort or another, I have come to appreciate the qualities which help make spiritual care effective in supporting those in vulnerable situations. That might be in a prison, a hospital or on the battlefield. A text that speaks to me of what it means to be a chaplain can be found in the Book of Job. In chapter 2 we hear how Job's friends learn of his distress, leave their homes, meet together and go to find him. When they encounter him they see how much he is suffering. Reflecting the frequent experience that words are inadequate to describe someone's pain, they get down on the ground beside Job and say nothing for seven days and nights because *'they saw how great his suffering was'*. (Job 2:13)[1] For a chaplain, knowing when not to speak matters at least as much as having something to say.

Being with people in suffering, loss or away from home, is a key part of chaplaincy. Spiritual care requires us to meet others and show by our actions that we recognise their experience. I'll never forget being called to be with a mother whose baby had died despite the best efforts of an A&E department. Entering the room I saw mum with her baby sitting on the floor in the middle of the space – it was obvious that there was only one place for me to be, and that was beside her. Great care with the words we use, an openness to silence, and the question of the right physical place to be – all matter for chaplaincy if it is to be useful and effective.

'Chaplains foster and sustain relationships ... which recognise our fundamental humanity.'

Both from personal experience and in my role at MHA, these are key approaches for supporting someone living with dementia. As Job's comforters found, there are no easy answers and our own willingness to recognise the inadequacy of words can help us make way for that most important quality of spiritual care: compassion. Chaplains foster and sustain relationships with the people in their care which recognise our fundamental humanity. In care homes we get alongside residents in a host of different ways, working with other staff members to ensure we do everything we can to help people make the most of life. While professional boundaries are important for chaplains, so too is our shared sense of belonging as 'children of the living God' – resident and chaplain alike.

Right from the start, MHA decided to be here for older people seeking our help whatever their faith or belief. The presence of our chaplains, our values and commitment to high-quality care, all stem from the determination of Walter Hall to see the needs of older people as a call to live out the vocation of Christian service. In doing this we have developed communities of care where every moment of life matters, up to and including the moment of death. After 75 years we continue to be a charity 'inspired by Christian concern', striving to discover new ways to help older people find the dignity and support they need.

1   The Holy Bible, New International Version®, NIV® Copyright © 1973, 1978, 1984, 2011 by Biblica, Inc.™ Used by permission. All rights reserved worldwide.

Rev Dr Chris Swift is Director of Chaplaincy & Spirituality for Methodist Homes (MHA), a charity founded in 1943 which provides care for almost 18,000 older people every year. MHA employs 140 chaplains to ensure that the spiritual needs of residents are met and staff are supported in their work. Before joining MHA in 2017, Chris spent 16 years in the role of Head of Chaplaincy at the Leeds Teaching Hospitals. He is a past-president of the College of Health Care Chaplains (2004–7) and author of Hospital Chaplaincy in the Twenty-first Century *(Routledge 2014). @ChrisSwift1*

Sharing the gift of hospitality

Angie Tunstall explores what it means to offer retreats from an urban home.

'Welcome to Saranam! Come on in, it's good to see you!' The retreatant steps through the door as we wheel their luggage down the hall, through the kitchen, turning left at the dining room and left again into the small private space that will be their room (their cell or cave) for the duration of their retreat. They arrive to wonderful smells of the delicious food Dave, my husband, makes as retreat 'head cook and bottle washer'. We offer a drink and an Eccles cake – our signature cake – here at Saranam, our home and tiny retreat space in Eccles, in the city of Salford, west of Manchester.

The word Saranam can be found in different faith traditions and is connected spiritually to a space of refuge, shelter, protection, surrender and rest. This sets the tone as we invite retreatants into a five-day silent individually guided retreat (IGR) – albeit we sometimes customise these to suit circumstances. Most retreatants are urban workers and again for most this is to be their first experience of being on retreat ... and receiving an invitation into silence.

We offer a gentle programme of settling, being introduced to the Examen and short daily one-to-one meetings with me – for listening and accompaniment. We also offer Ignatian prayer exercises, including stillness, imaginative prayer, lectio divina, praying with art and creation walks. Prayer spaces at Saranam include the retreatant's room, a reading room and an upstairs prayer room. Further, we have a fairly extensive range of craft activities available that are well used by some, and the garden offers a labyrinth experience, wood-making space, and gardeners are welcome to tend the garden if they are that way inclined!

Set in a quiet cul-de-sac, Saranam remains an ideal space for quietness and, living on the edge of Manchester and with good transportation links, it is also ideal for city centre sightseeing, museums and art galleries. We have a beautiful urban nature reserve, cycle paths and woodland all within walking distance and the local

A nature reserve and woodland are within walking distance of Saranam.

leisure centre provides free day passes to those who want to 'gym and swim'.

It really is a joy to offer this to others. Yet you may ask, Why? Why do we open up our urban home on a six-weekly rota, to offer IGRs to urban workers who simply could not (or would not) use the resource of money to pay to go on a retreat? Good question! Let me offer some reflections.

I personally have always valued going on retreat. Coming from a free church background, these first began for me when I was introduced to the Northumbria Community in the late 1980s. I soon developed a pattern of making an annual retreat, finding them nurturing to my soul and my relationship with God. Perhaps this was a precursor to us offering retreats?

My Ignatian journey began in 2008, receiving spiritual direction at the Loreto Centre, Llandudno, North Wales. Spiritual direction was followed by Ignatian retreats, themed movie retreats and gradually led to my undertaking the 30-day Spiritual Exercises retreat. Dave was also able to embrace Ignatian spirituality and we came

to see that we were constantly experiencing the welcome and generosity of God. Years later, we discerned we have the opportunity to share this welcome and generosity with others.

Why urban workers and why at no cost? Since 2010 I have served as a North West regional coordinator with Urban Expression (UE)[1] – an urban mission agency that recruits, equips, deploys and networks self-financing teams, pioneering creative and relevant expression of the Christian church in under-churched areas of the inner city, outer estates and marginalised communities. UE is a fairly reflective, questioning and activist missional community. Yet, I noticed quite early on that whilst many of my peers had a pattern of engagement in active service, there was not a natural pattern of withdrawal to be with God, a pattern I discern reflected in the life of Christ and his relationship with his Father.

Dave and I made a move 'home' to Eccles and became a UE team in 2012. We found ourselves part of a dispersed community who were living simply and, as self-funded

A labyrinth in the garden of Saranam.

teams, there was often little spare cash around on a daily basis. We also began to develop our local team values around hospitality, workplace and town centre ministry.

We began to see that the words 'hospitality' and 'welcome' are interchangeable as we started to hold weekly Sabbath meals (on Thursdays!) where we invite local people we 'do life with' to join us for a simple liturgy of bread, wine and table fellowship, alongside Dave's lovely food. Those who join us may or may not be people of faith and belief. We invite them to observe or participate. We find most participate whilst feeling welcomed but not coerced. Perhaps this was another precursor to us offering retreats?

We also began to serve as hosts with the Boaz Trust[2], a Christian organisation which supports destitute asylum seekers and refugees in Greater Manchester. Hosting generally involves welcoming someone into our home for three to four weeks, offering them sanctuary and a safe space whilst they make fresh asylum claims and await decisions. The hosting time is an incubating

time as they prepare to live in shared Boaz houses with other destitute asylum seekers and refugees.

Over the years we noticed the strands that were being drawn together: my own appreciation of IGRs; being part of an engaging, but not withdrawing, missional community; that retreats could be a luxury for those who could afford it; that urban workers are often more comfortable in an urban context, rather than a rural one (I like both myself!). Finally, as we received Boaz guests into our home, we noticed we were growing in our experience of hospitality and welcome. We discerned that as we had been graced with the hospitality of opening up our hearts and our home to others, God might just be asking us to offer retreats.

Reflecting as I write, there is joy in my spirit, that God would grace us and trust us to hold these tender ones on their journey towards and with God as they experience more of God's very own welcome.

1 For more on Urban Expression see www.urbanexpression.org.uk

2 For more on Boaz Trust see www.boaztrust.org.uk

Rev Angie Tunstall is a Baptist community minister and team leader of Urban Expression Eccles. Together with Dave, her husband, they run Saranam, in their Eccles home, creating space for other urban workers to meet with God on urban retreats. Angie is also a Healthcare Chaplain at Christie Oncology Trust.

An act of love

Amanda Kimberley describes how a retreat centre offers hospitality to all.

Whitchester Christian Centre has operated an interdenominational place of retreat for 34 years. Set up initially at Whitchester House near Duns, Berwickshire, its home has been at Borthaugh, just outside Hawick, nestled at the end of a valley in the stunning scenery of the Scottish Borders, for the last 27 years. The original vision, outlined in a prophecy given in 1984, is for a place where God's people will be built up, blessed, drawn apart and strengthened – somewhere from which individuals will go with a new vision and an assurance of God's presence and power within them – a place particularly where those in Christian ministry can find rest and refreshment.

The nineteenth-century house has 13 en suite rooms, a comfortable lounge (with an open fire in the winter months), conservatory, dining room, chapel and art room. There are also little nooks and crannies to sit and read, browse through books, choose cards and gifts to buy, or just enjoy the view. At the rear of the house are a walled vegetable garden and orchard –

rhubarb and apple crumbles feature on the menu regularly, and we also grow summer fruits, cucumbers, lettuce, tomatoes and onions. The garden at the front of the house with a pastoral view of sheep on the opposite hillside provides an oasis of rural tranquillity.

Whitchester is a place where there is a deep sense of being welcomed and cared for, somewhere to come apart and rest from the busyness and pressures of everyday life, where God's love can be made more real through offering hospitality.

This is worked out in numerous ways: from the initial contact, to the welcome on arrival, accommodating dietary needs and providing excellent food, to the comfortable rooms, the 'special' porridge, after-dinner chocolate mints and the unusual additional welcome to four-legged canines! Welcome is about receiving people gladly, finding out what will make each individual feel at home and relaxed, whatever their background and wherever they are coming from. At Whitchester we aim to provide a

Views of Whitchester Christian Centre.

place where God's presence is sensed in a real way: where you can just come and 'be'.

Helen Miller, who owns the house, received a vision in the form of a poem, which includes the following lines:

> My 'open door':
> A place of welcome,
> A place of peace,
> A place where the weary
> Can find release.
> A place of comfort,
> A place of balm,
> A place of caring,
> A place of calm.
> With a shoulder to cry on,
> And a hand to uphold,
> With ears ever open,
> And arms to enfold.[1]

This is very much the ethos of Whitchester: whilst it can be bedlam in the back of the house with all the normal challenges of life – such as laundry piling up, the dishwasher breaking down and so on – a very special peace reigns over the main house, which is remarked on by the vast majority of our guests and visitors.

As we are listed on accommodation websites, we take bookings from people in all walks of life. Our main focus is to provide a retreat for Christians in need of time out, quiet space, and the ministry of good food and hospitality. However, we are also glad to offer this welcome to church and clergy groups, reading groups, quilting groups, builders working in the area, families attending a nearby wedding, and anyone needing a few nights away from it all. As much as we are able, we encourage events that tie in with our ministry ethos: for example, a silent midweek Individually Guided Retreat run by the Ignatian Spirituality Centre from Glasgow. We also run our own events at Whitchester when resourcing allows. These have included house-parties, Advent retreats, bereavement and healing weekends.

As a team we pray together regularly, and an informal, interdenominational chapel time is held twice each day – in the morning after breakfast and again after the evening meal. Prayer requests are invited and this time provides an oasis of calm for the team as well as offering a ministry to guests.

The team and directors all share the values of

compassion and hospitality and are therefore sensitive to the differing needs of visitors. Some are looking for space and time apart, while others may be seeking pastoral support through attentive listening and prayer ministry, which are provided by the team as required.

All are welcome at Whitchester: Christians of any denomination, as well as those who may be searching; the wealthy and the not so wealthy (we are grateful for the donations to our 'access fund' which enables those with financial restrictions to stay). As well as financial supporters, without whom we would have difficulty operating, we also welcome volunteers who encourage us by coming and lending a willing hand, often with their own specific talents and abilities.

Since 2012 Joan Kinnings-Smith has been Head Warden with her husband Nigel and believes Whitchester is a very special place. In common with other Retreat Houses, it has been covered by prayer from the beginning of its ministry, and we guard this spiritual presence of God that is tangible to so many guests but also due in part to the way everyone is accepted as they are. As one visitor commented, 'People don't feel they have to tick boxes here.' The ministry is focused on guests, using the place for their own spiritual journey – which means people are free to dip in and out of chapel times or other activities with no pressure either way. It is recognised that some people just need space and in some cases silence; others a holiday in which they can share fellowship with others; some just need a bed to sleep in! However, for some the availability of a listening ear and prayer ministry are a key part of their stay.

Going with the flow of people's spiritual journey and offering practical support are all part of the welcome that we offer at Whitchester. There are too many responses to describe fully here, but they include: dancing in the rain with abandonment and laughter (it wasn't bucketing down!) with a group of guests who had all been facing difficulty; walking with guests in the countryside; to the more mundane – washing clothes, lifts to town, helping arrange visits to landmarks in the area and meeting people off the bus. All this takes place against a backdrop rhythm of chapel prayers and food (or no food for those fasting). In demonstrating God's love in both spiritual and practical ways, we strive to maintain our vision of hospitality for all.

1 Helen Miller, 'The Whitchester Vision', from a guest information pack at Whitchester, 2002.

Amanda Kimberley and her husband, Simon, started out married life in Uganda where the realisation that missionaries often can't get a break locally due to cultural expectations birthed a desire to provide retreats for people who give of themselves so generously. They spent 16 years on the Isle of Man and flew the nest promptly after their children did! Amanda is trained and experienced in both listening and prayer ministry; and a contemplative by preference. The couple joined Whitchester as Deputy Wardens at the end of May 2018 but by the time you are reading this (and if all goes to plan!), will have become the new Wardens.

Book reviews

We have included a range of titles in our reviews this year. Many of these resources are available to order from our website: **www.retreats.org.uk**. Any profits made from the sale of these resources will be used for the continuing work of the Retreat Association. We hope that you will find inspiration in the pages that follow.

Welcome

Magdalen Lawler
LOVE BADE ME WELCOME: Reflections on the Eucharist in the Art of Sieger Köder
Pauline Books and Media, 2016   ISBN 978 1 90478 571 2
Paperback, 64 pages

George Herbert's classic poem 'Love Bade Me Welcome' and the artwork of the late Sieger Köder form the inspiration for an extended meditation on God's unconditional love. This slender yet profound little book by Sr Magdalen Lawler SND weaves together Scripture, art, poetry and song to guide the reader through a series of reflections on the mystery of the Eucharist. By way of eight beautiful paintings, we travel with the once-exiled Israelites from Old Testament to New: via the gospels to the events of the crucifixion and resurrection.

Many of us have encountered the artist's painted homilies for the first time on retreat. Köder's works have such an evocative quality about them, an immediacy borne of the attention to detail and vivid colours that draw you into the narrative. I experience them like icons, to be prayed with as well as gazed upon and to be revisited time and again as my understanding deepens. Though each contributes to the book's overarching theme of God's unconditional welcome at his table, Sr Magdalen's reflections could also be read individually or as a series during Lent. I personally benefitted from using them as early-morning meditations during last summer's heatwave.

The author has a background in theology and art history. I found her explanation of the various recurring motifs in Köder's works illuminating. In particular, that of the reflection of the face of Christ which reminded me so much of the refrain from the old hymn: '*Turn your eyes upon Jesus, look full in his wonderful face*',[1] which for me so aptly sums up that moment of eucharistic encounter.

Love Bade Me Welcome is enhanced by the inclusion of several songs by Tom McGuinness SJ and an afterword by Gemma Simmonds CJ; the whole is beautifully designed by Mary Louise Winters FSP. There is much food for reflection here.

Jane Sigrist

1 Helen Howarth Lemmel, 'Turn your eyes upon Jesus'. Published in 57 Hymnals.

Arthur Howells, Foreword by David Winter
A FRANCISCAN WAY OF LIFE: Brother Ramon's quest for holiness
Bible Reading Fellowship, 2018   ISBN 978 0 85746 662 4
Paperback, 176 pages

As suggested by Rowan Williams on the cover of this accessible and attractive book, we can be most grateful to Arthur Howells for authoring the first biography of Brother Ramon.

Anyone who has not yet encountered Brother Ramon is in for a treat. I remember being astounded when, on retreat, I first heard Brother Ramon speaking on audio tape. He entered my consciousness as a whirlwind, and it took me a while to adjust to his tone. However, as soon as Ramon started to talk about his own journey, his voice changed, or rather it made sense, and then I was fully in step, gathered up in the energy and authenticity of the revelations from his time in prayer and solitude.

All of the authority of his teaching for me came from his personal experience, which he himself recognised was the way he needed to pursue. Arthur Howells has suggested that Ramon's humble spirit might not have approved of a book being written about him, but it was precisely this – his own life and being – that spoke to others.

And this is what Arthur Howells has captured so well: the balance of the man. A natural teacher and communicator of gregarious temperament and good humour who at the same time felt a strong call to prayer and solitude with God and who tested this desire on three occasions, at hermitages in Dorset, Wales and Glasshampton. He was able to tap into all of these resources to be a great source of strength and spiritual guidance to others.

The life of Ramon makes up the first third of this book in which we learn of his stable childhood, his early conversion at the age of 12 from which he said, *'there has been no looking back, only a deepening of commitment, a maturing of experience, a widening of horizons'*, his absolutist pacifist stance when called to register for national service, his ministry in the Baptist and Anglican churches and his call to the hermit life as a Franciscan brother.

There is a selection from the few still existing of Ramon's letters in Part 2 of the book dating from 1979 until 2000, the year of his death, and the final third of the book gives extracts from Ramon's many works. Ramon was and is a phenomenon whose wisdom and enthusiasm reaches us from the most remote and humble of external circumstances.

Susan Daniell

Christopher Chapman
EARTHED IN GOD: Four movements of spiritual growth
Canterbury Press, 2018   ISBN 978 1 78622 055 4
Paperback, 186 pages

Christopher Chapman's latest work, which parallels spiritual development with the growth cycle in nature, has emerged from the 'good soil' created from his ten years' experience as an allotment holder mixed with his background as a spiritual director, mentor, retreat giver and erstwhile parish priest. It has also been enriched by generously shared examples from the author's own spiritual journey, which ground it in authenticity.

A message from the book is the need for us to meet God half way in the gardening process. God desires that we have abundant lives and like a gardener sees what needs attending to in creating the conditions for fruitfulness, but it is a joint enterprise. If we begin by becoming 'earthed in God', and dig, plant, prune and harvest alongside God, we cannot help but be fruitful.

The first part of the book invites us to acknowledge the reality of our allotment in life. Just as Christopher's allotment wouldn't allow him to grow celery, but could produce basketfuls of lavender, so we need to get to know our own ground and actively invite God to work on it with us.

The second section teaches us how, as winter must give way to spring, we must allow what is within to find its way to the light. Beautiful words illustrate such ideas:

'God is present in the soul, within your depths, in the person you do not yet know. Somewhere in the dark depths of the wood a bud is breaking; a seed wakes; the turtle dove sings.' Just these two sentences generate hope, and this book has many such inspirations. We are encouraged to a *'holy daring'* of breaking out from our self-consciousness to co-create ourselves in God for others and the world.

Part three calls us to allow God to release within us all that constrains us, to prune and clear away unhelpful legacies from our past experiences, so that we can flourish and become fruitful. The fourth and final part contains the whole within it, and the author considers Jesus' parable of the grain of wheat, which in its dying ultimately bears much fruit.

Each chapter concludes with reflective exercises, biblical readings and practical suggestions that help us actively take on this process of growth. In gifting us these, there is a strong sense of the author nearby, loosening the soil, of expert assistance with this hard but eternally rewarding work.

Susan Daniell

John-Francis Friendship
ENFOLDED IN CHRIST: The inner life of a priest
Canterbury Press, 2018   ISBN 978 1 78622 046 2
Paperback, 218 pages

John-Francis Friendship has written this book as the fruit of many years' experience in ministry: as a brother of the Anglican Society of St Francis (SSF), as the rector of a 'back-streets' parish on the eastern edge of London, and as a spiritual director and trainer in the City of London. His concern is to help keep the inner core of the vocation to priestly ministry alive, so that the priest may remain close to the heart of Christ. She or he is thus enabled to be a 'threshold-minder', who 'holds open the door to the mysteries of God'.

John-Francis interweaves his own story with reflections on differing aspects of priesthood including prayer, service to others, eucharistic living, confession, way of life, and letting go. He is mindful of the dangers of priesthood lived out over time: over-activity, burn-out, the blurring between life and work, over-identification with the role and losing the sense of one's own being and identity before God. He offers much wise guidance based on broad experience, along with many helpful resources. There is an excellent section on the use and purpose of the Daily Office.

The book would be a useful gift for someone setting out on this road or for anyone who identifies the need to be called back to first principles, and it draws on the wisdom of those who have already trodden this path, such as George Herbert, Michael Ramsey and Bill Kirkpatrick. Finally, the book recognises that we are all called to share in the priesthood of Christ – and that we need to keep the flame of our own prayer and vocation alive with the assiduousness and loving care that this book recommends.

Jill Keegan

Reviews

Keith Ward
THE MYSTERY OF CHRIST: Meditations and prayers
SPCK, 2018   ISBN 978 0 28107 915 5
Paperback, 96 pages

I love writing that integrates substance and beauty, and Keith Ward's slender book does so with clarity. Thirty concise 'chapters' await the reader, none more than three pages in length – but don't be deceived. This book of meditations and prayers is not a selection of illustrative spiritual anecdotes or poems, but a contemporary devotional communication of biblical faith and thoughtful theology.

Ward's objective is to find an articulation of Christian spirituality for today. In the same way that Ignatius of Loyola or Julian of Norwich wrote of their spiritual experiences by employing the metaphors and language of their own contexts, Ward re-presents key gospel themes about the person of Jesus in a way that is suited to the very different narrative of our times. *'People now have what sometimes seems to be a new mythology, evoked by the scientific picture of a vast and evolving cosmos'*, suggests Ward. He insists that the ancient story of self-giving love is unchanged, and Jesus still reveals the truth of a God to us, but the story requires fresh expression for today's disciples.

Each chapter develops a key biblical idea such as 'God is love', or 'The way, the truth and the life', and explores it fearlessly, followed by a crafted prayer or two. Ward is a superb theologian and is able to condense complex truths into short and readable discussions. Sometimes when writers attempt this, depth and clarity are lost for the sake of simplicity, but Ward excels at finding ways of expressing doctrine in an accessible manner that is full of wonder. At college, I would encourage first-year students to read this book, since they often struggle to connect doctrine meaningfully with worship: Ward shows that it is a natural partnership.

Neither does Ward avoid the big controversies, offering explanatory 'asides'. For example, he informs readers about differing scholarly views of the virginal conception – in a 'scientific' age this is a key question – but whatever the topics, he always takes us back to the secure territory of Christ's identity as the second person of the Trinity. The chapters are thus not necessarily a quick read, since a lot is packed in, but they can be used one at a time for reflection.

Some spiritual accompaniers are wary of doctrine because they feel it is cerebral, and the knowledge of God is of the heart, not the head. This book does require the reader to use the intellect, but the heart is ever-present since Ward is a priest as well as a theologian. It is a mixture that feeds me – why not try it yourself?

Sally Nelson

Thomas Merton, Foreword by Sarah Coakley
WHERE PRAYER FLOURISHES
Canterbury Press, 2018   ISBN 978 1 78622 061 5
Paperback, 144 pages

This rich little book echoes with the distinctive, passionate voice of Thomas Merton, a Cistercian monk and prolific writer, who wrote it shortly before his untimely death. While the book is written particularly with the monastic community in mind, there are several sections which are both incisively helpful for anyone struggling to maintain a contemplative prayer life, and also prophetic for the wider church. The focus is the essence of contemplative prayer and its vital role in the life of anyone wishing to develop an authentic prayer life.

The main theme is not about techniques and methods of prayer but about the nature of prayer, its purpose and its pitfalls. Merton addresses the difficulties commonly encountered in a life of prayer such as dread, anxiety, ennui and excessive individualism as well as the struggles of the dark night. He draws constantly on the writings of numerous teachers of the historical tradition such as St John of the Cross and St Bernard of Clairvaux.

He also situates contemplative prayer firmly in the context of Christian life and worship, speaking of the necessity of a balance between action and contemplation. To quote him with regard to the latter, he speaks of the need *'to restore the ancient, harmonious and organic balance between the two. Both are necessary ... The answer is not liturgy alone, or meditation alone, but a full and many-sided life of prayer in which all things can receive their proper emphasis.'*

Merton writes firmly in the context of living as a Christian in the wider world. His strong call to maintain a contemplative dimension in the Christian community is a salutary, prophetic warning to the church in the twenty-first century when emphasis is sometimes directed more to managerial approaches than a solid life of prayer. There is therefore much to recommend this book both for the individual and for the church at large.

Mollie Robinson

Poetry

Kenneth Steven
LETTING IN THE LIGHT
SPCK, 2016   ISBN 978 0 28107 670 3
Paperback, 64 pages

There is much to be grateful for in this recent collection from Kenneth Steven, Scottish poet who writes poems which uncover the holiness of the natural world. The collection is dedicated to his young daughter, Willow, and we learn that the joy she brings him is accompanied by the sorrow of a marriage that has faltered and failed. However, the collection as a whole brings both tears and peace, as the poet contemplates the brokenness that lets in light.

The waiting is part of the journey. Cold December rain, misty November days, wakeful nights and the unopened rose all contain the possibility of the in-breaking of light. Kenneth's father, no longer alive, is very much a presence here, and readers of previous collections will recognise the reprise of the moment when he shows young Kenneth how to be alert and see the wild geese flying overhead.

Kenneth Steven has a creativity with words and images, and an ability to express truths through nature rather than doctrine, that make him one of our foremost Christian poets. His poems are always surprising, and spring from a deep contemplative outlook. His sharing of his own pain and suffering in this collection serves only to bring him closer to the reader, and makes these poems into small jewels to hold against the cold. Despite the pain, hope is evident throughout, whatever the season:

'Only somewhere on the wandering road at last, this morning, a flock of snowdrops their white cries risen, their voices clear.'

Jill Keegan

Choosing a retreat

The list of retreats in this section offers an enormous choice of venues and programmes. Common to all the retreats listed here are events that:
- are prayerful and rooted in the spirit of the Christian retreat tradition
- are open to everyone, including Christians and non-Christians, those belonging to the Church and those who are not a part of it
- include an element of silence and/or reflection.

The events listed include:
- retreats and days of reflection (quiet days, led meditations, theme retreats etc)
- workshops and courses promoting greater understanding of ourselves and others, and therefore deepening our relationship to God
- dialogues with other traditions
- holidays and house parties sharing Christian community life.

Here are some considerations when selecting a retreat:
- Location – the houses are listed by county and are to be found across the UK, with a small selection overseas (please see regional maps on pages 60–63). Some are more difficult to reach by public transport. Please check with the retreat house for further information.
- Size – the retreat houses range in size from one room to large Christian conference centres. See each individual listing for detailed information.
- Denomination – some retreat houses are affiliated to a particular denomination, others are ecumenical. Use the notes to each listing for detailed information or contact the house direct.
- Programme of events – the majority of the retreat houses have included their programme for 2019. Please note that others may have been added since *Retreats* was published.
- Individual retreats and requirements – many retreat houses welcome individuals to make their own retreat and are able to cater for individual needs. Please contact the particular retreat house for further information.

Retreat List 2019

ORDER OF ENTRIES

Retreat houses are listed alphabetically by county, in this order: England, Scotland, Wales, Ireland and other countries.

RETREAT HOUSES

All of the retreat houses listed are Christian, and welcome people of any denomination. Most, though not all, are members of one of the Retreat Association's constituent member groups (see page 7). For tariffs, bookings and additional information, please contact the individual retreat houses directly.

SEARCH FOR A RETREAT ONLINE

In 2019 a number of retreat centres are making their events available to view on an online calendar, which will be updated during the year, making it easier to browse by date or type of retreat. To view the calendar, please go to **www.retreats.org.uk/retreatdiary.php** The full calendar is only accessible to people with a copy of the handbook, using the following password: **welcome19**

KEY TO ABBREVIATIONS

❏   Advertisement
CARM   Creative Arts Retreat Movement
IGR   Individually guided retreat
MBTI®   Myers-Briggs Typology Indicator®
tba   To be announced
tbc   To be confirmed

QUICK REFERENCE GUIDE
(B, C, Ch, Co, D, E, I, P, Pe, Q, S, V, W, Wf, Y)

To help you find the retreat to suit you, we have included a list of abbreviated letters at the beginning of each entry, where relevant. These indicate any particular type of retreat offered by that retreat house.

B   Beginners' retreat
C   Creative retreat
Ch   Christmas programme
Co   Counselling available
D   Disabled access
E   Easter programme
I   Individually guided retreat (IGR)
P   Welcoming private retreatants
Pe   Pets welcome
Q   Quiet days
S   Spiritual direction available
V   Volunteers welcome
W   Walking retreat/access to walks
Wf   Wifi available
Y   Welcoming youth and/or families

England

The map and list below indicates the retreat house number and location. See index on pages 146–148 for an alphabetical list of houses with page references.

1 **Priory of Our Lady of Peace** Turvey Abbey, Beds
2 **Ascot Priory** Ascot, Berks
3 **Cold Ash Retreat & Conference Centre** Thatcham, Berks
4 **Douai Abbey** Reading, Berks
5 **St Cassian's Centre** Hungerford, Berks
6 **Well, Centre for Spirituality, The** Westbury-on-Trym, Bristol
7 **Bridgettine Convent** Iver Heath, Bucks
8 **Community of the Sisters of the Church** Gerrards Cross, Bucks
9 **Jordans Quaker Centre** Jordans, Bucks
10 **Lee Common Methodist Chapel** Lee Common, Bucks
11 **Prophet's Chamber** Milton Keynes, Bucks
12 **Quiet Garden Movement, The** Beaconsfield, Bucks
13 **St Micheal's Priory** Milton Keynes, Bucks
14 **Bishop Woodford House** Ely, Cambs
15 **St Claret Centre** Buckden, Cambs
16 **Foxhill House & Woodlands** Frodsham, Cheshire
17 **Oblate Retreat Centre** Crewe, Cheshire
18 **Retreat House Chester** Cheshire
19 **Epiphany House, Truro** Cornwall
20 **Fowey Retreat** Fowey, Cornwall
21 **Sclerder Abbey** Looe, Cornwall
22 **Treargel Retreats** Portlooe, Cornwall
23 **Trelowarren Retreat** Helston, Cornwall
24 **Withy Barn Retreat** Helston, Cornwall
25 **Minsteracres Retreat Centre** Consett, Co Durham
26 **St Antony's Priory** Durham
27 **Sanctuary Christian Retreat & Counselling Centre, The** Darlington, Co Durham
28 **Glenthorne Quaker Centre & Guest House** Grasmere, Cumbria
29 **Rydal Hall** Ambleside, Cumbria
30 **Sacred Space Foundation** Mungrisdale, Cumbria
31 **Stillpoints@Elterwater** Ambleside, Cumbria
32 **Swarthmoor Hall** Ulverston, Cumbria
33 **Upper Room, The** Ambleside, Cumbria
34 **Boylestone Methodist Church** Ashbourne, Derbys
35 **Convent of the Holy Name** Oakwood, Derby
36 **Portiuncula, The** Clay Cross, Derbys
37 **Sōzein** Ilkeston, Derbys
38 **Whaley Hall** High Peak, Derbys
39 **Buckfast Abbey** Buckfastleigh, Devon
40 **Lee Abbey** Lynton, Devon
41 **Lowerfield House** Crediton, Devon
42 **Mill House Retreats** Tiverton, Devon
43 **Retreat by the Dart** Totnes, Devon
44 **St Rita's Centre** Honiton, Devon
45 **Society of Mary & Martha, The** Sheldon, Devon
46 **Tinhay Retreats** Lifton, Devon
47 **Greenhouse Christian Centre, The** Poole, Dorset
48 **Hilfield Friary** Dorchester, Dorset

49 **Othona West Dorset** Burton Bradstock, Dorset
50 **Pilsdon Community, The** Bridport, Dorset
51 **Bowling Green, The** Great Dunmow, Essex
52 **Chelmsford Diocesan House of Retreat, Pleshey** Chelmsford, Essex
53 **St Peter's Chapel** Bradwell-on-Sea, Essex
54 **Marist Retreat Centre** Nympsfield, Gloucs
55 **Monastery of Our Lady & St Bernard** Stroud, Gloucs
56 **Community of the Word of God** Homerton, G London
57 **Edgware Abbey St Mary at the Cross** Edgware, Middlesex
58 **Guild of Health & St Raphael** Oakleigh Park, G London
59 **Kairos Centre, The** Roehampton, G London
60 **Mount Street Jesuit Centre** Mayfair, G London
61 **Oasis Days** Holborn, G London
62 **Penlar** Pinner, Middlesex
63 **Royal Foundation of St Katharine, The** Limehouse, G London
64 **St Peter's Bourne** Whetstone, G London
65 **Sisters of St Andrew** Lewisham, G London
66 **Katherine House** Salford
67 **Salford Prayer Guides** G Manchester area
68 **Community of Hopeweavers, The** Southampton, Hants
69 **Grail, The** Winchester, Hants
70 **High House, The** Petersfield, Hants
71 **Sisters of Bethany** Southsea, Hants
72 **Wisdom Centre** Romsey, Hants
73 **Belmont Abbey** Hereford
74 **Knight's Retreat** Eaton Bishop, Herefordshire
75 **Travelling Light** Ross-on-Wye, Herefordshire
76 **Watton at Stone Methodist Church** Hertford, Herts
77 **Haven Hall** Shanklin, Isle of Wight
78 **St Cecilia's Abbey** Ryde, Isle of Wight
79 **Burrswood Health & Wellbeing** Tunbridge Wells, Kent
80 **Friars, The** Aylesford, Kent
81 **Living Well, The** Dover, Kent
82 **Quiet View, The** Canterbury, Kent
83 **Monastery of Our Lady of Hyning** Carnforth, Lancs
84 **Whalley Abbey** Whalley, Lancs
85 **Launde Abbey** East Norton, Leics
86 **Rosmini Centre House of Prayer** Ratcliffe on the Wreake, Leics
87 **Community of St Francis, The** Metheringham, Lincs
88 **Edenham Regional House** Bourne, Lincs
89 **Epworth Old Rectory** Epworth, North Lincs
90 **Cenacle Retreat House** Liverpool
91 **St Joseph's Prayer Centre** Formby, Liverpool
92 **The Shrine of Our Lady of Walsingham** Norfolk

93 **Walsingham Retreats** Walsingham, Norfolk
94 **Wigwam Retreat Centre** Diss, Norfolk
95 **Even Sparrows Retreats** Holy Island, Northumb
96 **Friary of Saint Francis, The** Alnmouth, Northumb
97 **Marygate House** Holy Island, Northumb
98 **Open Gate Retreat House, The** Holy Island, Northumb
99 **St Cuthbert's Centre** Holy Island, Northumb
100 **Shepherds Dene Retreat House** Riding Mill, Northumb
101 **Sacrista Prebend Retreat House** Southwell, Notts
102 **Abbey, The** Sutton Courtenay, Oxon
103 **Carmelite Priory** Boars Hill, Oxford
104 **Charney Manor** Wantage, Oxon
105 **Community of St Mary the Virgin** Wantage, Oxon
106 **Newman's College at Littlemore** Oxford
107 **Ripon College Cuddesdon** Oxon
108 **St Katharine's Parmoor** Henley on Thames, Oxon
109 **St Stephen's House** Oxford
110 **Stanton House** Stanton St John, Oxford
111 **Little Detton** Kidderminster, Shropshire
112 **Ammerdown Centre, The** Radstock, Somerset
113 **House of Prayer** Butleigh, Somerset
114 **St Nicholas Wayfarer's Church** Kilton, Somerset
115 **Reflections/Hermitage** Rugeley, Staffs
116 **St Chad's House** Leek, Staffs
117 **Shallowford House** Stone, Staffs
118 **Clare Priory** Clare, Suffolk
119 **HOME Retreat Centre** Monks Eleigh, Suffolk
120 **Quiet Waters Christian Retreat House** Bungay, Suffolk
121 **Ringsfield Hall** Beccles, Suffolk
122 **Claridge House** Lingfield, Surrey
123 **House of Prayer** East Molesey, Surrey
124 **Ladywell Retreat & Spirituality Centre** Godalming, Surrey
125 **Saint Columba's House** Woking, Surrey
126 **Wychcroft House Retreat & Resource Centre** Redhill, Surrey
127 **Penhurst Retreat Centre** Battle, E Sussex
128 **Chichester Cathedral** Chichester, W Sussex
129 **Monastery of the Holy Trinity** Crawley, W Sussex
130 **Open Cloister, Worth Abbey, The** Crawley, W Sussex
131 **Priory, Storrington, The** W Sussex
132 **TS Resolute/CYE Retreats** Chichester, W Sussex
133 **St Mary's Convent** Handsworth, Birmingham
134 **Woodbrooke** Selly Oak, Birmingham
135 **Sarum College** Salisbury, Wilts
136 **Barnes Close, Community for Reconciliation** Bromsgrove, Worcs
137 **Holland House** Pershore, Worcs

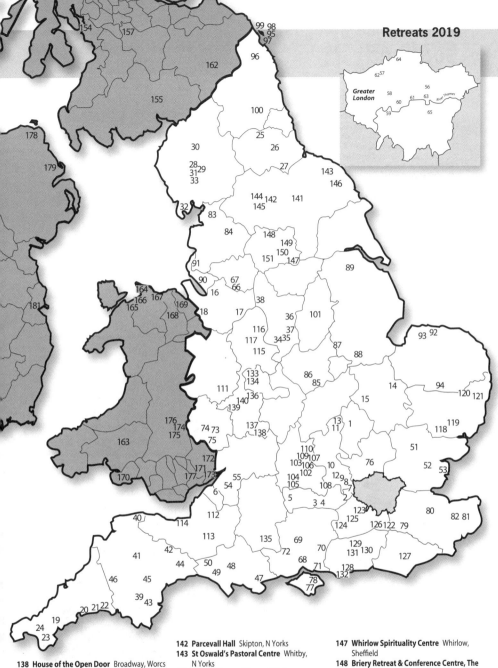

Greater London

138 **House of the Open Door** Broadway, Worcs
139 **The Retreat** Tenbury Wells, Worcs
140 **Society of St Francis, The** Glasshampton, Worcs
141 **Holy Rood House, Centre for Health & Pastoral Care** Thirsk, N Yorks

142 **Parcevall Hall** Skipton, N Yorks
143 **St Oswald's Pastoral Centre** Whitby, N Yorks
144 **Scargill House** Skipton, N Yorks
145 **Summerscales Quiet Garden** Skipton, N Yorks
146 **Wydale Hall & the Emmaus Centre** Scarborough, N Yorks

147 **Whirlow Spirituality Centre** Whirlow, Sheffield
148 **Briery Retreat & Conference Centre, The** Ilkley, W Yorks
149 **Hinsley Hall** Leeds
150 **House of the Resurrection** Mirfield, W Yorks
151 **Westwood Christian Centre** Huddersfield, W Yorks

Scotland

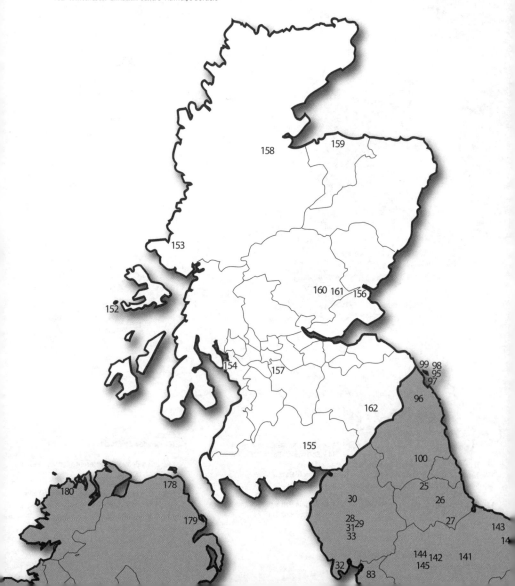

Wales

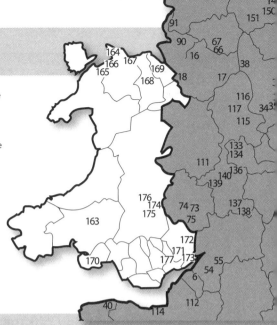

163 **Bryndolau & Kites' Nest Cottage** Llandeilo, Carmarthenshire
164 **Loreto Centre** Llandudno, Conwy
165 **Noddfa Spirituality Centre** Penmaenmawr, Conwy
166 **Ruach Retreat** Dwygyfylchi, Conwy
167 **St Augustine's Priory, House of Prayer** Conwy
168 **St Beuno's Jesuit Spirituality Centre** St Asaph, Denbighshire
169 **Gladstone's Library** Hawarden, Flintshire
170 **Nicholaston House Christian Retreat & Conference Centre**
    Penmaen, Gower, Swansea
171 **Lansôr Mill** Caerleon, Newport
172 **Society of the Sacred Cross, The** Lydart, Monmouthshire
173 **Tabernacle United Reformed Church** Newport, Gwent
174 **Coleg Trefeca** Talgarth, Brecon, Powys
175 **Llangasty Retreat House** Brecon, Powys
176 **Llannerchwen (Society of the Sacred Heart)** Brecon, Powys
177 **Ty Croeso Centre** Cwmbran, Torfaen

Ireland

178 **Corrymeela** Ballycastle, Co Antrim
179 **Drumalis Retreat & Conference Centre** Larne,
    Co Antrim
180 **Ards Friary Retreat & Conference Centre**
    Creeslough, Co Donegal
181 **Manresa Jesuit Centre of Spirituality**
    Dollymount, Dublin
182 **Hermitage, The** Lower Newcastle, Galway
183 **Jesuit Centre of Spirituality & Culture** Galway
184 **Ardfert Retreat Centre** Ardfert, Co Kerry

Retreat Association
Gift Token Scheme

Give the gift of a retreat!

A Retreat Association gift token could be exactly what you are looking for!

These tokens, available in £5, £10 and £20 units, can be used to pay for part or all of a quiet day or retreat* and are supplied in an attractive card with envelope.

Ascot Priory

Bield at Blackruthven

Bishop Woodford House

Boylestone Methodist Church

Bryndolau & Kites' Nest Cottage

Chelmsford Diocesan House of Retreat, Pleshey

Clare Priory

The Coach House Kilmuir Trust

College of The Holy Spirit

Community of St Mary the Virgin

Edenham Regional House

Greenhouse Christian Centre

Hilfield Friary

Holland House

Holy Rood House

Kairos Centre

Katherine House

Priory of Our Lady of Peace

The Priory, Storrington

Royal Foundation of St Katharine

St Beuno's Jesuit Spirituality Centre

St Nicholas Wayfarer's Church

Sclerder Abbey

Shallowford House

Shepherds Dene

Sisters of Bethany

Society of Mary & Martha

Swarthmoor Hall

Te Deum

Tinhay Retreats

Treargel Retreats

TS Resolute/CYE Retreats

Whitchester Christian Centre

*This excludes payment for any Retreat Association quiet day or training day. The cost of retreats and quiet days will vary. Please contact participating retreat houses for further details.

For more information please go to www.retreats.org.uk/gift-tokens.php or contact the Retreat Association on: info@retreats.org.uk, 01494 569056.

ENGLAND

BEDFORDSHIRE

1 Priory of Our Lady of Peace

Turvey Abbey, Turvey, Bedfordshire
MK43 8DE   01234 881432
                                    fax 01234 882300
                      email info@turveyabbey.org.uk
C, D, P   *website* www.turveyabbey.org.uk

Rooms 3 single, 1 single *en suite*, 1 twin *en suite*.
Notes We are a community of nuns living according to
the Rule of St Benedict. We belong to the Vita et Pax (Life
and Peace) Foundation, whose main charisms are liturgy
and ecumenism. By offering hospitality we hope to share
the riches of our Christian monastic heritage. By
developing an awareness of the presence of God in daily
life, we seek in our work and prayer to radiate God's life
and peace to all who visit our monastery. Not only
Christians but people of every faith and spiritual tradition,
all who 'truly seek God' (Rule of St Benedict), are warmly
welcome to visit and to join us in prayer. Private guests
and residential groups. Both resident and non-resident
events. Private retreats.
Contact The Retreat Secretary.
Information about Icon painting courses and other events
are posted on our website. Unless otherwise stated, events
are led by the Turvey Nuns.

BERKSHIRE

2 Ascot Priory

Priory Road, Ascot, Berkshire
SL5 8RT   01344 882067
                      email mclarencook@btinternet.com
B, D, E, I, P, Q, S, Wf   *website* www.ascotpriory.org

Rooms 8 *en suite* rooms. 20 rooms with shared facilities.
Notes A retreat house in the Anglo-Catholic tradition, but
all are welcome. We can provide 2 large meeting rooms, a
chapel, library, dining room (full catering is available). We
offer conducted retreats for groups or individuals. Parish
groups are welcome for PCC awaydays, Alpha weekends or
retreats. A self-contained flat is available for long or short
stays. Clergy in full-time ministry can be offered a bursary.
Day conferences can also be catered for and the acoustics
of the church make it a great place for concerts or
recording.
Contact The Warden, Fr Paul McLaren-Cook.

YOUR FIRST RETREAT?

Choosing a retreat – see page 58

---

3 Cold Ash Retreat and Conference Centre

The Ridge, Cold Ash, Thatcham, Berkshire
RG18 9HU   01635 865353
                      email coldashcentre@hotmail.co.uk
B, C, I, P, S, V, W, Wf   *website* www.coldashcentre.org

Rooms In the main building there are 12 standard rooms,
1 standard with 2 beds, 8 studio rooms, 1 plus dormitories:
large (1–3 adults/14 youth); normal (1–2 adults/4 youths);
small (1–2 adults/4 youths). Cold Ash Centre is also an ideal
location for conferences with natural light function and 5
breakout rooms. We have spacious facilities to
accommodate conferences for up to 40 people. As part of
this we can offer hearty home-cooked buffets or sit-down
meals in our bright and airy dining room. The conference
room has projector, extra-large TV screen, complimentary
Wifi connection and loop sound system.
Notes Centred in our relationship with God as a
community of Franciscan sisters (Franciscan Missionaries of
Mary), we desire to offer to all who come to us a place of
welcome where they may discover a loving God in their
lives and in the beauty of creation. Cold Ash Centre is an
ideal venue for workshops and conferences, parish groups,
schools, confirmation preparation, adult retreats, quiet
days. We also offer spiritual direction by appointment.
Contact The Team. Please take a look at our website and
send us an enquiry email or contact us by phone.
Confirmation group retreats, schools retreats, silent and
Individually Guided Retreats (IGRs) throughout the year by
arrangement.
Seeking wholeness In response to this gift and task, we
offer a shortened version of the seven weeks seeking
wholeness programme. Directed by Sr Margaret Taylor
FMM & guest speakers.
      February
11–14 Seeking wholeness module 2. How our personality
      is formed early in life and how we are today.
      March
14–17 Seeking wholeness module 3. Reuniting spirituality
      and sexuality (owning the sacredness of our
      sexuality).
      April
4–7   Seeking wholeness module 4. Healing the
      wounded often traumatised self. Transitions in life.
      May
2–7   Seeking wholeness module 5. Gospel leadership.

4 Douai Abbey

Woolhampton, Reading, Berkshire RG7 5TQ
                  0118 971 5310 / 0118 971 5399
                      email gabriel@douaiabbey.org.uk
B, C, I, P, Q, W, Wf, Y   *website* www.douaiabbey.org.uk

Rooms 1 family room (double and 2 singles), 5 double,
3 twin, 13 single. Lift for disabled access to guest rooms. All
rooms *en suite*.
Notes Benedictine monastery (Roman Catholic) with daily
divine office and Mass. ❏ *p 3*

❱ *p. 67*

archway

A network of encouragement, support, information, sharing and prayer

Archway is an organisation of those who have responsibility for running Christian Retreat and Conference Houses and aims to support members in their work, provide appropriate information wherever possible and facilitate the work of Retreat Houses into the structure of the church

President: The Rt Revd Alison White
Chairperson: Ron Blackmore, Bishop Woodford House
Administrator: Jeff Witts

admin@archwaywardens.org.uk
www.archwaywardens.org.uk
or find us on Facebook & Twitter

CREATIVE ARTS RETREAT MOVEMENT

Join us at a CARM Retreat: held in selected Houses in Britain and overseas; led by chaplain and tutor; open to beginners and the more experienced; includes worship and silence; ecumenical.

Painting Poetry
Calligraphy Photography
Music in Worship Embroidery
Creative Writing

www.carmretreats.org or on
Facebook or Twitter
Tel: 024 7786 3014

Registered Charity No. 1149636

Contact Fr Gabriel Wilson OSB for information about retreats and courses, and Fr Finbar Kealy for guest house and retreat bookings (guestmaster@douaiabbey.org.uk).
February
15–17 Weekend course. The golden age of Old Testament prophecy. Br Simon Hill OSB
March
8–10 Start of Lent silent group retreat for those who wish to make a silent retreat with the support of others.
22–24 Weekend course. Some English medieval mystics in their context. Dr Santha Bhattacharji
April
18–21 Easter Triduum retreat. Love's confession, love's renewal. Euan Tait
May
10–12 Weekend retreat. From addiction to grace (the 12-Step path through the Psalms). Fr David Barrett
June
7–9 Weekend retreat. Finding God through your smartphone camera. Steve Radley
14–16 Monastic experience weekend for men 18–40 yrs interested in Douai Abbey's Alongsider programme. Gabriel Wilson OSB & Fr Alban Hood OSB
20–23 Lectio divina retreat. Gervase Holdaway OSB
July
5–7 Weekend retreat. Spirituality of the heart. Fr Francis Preston & Fr Hugh Preston
19–21 Weekend course. How to write a gospel. John Huntriss
26–28 Weekend retreat. Mercy's laughter (with music from *The Marriage of Figaro*). Euan Tait
September
20–22 Christian Mindfulness Forum weekend. Martin Zetter & Br Christopher Greener OSB
27–29 Weekend retreat. To God through music. Gervase Holdaway OSB
October
4–6 Weekend retreat. Visions of redemption. Br Christopher Greener OSB & Nick Gurr
18–20 Monastic experience weekend. Fr Gabriel Wilson OSB & Fr Alban Hood OSB
November
8–10 Weekend retreat. Living the Beatitudes. Sr Tamsin Geach OP
15–17 Weekend course. Church History Part III (The Reformation). Abbot Geoffrey Scott OSB
22–24 Weekend course. The Mayfly Mass (The Lost Liturgy of Vat II). Fr Hugh Somerville Knapman OSB
November–December
29–1 Start of Advent weekend retreat. Fr Alban Hood OSB
December
10–13 Lectio divina retreat. Gervase Holdaway OSB

LOOKING FOR A SPIRITUAL DIRECTOR?
The Retreat Association can help you find one.
Call 01494 569056, email info@retreats.org.uk
or visit our website www.retreats.org.uk

---

5 St Cassian's Centre

Wallingtons Road, Kintbury, Hungerford, Berkshire RG17 9SR　　　01488 658267
fax 01488 657292
email kintbury@aol.com
C, Ch, E, P, W, Y　　*website* www.thekintburyexperience.com

Rooms 5 single, 23 double, 6 triple.
Notes Run by the De La Salle Brothers, St Cassian's caters mainly for school groups in years 10, 11 and sixth form. There are also family weekends and Advent and Lent retreats for adults. 'Yes' weeks are held in July for young people 16+. Other residential groups can be accommodated, with or without centre input, depending on availability. Day groups can also be accommodated throughout the year, either with or without centre input. We also have conference facilities for use by residential and non-residential groups. We do not have facilities for individual retreats other than those mentioned. Please contact us or check the website for more information.
Contact Kevin Humphrey.

BRISTOL

6 The Well, Centre for Spirituality, at Elsie Briggs House

38 Church Road, Westbury-on-Trym, Bristol BS9 3EQ　　　0117 950 7242
email warden@thewellcentreforspirituality.org.uk
C, P, Q, V, Wf　　*website* www.thewellcentreforspirituality.org.uk

Rooms 2 meeting rooms, each for individuals and groups of up to 20 people, 1 on the ground floor and 1 on the first floor. 2 small, single bedrooms. Self-catering kitchen.
Notes We welcome everyone from wherever they come to contemplative spirituality in a medieval setting. Ecumenical, open-minded and using imaginative spiritual practices.
Open House visit the House and receive a warm welcome with tea and chat, 3–5pm every Tuesday, followed by silent meditation hour.
Julian Group 2–3pm, 1st and 3rd Tuesday of month.
Centering Prayer Group 7.15–8.45pm every Wednesday. Beginners are encouraged to come on the 1st Wednesday of the month.
WCCM Christian Meditation 8–9pm every Thursday.
Taizé Group 7.45–9pm, 1st Friday of month.
Reading Group 7.30–9pm, 1st Wednesday of month.
Film Night with shared supper 7pm last Wednesday of month.
Plus a regular programme of events. For a programme or for an individual or group wanting to use our facilities, please contact the Warden. We are members of the Quiet Garden Movement and encourage a green outlook. We are members of the Small Pilgrim Places Network, encouraging people to find space and silence.
Contact Frances Henley Lock, Warden.

Retreat Association
Stop! In the name of God

12–14 July 2019

Since 1993 the Retreat Association has encouraged setting aside a day or weekend in the summer to stop and take some time out.

The vision behind the event is to encourage as many people as possible, in whatever ways they can, to organise or take part in some time of reflection. A quiet day or retreat can be a welcome oasis in the midst of a busy routine and a place where we can become better aware of the presence of God in our lives.

A number of retreat centres are organising events during the weekend including:

Venue	House No	Date	Event type
Boylestone Methodist Church	34	14	Sunday worship 10am
Buckfast Abbey	39	12–14	Weekend retreat
Community of the Sisters of the Church	8	12–14	Circle dance & prayer
Convent of the Holy Name	35	13	Poetry quiet day
The Greenhouse Christian Centre	47	12–14	Silent retreat
Sisters of Bethany	71	13	Open quiet day
Whaley Hall	38	12–14	House & church available for pilgrims

Please contact the retreat centre directly for further information.

If you would like organise an event in your local area please let us know so that we can add your event to our online programme. Please see our website **www.retreats.org.uk** for a full list of events.

To order a **Quiet Day Pack** or **Introducing Retreats & Prayer Pack** to help you organise the day please see pages 76 and 127.

English Retreats in Norway

2019 IGRs:
- 28 Jan – 3 Feb
- 12 – 18 August
- 8 – 11 April
- 5 – 14 September
- 13 – 22 May
- 2 – 7 December

5 – 8 May	Advanced Enneagram Workshop: Andreas Ebert
9 – 12 May	Advanced Enneagram Workshop – Healing the family tree: Andreas Ebert

All the above retreats are available in English. Lia Gard is a delightful retreat house with modern facilities, set in woodland with lake and mountains. Train from Oslo Gardermoen airport to Koppang.

Enquiries to: **Lia Gard, Post Box 106, 2481 Koppang, Norway** • Tel: 00 47 62 466500 Email: retreat@liagard.no • www.liagard.no

LIA GÅRD

BUCKINGHAMSHIRE

7 Bridgettine Convent

**Fulmer Common Road, Iver Heath,
Buckinghamshire SL0 0NR**   01753 663520
email bridgettineiver@icloud.com
Ch, D, E, P, Q, W, Wf *website* www.bridgettineguesthouse.co.uk

Rooms 5 twin, 1 single, 1 disabled access with single sofa bed, 3 family (on 2 floors). All rooms *en suite*.
Notes The Bridgettine Guesthouse, newly renovated, is located in the beautiful countryside of Buckinghamshire and is a pretty construction in Tudor style close to the village of Iver Heath. TV and Wifi. The house has a chapel, conference room, dining room, large garden and fruit orchard.
Contact Mother Superior.

8 Community of the Sisters of the Church

**St Michael's Convent, Vicarage Way, Gerrards
Cross, Buckinghamshire SL9 8AT**
0330 120 0631 Hospitality / 0330 120 0630 Convent
email hospitality@sistersofthechurch.org.uk
website www.sistersofthechurch.org/retreats
B, C, Ch, Co, D, E, I, P, Q, S, V, W, Wf

Rooms 3 single (*en suite* shower/WC, lift accessible), 4 single (lift accessible), 1 twin (lift accessible), 1 double (*en suite* bath/shower/WC, second floor not accessible by lift), 1 twin (second floor not accessible by lift), 2 single (second floor not accessible by lift). 2 meeting rooms (ground floor), 3 one-to-one rooms (lift accessible), library (lift accessible), creativity room (lift accessible), oratory (second floor not accessible by lift), chapel (ground floor).
Notes Our new Convent and Retreat House at Gerrards Cross, with its 2-acre mature garden, is now open to guests – offering space in which to rest and recharge the spirit. (St Michael's Convent, Ham Common is now closed.) Private retreats may be booked by the day or residentially, for individuals or small groups (up to 12 residentially or around 20 by the day). Individual retreatants are allocated a bedroom that is simply but comfortably furnished. Small kitchenettes are stocked for breakfast and 'tea times'. Day guests may also choose to have a midday meal with us. Further information is available on our website.
Contact Hospitality Team. ❏ *p 82*

March
16 Quiet day. 'Love bade me welcome.' Reflecting on George Herbert's poem, his life and poetry as a way into prayer. Sr Hilda Mary CSC
29–31 Introduction to Myers Briggs Type Indicator (MBTI®). Discover and explore your personality type, your unique gifts and how you interact with others. Anne East & Sr Catherine CSC
April
14–21 Liturgical journey through Holy Week and Easter with the Sisters.
May
3–5 Vocations weekend. Might God be calling you to the religious life? Consider this question through

discussion, prayer and participation in our way of life. Sr Anita CSC
June
7–9 First-time retreat. A weekend of reflection and silence suitable for those who have not been on retreat before. Sr Catherine CSC
July
12–14 Moving into stillness: circle dance – a way into prayer. Sue King
16–20 Garden days. Come and enjoy working in our garden, helping us to prepare for our NGS 'Yellow Book' Open Garden day. Free board and lodging!
July–August
27–3 6-day IGR. Scripture-based residential silent retreat, with one-to-one guidance. Sr Aileen CSC
October
19 Quiet day. The woman at the well. Jesus' encounter with the Samaritan woman, getting in touch with our own thirsts and hearing Jesus say 'Give me a drink'. Sr Hilda Mary CSC
November
22–24 Music and spirituality. Comparing the spiritual experience involving music within Christianity with other faiths and spirituality, through music. No musical skills necessary. Rev Dr June Boyce-Tillman, MBE
December
24–27 Christmas with the Community of the Sisters of the Church.

9 Jordans Quaker Centre

**Welders Lane, Jordans, Buckinghamshire
HP9 2SN**   01494 876594
email office@jordansquakercentre.org
Co, D, P, Q, Wf   *website* www.jordansquakercentre.org

Non-residential.
Rooms An ideal venue for groups wishing to run their own day retreats, for solo day retreatants and for awaydays for gatherings and small conferences. We offer 2 large and 2 smaller rooms. The Meeting House holds up to 100, the Penn Room (with small kitchen attached) takes 40 lecture-style, or 24 in a comfortable circle; our smaller rooms suitable for groups of 4–12 people. Catering can be arranged. Wheelchair access and hearing loop in main rooms. Conference equipment, broadband and Wifi access.
Notes Jordans Quaker Meeting House, built in 1688, is situated in a tranquil and secluded spot near Beaconsfield, Buckinghamshire. The surrounding burial grounds and gardens are ideal for reflective walking and time in nature. The Meeting House, described by Simon Jenkins as 'the Quaker Westminster Abbey', is striking for its plain and tranquil atmosphere. Yet it is just 5 mins by car from M40/J2 and M25/J16 is 10 mins away. Fast rail link from Marylebone or Birmingham to Seer Green and Jordans, half a mile from the Meeting House (with taxis available at the station). On-site parking for up to 20 cars. Basic dormitory accommodation is available at Jordans Youth Hostel (www.yha.org) next door. List of local B&Bs can be supplied. We also run our own programme of day retreats: see our website for details or email us.
Contact The Manager.

69

Buckfast Abbey

Spiritual vacations at Buckfast Abbey

The Monastery Guestquarters

When you stay in the Monastery Guestquarters, you can follow the age-old rhythm of life lived according to the Rule of St Benedict, with its emphasis on balance, quietness and "moderation in all things", under the care of the Monastery Guestmaster.

Southgate

Southgate was established to make the Monastery Guestquarters available to women and couples. Southgate has its own chapel, lounge/dining room and grounds; providing for the needs of those following personal retreats or simply wishing to experience a change from their normal routine.

Some en-suite rooms available.

Group and family stays at Buckfast Abbey

Grangehurst House
15 rooms 50 people

Avila House
4 rooms 7 people

Spacious lawn for use by all groups

For bookings and further information please contact.....
Monastery: Br Daniel, 01364 645622 or brdaniel@buckfast.org.uk
Southgate: Br Stephen, 01364 645521 or brstephen@buckfast.org.uk
Groups: Mr Geoff Pring, 01364 645532 or warden@buckfast.org.uk
www.buckfast.org.uk

10 Lee Common Methodist Chapel

Oxford Street, Lee Common, Buckinghamshire
HP16 9JP   01494 580016
P, W   email susan.evans100@ntlworld.com

Non-residential.

Rooms Available for day groups of up to 30 people to run their own retreats or quiet days. In addition to the chapel, which can be used as the main meeting room, there are 2 other rooms and a small, self-catering kitchen.

Notes The Methodist chapel is situated in the lovely, peaceful setting of Lee Common village, in the beautiful Buckinghamshire countryside. A quiet, private garden surrounds the chapel. Nearby there are several short woodland and country walks for those wishing to stretch their legs.

Contact Susan Evans.

11 Prophet's Chamber

Paddock House, 6 Linford Lane, Willen, Milton
Keynes, Buckinghamshire MK15 9DL
                           01908 397267 / 07889 654881
P, Wf   email hazel.s35@talktalk.net

Rooms A converted attic adjoining Paddock House, day or residential use for 1 person with own toilet and washbasin, access to shower in adjacent house, fridge, microwave and kettle. Guests may be self-catering and a main meal can be provided with prior arrangement.

Notes The Prophet's Chamber is a welcoming space for anyone wishing to spend time in quiet reflection. The room overlooks and has access to a garden and is a few minutes' walk from Willen Lakes with its many walkways and open-air labyrinth. It is also neighbour to St Michael's Priory, an Anglican religious order where guests are welcome to join in with the daily Eucharist and the fourfold office if they wish.

Contact Sister Hazel.

12 The Quiet Garden Movement

Copse End, Copse Lane, Jordans, Beaconsfield,
Buckinghamshire HP9 2TA   01494 578909
                            email info@quietgarden.org
P, Q   website www.quietgarden.org

Non-residential.

Notes Sharing outdoor space for the inner journey – The Quiet Garden Movement nurtures the sharing of gardens and outdoor space for prayer, contemplation, rest and inspiration. Quiet Gardens are in a variety of settings, such as private homes, churches, retreat centres, schools and hospitals. There are over 300 Quiet Gardens in the UK and around the world which offer quiet days and space for individual quiet time. To find a Quiet Garden near you, and a list of quiet days and events, visit our website or contact us.

Contact Mary-Anne Hall.

May
11 Quiet Garden annual gathering in Merseyside. See our website for details and booking.

13 St Michael's Priory

Newport Road, Willen, Milton Keynes,
Buckinghamshire MK15 9AA   01908 242190
                         email bookings@stmichaelspriory.org.uk
D, E, I, P, Q, S, V, Wf, Y   website www.stmichaelspriory.org.uk

Rooms 5 single and 1 double room, shared shower and toilet. 2 en suite ground-floor rooms. Twin rooms available on request.

Notes An Anglican religious community on the edge of Milton Keynes, set in 3 acres of ground and close to Willen Lake and the 17th-century church of St Mary Magdalene. Daily offices and Eucharists, open to all, are celebrated by the religious community. Wednesday and Friday Eucharists at 12.15pm are followed by lunch, to which all are welcome. The Priory offers quiet days and study days on a diverse range of topics. The library is also a much-loved and well-used resource and the Thomas Merton Archive is now held at the Priory. Both are open to the public. The library arranges lectures and conversations with authors. Working retreats are available by arrangement.

Contact email address above.

CAMBRIDGESHIRE

14 Bishop Woodford House

Retreat & Conference Centre,
Barton Road, Ely, Cambridgeshire CB7 4DX
                                    01353 663039
                         email office@bishopwoodfordhouse.com
B, C, D, P, Q, Wf   website www.bishopwoodfordhouse.com

Rooms 27 rooms in total, comprising 10 single en suite. (2 on ground floor), 4 twin en suite (2 on ground floor) and 13 single rooms.

Notes In addition, we have 2 large meeting rooms for 20 and 45 people, 1 small meeting room for 6 people and numerous smaller rooms for one-to-ones or for 2–4 people. The chapel holds 70 and the dining room 50. We welcome up to 50 people for day events and meetings. The beautiful and interesting garden offers a number of quiet spaces and being close to the centre of Ely we are able to offer a retreat within close proximity of good road and rail links and the city centre.

Contact Tim Shorey and Ron Blackmore.

Days of Reflection and Quiet Days A monthly opportunity to have some space contemplating our own leader's subject. Please stay over before and/or after the day to create a mini retreat.

CARM Retreats Art-based week-long residential retreats.

September
6 Day of Reflection with Retreat Association Icon.

**FOR A LIST OF LEAFLETS ON PRAYER,
RETREATS AND SPIRITUAL DIRECTION
SEE OUR WEBSITE**

www.retreats.org.uk/leaflets.php

Find Peace and Rest at Umbrian Retreats in 2019

5th to 12th June *Listen to your life* – Rev Dave Tomlinson, Enneagram teacher, spiritual director and author leads this holiday retreat that aims to help participants develop a comprehensive working knowledge of the Enneagram.

19th to 26th June *Ponder with Piero* led by Rev Nicholas Gandy, experienced spiritual director, enthusiastic cook and lover of good wine. With Nicholas a small group will explore 'The Piero della Francesca Trail' and enjoy times of spiritual reflection.

4th to 11th September *Being Human, Being Spiritual – the art of letting go of non-essentials and making room for the essential you!* led by David McCormick, life coach and NLP practitioner. Specialising in creating life-balance & mindset change, he also offers spiritual direction.

18th to 25th September *A Pilgrimage with St Francis of Assisi* led by Rev Canon Andrew Hawes, experienced pilgrimage / retreat leader and spiritual director.

Umbrian Retreats is also available to rent for holidays and church retreats
www.umbrianretreats.com   florence.morton1@btinternet.com   01733 552535 / 07702 341041

You are guaranteed a warm welcome at St Rita's Retreat & Conference Centre, which is set in the beautiful vale of Honiton, famous for its market and lace.

East Devon Retreat and Conference Centre Facilities

With its excellent accommodation St Rita's Retreat & Conference Centre is ideal for residential gatherings, community chapters and assemblies, small group conferences, parish and group retreats, workshops and prayer days.

Visit our web site

www.stritascentre.org.uk

Tel: 01404 42635 • stritas@btinternet.com

Find us on Facebook

The House of Retreat, Pleshey

A quiet place in the heart of Essex where through encounter with God we are inspired to holy living. An ideal setting for retreat, prayer and refreshment for groups and individuals.

**Details from: The Manager,
The House of Retreat, The Street,
Pleshey, Essex. CM3 1HA**

Tel: 01245 237251
Email: retreathouse@chelmsford.anglican.org

www.retreathousepleshey.com

15 St Claret Centre

The Towers, High Street, Buckden, St Neots,
Cambridgeshire PE19 5TA   01480 810344
email claret_centre@claret.org.uk
Ch, E, D, P, Q, W, Wf, Y   *website* www.buckden-towers.org.uk

Rooms 2 single, 10 twin and 3 treble in Victorian house
with 3 conference rooms. 4 self-catering apartments in
15th-century Gatehouse. 40 beds in dormitory
accommodation for young people and 4 turret rooms for
leaders in 15th-century Tower. All set in 15 acres of
pleasant parkland. Events self-catered or full catering can
be provided.
Notes Space offered for groups to run their own courses.
Contact Office administrator for more information.

CHESHIRE

16 Foxhill House and Woodlands

Tarvin Road, Frodsham, Cheshire WA6 6XB
01928 733777
email foxhill@chester.anglican.org
B, C, D, I, P, Q, S, W, Wf, Y   *website* www.foxhillchester.co.uk

Rooms 17 single *en suite*, 2 twin *en suite*, 1 single, 2 twin.
Halfpenny Suite (double bedroom, lounge, kitchenette and
bathroom).
Notes Foxhill is the Diocese of Chester centre for prayer,
study and mission. We are set within 70 acres of beautiful
Cheshire woodland, and offer a programme of retreats,
study days and training. As Jesus promises to be a well of
life to all who come to Him, our commitment is to be a
place of refreshment, restoration and renewal for all who
visit us. Whether you come on your own or with others,
whether you are a frequent visitor or coming for the first
time, whether you are joining one of our events or using
our facilities for your own programme, we look forward to
welcoming you to Foxhill.
By Still Waters A series of reflections on the Psalms. Every
second Monday of the month 9.30am-4pm. For more
information and bookings please visit our website.
Tools to Pray Every first Saturday of the month except
January, with an extended time over the August weekend.
Led by the Foxhill Prayer Team.
Contact Rev Jonathon Green, Director.

March
11–13 Lent retreat.
April
15–17 Holy Week. Chris Duffett
April–May
29–3 Icon painting retreat. Christopher Perrins
May
29–31 Prayer retreat. Thy Kingdom Come Team
August
2–4 Tools to Pray Summer School. Foxhill Prayer Team
17–24 Foxhill holiday week. Hosted by the Friends of
Foxhill
September
16–18 Picking up the pieces. Wes Sutton

September–October
30–3 Painting and prayer. Maggie and Keith Hilditch
November
8–10 Taizé weekend.
25–28 IGR. Diocesan Spirituality Team
November–December
29–1 Advent retreat.

17 Oblate Retreat Centre

Wistaston Hall, 89 Broughton Lane, Crewe,
Cheshire CW2 8JS   01270 568653
email director@oblateretreatcentre.org.uk
C, D, E, I, P, Q, S Wf   *website* www.orc-crewe.org

Rooms 25 rooms (21 *en suite*), 3 ground-floor rooms
adapted for use by people with reduced mobility.
2 conference rooms.
Notes Wistaston Hall is set in 5 acres of grounds, a 25-min
walk from Crewe railway station. It is a modern, well-
equipped facility. As well as running our own events, we
welcome groups for retreats, workshops and courses. Our
mission is to promote adult faith formation and justice,
peace and integrity of creation.
Contact Brian Maher OMI.
All events listed are run by the Oblate Retreat Team unless
otherwise stated.

January
26 Reflection day (1).
February–March
25–1 3-day IGR.
March
9 Reflection day (2).
19 Lenten day retreat.
April
12–14 Weekend Lenten retreat.
14–21 Holy Week IGR.
18–21 Triduum retreat.
May
11 Reflection day (3).
July
8–12 Art and prayer workshop. Shelia Gosney RJM
13 Discovering the mystics through contemplative
creativity. Julian of Norwich. Shelia Gosney RJM &
Joan Brown SND
13–22 8-day IGR.
August
21–28 6-day IGR.
21–30 8-day IGR.
September
13–20 6-day preached retreat.
28 Reflection day (4).
October
26 Reflection day (5).
November
16 Reflection day (6).
December
4 Advent day retreat.
9–11 Advent retreat.
13–15 Weekend Advent retreat.

18 Retreat House Chester

9 Abbey Square, Chester, Cheshire CH1 2HU
07514 357427
email admin@retreathousechester.co.uk
B, C, I, Q, S, V, W   *website* www.retreathousechester.co.uk

Non-residential.
Notes Retreat House Chester offers the benefits of retreat in the city. Non-denominational and rooted gently and deeply in Christian spiritual tradition, we offer non-residential ways of retreating in daily life. Our programme runs in various locations in the city, including the Cathedral, while we also develop our own retreat space, which we hope will be fully ready at some point in 2019: please see our website or contact us for full details.
Contact Clare Black. Please note that the above address is primarily a postal address for contact purposes.

CORNWALL

19 Epiphany House, Truro

Kenwyn, Church Road, Truro, Cornwall TR1 3DR
01872 272249
email info@epiphanyhouse.co.uk
B, C, D, I, P, Q, S, V, W, Wf   *website* www.epiphanyhouse.co.uk

Rooms Up to 13 rooms are available: 8 single (3 with ground-floor access), 3 double and 2 twin.
Notes An ecumenical retreat venue set in a comfortable historic house in beautiful grounds adjoining open countryside yet within walking distance of central Truro and the Cathedral. We offer facilities for groups or for individuals seeking quiet space for prayer, reflection or study. We have become a centre for spiritual accompaniment and direction. Epiphany House offers a wide range of retreats, quiet days, study days and workshops. Please visit our website for details of our current programme which is updated throughout the year.
Contact Janette Mullett, Director.

20 Fowey Retreat

17 Lankelly Lane, Fowey, Cornwall PL23 1HN
01208 871517
email saralow@btconnect.com
B, I, P, Q, S, Wf   *website* www.foweyretreat.co.uk

Rooms 6 bedrooms (3 on ground floor): 2 singles, 3 twin, 1 double, 3 bath/shower, family kitchen, dining room, sitting room, conservatory, chapel. Large private garden with sea views.
Notes Beautiful, peaceful, secluded setting above historic harbour town. Near beaches and coastal path walks. Ideal for individuals, small prayer groups, cell groups, study days, priests and religious, holidays. Outside peak holiday season we are usually able to offer these courses at a time that would suit your group. Retreats are silent and traditional. Clergy, religious and missionaries welcome for private retreats, respite, cell groups and study days. There is no set programme of teaching retreats. Please contact us to discuss your needs. Individuals and small groups welcome.
Contact Fr Robbie Low.

21 Sclerder Abbey

Sclerder Lane, Nr Looe, Cornwall PL13 2JD
01503 272238
email sclerder@chemin-neuf.org
B, C, D, I, P, Q, S, V, W, Wf, Y   *website* www.chemin-neuf.org.uk

Rooms 30 rooms accommodating 47 people.
Notes The Chemin Neuf Community is an international Roman Catholic community with an ecumenical vocation and with members from many different Christian denominations. It was founded in France in 1973 and stems from the charismatic renewal and Ignatian spirituality. The community offers a friendly welcome at Sclerder in the beautiful Cornish countryside with sea views. IGRs on request according to availability. Unless specified otherwise, all retreats are led by members of Chemin Neuf. The house with its chapel is also available for day events accommodating up to 80 people.
Contact Sr Jacqueline.

February
16–23 Spiritual Exercises of St Ignatius. Guided silent retreat to know Christ more intimately in order to love and serve him better and to recognise God's call.
27 Quiet day. Silent time with guided prayer. Accompaniment available if required.
April
24 Quiet day (see 27 February).
May
4–10 Pray and fast. A 6-day journey to seek and find the presence of God through fasting, silence and prayer. Applicants will need previous experience of a silent retreat.
May–June
25–1 Spiritual Exercises retreat (see 16–23 February).
June
5 Quiet day (see 27 February).
July–August
28–3 CANA week for couples and children. A week-long retreat for couples while their children follow their own programme.
October
tbc Quiet day (see 27 February).
tbc Siloam cycle. First of three 4-day retreats (subsequent sessions in February and April 2020). An inner healing and reconciliation programme which includes spiritual accompaniment throughout the year. Applicants need previous experience of a silent retreat and may be interviewed.

22 Treargel Retreats

The Barn, Hendersick Farm, Portlooe, Cornwall PL13 2HZ   01503 598932 / 07711 924211
email info@treargel.com
B, Ch, I, P, Q, S, Wf   *website* www.treargel.com

Rooms
Piggery 1 double *en suite*, lounge, dining room, kitchen.
Byre 1 double, 1 twin, bathroom, lounge/diner /kitchen.

▶ *p. 77*

Hermitage 1 single, 1 compost toilet, no running water or electricity.
Notes Treargel is a Cornish home of retreat. Located in 5 acres of farmland with sea views and access to surrounding area of outstanding natural beauty. 3 different self-contained units with access to a labyrinth, woods, a pond and a hermitage. Self-guided or guided retreats on offer as well as optional part/self-catering.
Main Contact Clare Shearman.
Please check our website for upcoming events. WCCM meditation group runs most Monday evenings 6–7pm and is open to retreat guests.
Spiritual direction on offer to all guests.
Labyrinth on site and is open for guests and for day use.
Hermitage is open for guests and for day use.

23 Trelowarren Retreat Christian Resource Centre and Chapel
The Mansion House, Mawgan, Helston, Cornwall TR12 6AF   01326 221366
email elaine@trelowarrenretreat.org.uk
C, Ch, I, P, Q, S, V, W   *website* www.trelowarrenretreat.org.uk

Rooms 1 super king bed *en suite*, 1 super king bed with 2 bed settees *en suite*, 1 twin *en suite*, 1 single *en suite*, 1 double with shared bathroom.
Notes Trelowarren is the ideal place to take time out and seek God: a great location to rest, relax or simply to be. Offering individual or guided retreats, prayer ministry also available. We also have an ongoing events programme hosting a variety of conferences and events which includes soaking and communion every Wednesday and worship every day. We are an interdenominational centre.
Contact Elaine Clarke.
Please visit our website for details or telephone 01326 221366 for information.

24 Withy Barn Retreat
Rockville, Coverack Bridges, Helston, Cornwall TR13 0LY   01326 561792
email withybarnretreats@btinternet.com
B, I, P, Q, S, W, Wf   *website* www.withybarnretreat.co.uk

Rooms 1 double and 1 twin (which can become a double) with a separate bathroom and extra WC. Open-plan living with kitchen and dining and woodburning stove. Prayer room. Self-catering but we can provide you with an evening meal if requested.
Notes Set in a rural valley 5 miles from the coast, Withy Barn is a place set apart for you. It is detached with 4 acres of woodland garden, riverside prayer cabins for you to explore your spiritual path, or to study, walk and be. The ideal place to make a private retreat yet prayer accompaniment is available if desired.
Contact Rev Amanda Stevens.

FOR A LIST OF COURSES IN SPIRITUAL DIRECTION
email: info@retreats.org.uk
or phone: 01494 569056

CO DURHAM

25 Minsteracres Retreat Centre
Minsteracres, Nr Consett, Co Durham DH8 9RT
01434 673248
email info@minsteracres.org
B, C, D, E, I, P, Q, S, W, Wf, Y   *website* www.minsteracres.org

Rooms Sleeps 80 people in single, twin and double rooms. Limited *en suite* disabled facilities. Self-catering, self-contained youth centre with dormitory accommodation for 36.
Notes We offer a wide variety of residential and day retreats for parishes, groups and individuals, as well as conference and meeting rooms for hire. You are also welcome to make your own retreat or bring a self-led group. If you are looking for solitude, we have self-contained accommodation in a poustinia with its own chapel. Spiritual direction is available. We are situated in beautiful Northumberland countryside in the land of the Northern Saints within easy reach of Hexham, Durham and Hadrian's Wall. Our extensive grounds include lawns, gardens, parkland and woodland. Minsteracres has a resident community of Passionist priests, Cross and Passion sisters and lay people, as well as staff and a large body of volunteers.
Contact Margo Mooney, Retreat Centre Administrator.

March
1–3   Friends of Minsteracres. Retreat for Volunteers and Friends of Minsteracres at the start of a new season. Minsteracres Team
9   Walking retreat. Enjoy a walk of 7–10 miles through beautiful countryside around Minsteracres. Bring suitable walking boots, warm weatherproof clothing and a packed lunch. Minsteracres Team
13   Quiet day of reflection during Lent. Kathryn Turner
20   Quiet day of reflection during Lent. Sheelagh McNamara RSCJ
27   Quiet day of reflection during Lent. Anne McCarthy RSCJ
April
3   Study day. The spirituality of *The Book of Hours* by Rainer Maria Rilke. Explore his life, inspiration, key poetry themes and influences on the Jewish Holocaust diarist Etty Hillesum. Patrick Woodhouse
10   Walking retreat (see 9 March).
18–21   Holy Week retreat. Join the community on their journey towards Easter, with time for reflection and the opportunity to take part in Holy Week ceremonies. Minsteracres Team
May
6   Open day. An opportunity to look around our house and grounds at Minsteracres. With exhibitions, tours, moments of reflection. Tea, coffee and home cooking provided.
8   Day of prayer. Experience different ways of praying in a beautiful setting with time for personal prayer. Lunch, tea and coffee provided. Rosarie Spence RSM

Retreat Association Icon

The Retreat Association Icon will be on display in a number of retreat centres, churches and cathedrals in 2019. Please see below for details of venues and related events.

Further dates to be added – please contact the office or see our website for further information.

Date	House no	Venue, Event and Contact
7–27 January	68	Community of Hopeweavers, West End, Southampton
19 January		Quiet Day based on the Icon.
15 February–6 March	39	Buckfast Abbey, Buckfastleigh, Devon
7–21 March		All Saints Church, Berkhamstead, Hertfordshire
13 March		Morning Reflection & worship.
13 May–10 June		Rochester Cathedral, Kent
11–30 June	85	Launde Abbey, East Norton, Leicestershire
1–16 July	63	Royal Foundation of St Katharine, Limehouse, London
17 July–6 August	147	Whirlow Spirituality Centre, Sheffield
7–28 August		Exeter Cathedral, Devon
29 August–15 September	14	Bishop Woodford House, Ely, Cambridgeshire
6 September		Day of Reflection with the Icon.
16–30 September	18	Retreat House Chester & Chester Cathedral, Cheshire
1–31 October		Southwark Cathedral, London
1–30 November		Luther King House & Manchester Cathedral

10–12 Our relationship with nature. The challenge to Christians in a time of degradation of the natural world. Finding joy and sustenance to bring about a better world. Mary Colwell

17–19 Weekend retreat. Daring disciples. Prayer, reflection and nourishment on our journey of discipleship. For groups from parishes and partnerships. Individuals also welcome. Minsteracres Team

21–23 Workshop. Sacred calligraphy. Building on the ancient art of illuminating manuscripts, we reflect creatively on the Word of God. Experience with calligraphy is not required. Maureen Rimmer

22 Walking retreat (see 9 March).

June

7–9 Pentecost renewal retreat. Weekend of praise, worship and reflection in preparation for the coming of the Holy Spirit. Maria Natella OP

10–14 Following in the footsteps of the Northern Saints. Early Celtic spirituality and its motivation. Includes visits to Holy Island, Bamburgh, Durham and Hadrian's wall. Minsteracres Team

12 Quiet day. Step aside and listen to God in Scripture and enjoy the peace of the countryside. Coffee and tea provided. Please bring a packed lunch. Rosarie Spence RSM

21–23 Themed retreat. Daring disciples (see 17–19 May).

July

9–11 3-day walking retreat. Walks of 8–10 miles through beautiful countryside around Minsteracres. Every day starts with reflection. Bring suitable walking boots and weatherproofs. Minsteracres Team

July–August

29–4 Music workshop. With songs that invite you to look at the world and appreciate the beauty of God's creation. Monique van den Hoogen

August

10 Rosary rally. A prayerful day out at Minsteracres with celebration of the Eucharist, rosary procession through the grounds and benediction.

August–September

30–6 6-day IGR. Ignatian silent retreat. Ignatian Spirituality Centre, Glasgow & Minsteracres Team

30–6 The Beatitudes under the rainbow of God's healing love. Exploring the Beatitudes and colour through our spiritual and psychological growth and development. Silent retreat. Treasa Ridge PBVM

September

7 Walking retreat (see 9 March).

11 Day of prayer (see 8 May).

13–15 Themed retreat. Daring disciples (see 17–19 May).

16–20 Love and suffering. Exploring the memory of the Passion. Theological seminar for clergy, religious and laity exploring the heart of the Passionist charism from several perspectives.

27–29 The way of the embodied contemplative. Christian meditation through the language of the body, using breathing exercises, gentle stretching and slow Tai Chi movements. Suitable for all. Terry Doyle

October

4–6 Themed retreat. Daring disciples (see 17–19 May).

9 Walking retreat (see 9 March).

16 Quiet day (see 12 June).

November

1–3 Circle dance retreat. Disciplined and free. Exploring what it means to be both disciplined and free through dance, music and words. Suitable for beginners. Janette Blakemore

16 Walking retreat (see 9 March).

20 Quiet day (see 12 June).

November–December

29–1 Advent retreat. The time is now. Will you come – how willing am I to be the manger? Pat Kennedy

26 St Antony's Priory

74 Claypath, Durham DH1 1QT   0191 384 3747
email admin@stantonyspriory.org
Ch, E, P, Q, S, V, Wf   *website* www.stantonyspriory.org

Rooms We have 4 self-contained guest rooms for people wishing to make a retreat with us (3 double and 1 single). Each room has an *en suite* shower/toilet and small kitchen facilities for self-catering.
Notes St Antony's Priory is part of the Society of the Sacred Mission, an Anglican Religious Order established towards the end of the 19th century. Today the Priory offers a place for groups and individuals to enjoy spiritual refreshment away from the busyness of everyday life, as well as providing spiritual direction and a variety of other courses and activities. It also offers training and mentoring for people interested in offering spiritual direction. These events and activities form part of a changing programme, though this may be affected by planned building works during 2019. A rhythm of daily prayer is being established and in time it is hoped that this will be sustained by a small residential community living on site.
Contact Rev Dr Nicholas Buxton, Director.

27 The Sanctuary Christian Retreat and Counselling Centre

21 Westbrook, Darlington, County Durham
DL3 6TD   01325 484212
email info@christian-retreat.co.uk
Co, I, P, Pe, Q, S, V, Wf   *website* www.christian-retreat.co.uk

Rooms 3 twin, 1 single, 1 single with study/lounge area.
Notes Personal and guided retreats. Christian and secular counselling for adults, young people and children. Training in counselling skills. Hire of house/rooms for awaydays, groups and training courses. Base for holiday break. Exclusive use of house and gardens. 10 mins from Darlington town centre. Please contact the centre for details of guided retreat sessions for 2019.
Contact Judith Barrett; contact by post, phone or email.

Retreat Association Summer Event

The Royal Foundation of St Katharine, London E14 8DS
Wednesday 3 July 2019   10.00am–4.30pm

Guest speakers:
Father Anastasios Salapatas, Greek Orthodox
and **Father Stephen Platt,** Russian Orthodox

Reflecting on the **Retreat Association Icon**
and **How Icons speak to us in our contemporary world**

Join patrons, trustees and staff for a day of talks,
discussion, worship and opportunities to network!

Further details to follow on our website **www.retreats.org.uk**
or contact us to reserve your place **info@retreats.org.uk**

HOUSE OF PRAYER
A BREATHING SPACE IN THE HUBBUB OF LIFE
A PRAYERFUL SPACE FOR SOLITUDE AND SILENCE

For our programme please see our listing or contact:
House of Prayer, 35 Seymour Rd, East Molesey, KT8 0PB
T. 020 8941 2313 ~ E. admin@christian-retreat.org
or visit our website: www.christian-retreat.org

CUMBRIA

28 Glenthorne Quaker Centre and Guest House

Easedale Road, Grasmere, Cumbria LA22 9QH

015394 35389

email info@glenthorne.org

C, Co, D, S, Wf, Y   website www.glenthorne.org

Rooms 26 rooms in total, 46 beds: 3 single standard, 4 single en suite, 1 twin standard ground floor, 12 twin en suite (3 disabled-friendly ground floor), 6 double en suite.
Notes Glenthorne is a long-established guest house and meeting place in Grasmere. It is open to anyone who is seeking a relaxed welcoming atmosphere, comfortable accommodation, and delicious home-cooked meals in stunning surroundings. We aim to meet the differing needs of all our guests in a peaceful atmosphere with Quaker values and ethos. At Glenthorne we welcome families and individuals of all ages for holidays or short breaks in the heart of the English Lake District. There is newly-built ground-floor accommodation for disabled visitors and well-appointed single and double rooms – mostly en suite – in the main house and adjacent Bankside. Most rooms have access to free Wifi.
Contact Terry Winterton, Friend in Residence.

March
11–15 Patchwork for fun. Gillian Waddilove
25–29 Musical encounters. Jeff Dershin
April
1–5 Creative writing. Tony Rossiter
8–12 Boot, boat and goat. T Winterton & G Ogilvie
26–28 Finding out about Quakers. Quaker Quest Team
April–May
29–3 Walking holiday. Alan Robinson
May
6–10 Creative textiles. Jenni Simmons
10–12 Tai Chi and Chi Kung silk reeling. Kim Noy-Man Jackson
17–19 The spirituality of travel. Ben Pink Dandelion
27–31 Circle dancing. Anne-Lise Kryger
June
3–7 Alexander Technique and walking holiday. Hilary Cooke
7–9 Guide to the mindful way of life. Adam Dacey
10–14 Knitted shawls to love and treasure. Hilary Grundy
24–28 Finding peace through yoga. Leah Barnet
July
5–7 Jesus and religion in Mark's Gospel. Janet Scott
19–21 Allowing forgiveness. M Partington & B Davey
26–28 Soul, silence and song. Meri Goad
July–August
29–2 Sketching and painting the Cumbrian landscape. Sue Ford
August
2–4 A language for the inner landscape. Brian Drayton
5–9 Yoga. Julia Slater
9–11 Walking with trees. Letta Jones
26–30 Sketching and painting the Cumbrian landscape. Sue Ford

August–September
30–1 Exploring Waiting in the Light. EWL Team
September
2–6 Circle dancing. Anne-Lise Kryger
6–8 Where do we come from? A Wildwood & M Goad
16–20 Encountering the Divine in nature. T Winterton & M Calvert
27–29 Awareness. Roswitha Jarman
October
7–11 Boot, boat and goat. T Winterton & G Ogilvie
11–13 Zen mindfulness retreat. Adam Dacey
14–18 Spiritual wellbeing in later life. Rhonda Riachi
18–21 Sketching and painting the Cumbrian landscape. Sue Ford
21–25 What has Wordsworth to offer us today? Barbara Windle
25–27 Tai Chi and Chi Kung silk reeling. Kim Noy-Man Jackson
November
22–24 Mysticism and the Quaker tradition. J Arriens & C Bentley

29 Rydal Hall

Rydal, Ambleside, Cumbria LA22 9LX

01539 432050

email mail@rydalhall.org

C, Ch, E, P, Q, S, W   website www.rydalhall.org

Rooms 11 single, 5 double, 14 twin. All rooms have private facilities.
Notes Resident and non-resident groups, and individual bookings welcomed. Led retreats and activity retreats. Set in the very heart of the Lake District. Easy footpath walking to Grasmere and Ambleside, or straight on to the fells for the more adventurous.
Contact The Bookings Office 01539 432050.
Quiet days 9.30am–4pm Quarterly, our first being 1st March. Please contact us for details.
April
1–5 Mixed media art holiday. Robert Dutton
23–25 Lakeland writing retreat. Angela Locke
October
21–25 Painting and daily reflections. Linda Birch & Trevor Pitt
November
18–22 Autumn expressive painting with mixed media. Robert Dutton
December
23–27 Christmas House Party. Dinner, B&B and full-board on Christmas day.
For more details please see our website.

30 Sacred Space Foundation

Fell End, Mungrisdale, Cumbria CA11 0XR

01768 779831

email admin@sacredspace.org.uk

I, P, S, V, Wf   website www.sacredspace.org.uk

Rooms 3 separate and self-contained sanctuaries on 2 sites. All 3 are en suite with private kitchen and sitting areas. Extra rooms are available for small groups by arrangement.   ▶ p. 83

81

The Julian Meetings

Groups meeting for silent contemplative prayer

Explore praying silently.
Find ways that are natural for you.

Christian Ecumenical
350 groups in the UK.
Quiet days

The Julian Meetings,
263 Park Lodge Lane,
Wakefield,
West Yorkshire
WF1 4HY
(SAE please)

www.thejulianmeetings.net

JESUIT CENTRE OF SPIRITUALITY

Easily accessed from Dublin city centre, airport or ferry port, Manresa - Ireland's Jesuit retreat house - offers a range of retreats and training in spiritual direction in a modern facility located in Dublin Bay's UNESCO biosphere reserve.

426 Clontarf Road
Dollymount
Dublin
D03 FP52
Ireland

+353 1 833 1352
reception@manresa.ie
www.manresa.ie

the JESUITS in IRELAND **ihs**

Breathing Space Retreats

Silent retreats with individual guidance

13 – 17 April
12 – 14 July
29 Nov – 1st Dec

The Greenhouse Christian Centre Dorset

www.the-greenhouse.org

Labyrinths...

A *labyrinth for your quiet day, retreat, course or other events.*

Indoors or outdoors, we bring the labyrinth to you, with an experienced and trained facilitator. Also available: workshops, introductory walks, consultancy and initial training.

All enquiries welcome: www.jansellers.com

Our new Convent and Retreat House at Gerrards Cross is now open to Guests – offering space in which to rest and re-charge the spirit.

Community of the Sisters of the Church
St. Michael's Convent
Vicarage Way, Gerrards Cross
Buckinghamshire SL9 8AT

0330 120 0631
hospitality@sistersofthechurch.org.uk
www.sistersofthechurch.org/retreats

A CONTEMPLATIVE RETREAT

An introduction to the Contemplative Way of Life and to the Jesus Prayer in the way of Franz Jalics SJ (Haus Gries)
at
St. Augustine's Priory, House of Prayer Old Colwyn, North Wales

20th – 29th March 2019, 20th – 29th May 2019
19th – 28th September 2019

Led by Fr Anton Altnoder SJ
Director, Haus Gries, Wilhelmsthal, Germany.

For further information please contact The Administrator at the above address, or by telephone: 01492 514223

82

Notes Private gardens, labyrinths, meditation rooms, access to libraries and a resident spiritual director at each site amidst beautiful open country. SSF was set up by a group of NHS staff and supporters in the 1980s to provide teaching in the healing arts and accommodation for those stressed and burned out. The facilities are now available to anyone seeking rest, retreat and reflection. We have developed expertise in supporting those in burnout, especially carers of all kinds including ministers, social workers, teachers, doctors, nurses and so on. We welcome people from all faiths and none to our 2 sites, for one-to-one attention. Our spiritual directors all have training in healthcare, interfaith ministry, counselling and spiritual direction and offer an open, inclusive and confidential service. See our website for more information.
Contact Jean Sayre-Adams.
Regular 1-day courses and events held, please see website for details.

31 Stillpoints@Elterwater

Elterwater Park Guest House, Skelwith, Ambleside, Cumbria LA22 9NP
01539 432414 / 07930 177423
email enquiries@elterwaterparkguesthouse.co.uk
website www.elterwaterparkguesthouse.co.uk
B, C, I, P, Pe, Q, S, W, Wf

Rooms All rooms are *en suite*. Barn rooms have ground-floor access. 4 single, 2 double, 2 twin, 1 self-catering.
Notes Situated on an old farm with private garden, nestled by the surrounding fells, Stillpoints@Elterwater offers a peaceful, rural setting for holidays, quiet days and retreats. Ecumenical in ethos but with Anglican roots, we are open to people of all faiths and none. This unique hospitable house offers a place of encounter, an opportunity to meet God in the beauty, stillness and peace of the landscape and to experience the fullness of God's generosity and welcome. The guest house is in private parkland with walks to Elterwater Lake. Whether on holiday or a formal retreat, this is a place of relaxation and refreshment. Day groups (max 12) welcome – we can provide leadership if necessary. Spiritual direction is offered on retreats and at other times. Please contact Lesley for details.
Contact Lesley McCririe.
Please see the website for details of our programme for 2019.

32 Swarthmoor Hall

Swarthmoor Hall Lane, Ulverston, Lancashire LA12 0JQ   01229 583204
email info@swarthmoorhall.co.uk
C, D, I, Q, S, W, Wf, V, Y   *website* www.swarthmoorhall.co.uk

Rooms 4 single *en suite* (1 ground-floor access), 2 twin *en suite* (1 ground-floor and accessible), 2 twin shared bathroom (accessible), 6 double *en suite*. Self-catering, B&B and camping available.
Notes Swarthmoor Hall is a historic house in the Lake District, built in the 16th century. It is surrounded by calm and peaceful gardens and grounds, and is only 2 miles from the coast. There is also a café onsite which uses organic and locally produced ingredients in its menu.

The tranquil setting lends itself to the courses and retreats held at Swarthmoor Hall, which are open to everyone. The cradle of the Quaker movement, visitors leave feeling settled and revitalised. Courses and retreats are held throughout the year at Swarthmoor Hall, as well as day events. The Hall can also be used for organising group events or for holiday accommodation.
Contact Jane Pearson, Manager.
April
7–12 Writing retreat. Open to anyone looking for space and time for writing, to start or complete a project. Ben Pink Dandelion & John Gray
May
3–5 A place for Scriptures. Part of a continuing exploration of how Friends today relate to the Bible without compromising Quaker insights. Timothy Ashworth
10–12 The inner light. Studying the thought and style of texts from pre-history to the Middle Ages and how they may assist our spiritual development and understanding. Peter Brennan
June
7–9 Journalling: a way to the centre. Course for those who wish to use journalling as a tool to deepen spiritual life. Prayer and worship are part of the course. Gerald Hewitson
21–24 Retreat using art as a technique to reflect and share experiences. No previous art experience required, art equipment provided. Helen Meads, Andrea Freeman & Rae Maysie
July
1–5 In Fox's footsteps: 1652 Quaker pilgrimage. Learn about the early history of Quakerism and how it relates to our faith today. Gordon Matthews
12–14 Revitalizing your meeting: co-creating Spirit-led Quaker communities. How Quakers can care for their members' spirituality and physical needs, and nurture young Quakers. Wendy Hampton & Deborah Shaw
September
13–15 Developing a practice of Christian meditation. An introduction to prayer beyond words, as taught by Benedictine monks John Main and Laurence Freeman. Liz Watson
16–20 In Fox's footsteps: 1652 Quaker pilgrimage. Become part of an organised pilgrimage and worshipping group. Includes a tour of the Hall and travel to other sites. Leader tbc
27–29 Mothers of Israel. Explore the lives and writings of some important Seventeenth-century Quaker women, including Margaret Fell, Martha Simmonds and Dorothy White. Stuart Masters
October
18–20 Quaker nominations. For members of Quaker nominations committees. Rooting ourselves in good practices of discernment whilst responding to the issues that face us. Nominations Trust Team tutor
November
1–3 Frances Howgill and the Valiant Sixty. What can we learn from the Sixty and from Francis Howgill? How can we be valiant for the truth? Gordon Matthews

33 The Upper Room

Hawkshead Hill Baptist Chapel, Hawkshead Hill, Ambleside, Cumbria LA22 0PW
01539 436451 / 07827 793118
email kath.dodd@btinternet.com
website www.hawksheadhillbaptistchurch.org.uk
Co, I, P, Q, S, Wf

Rooms 1 double guest room with kitchen, shower room and toilet. Self-catering.
Notes Guests are free to make use of the adjoining historic, but modernised, chapel, as well as the extensive grounds. Seats are scattered around the grounds, and can be found in the graveyard, the poustinia (prayer place), the sensory garden, overlooking the orchard, and in the summerhouse which is sited near an outdoor baptistry. The chapel is situated in the heart of the Lake District near Tarn Hows (a famous beauty spot) and the village of Hawkshead. There are many walks from the chapel, as well as mountains and lakes within easy striking distance. There is parking space for cars. Local buses stop right outside the chapel.
Contact Rev Kath Dodd.

DERBYSHIRE

34 Boylestone Methodist Church

Chapel Lane, Boylestone, Ashbourne, Derbyshire DE6 5AA   01283 820110
email stella.mills@methodist.org.uk
B, D, P, Pe, Q, W *website* www.trentanddovemethodistcircuit.com

Non-residential.
Rooms A Methodist church registered for marriages and used weekly for worship, seating about 50 people and a good-sized quiet room with 12 very comfortable chairs, a new dining table and smaller folding tables, together with chairs for inside or outside use. There are blinds at all the windows and heating is efficient by gas and electricity. There is a toilet with washbasin and a completely refurbished kitchen for preparing food and hot drinks etc. Disabled access via a ramp.
Notes The church and adjoining rooms are situated in a very rural and quiet part of southern Derbyshire with extensive field walks from the door. There is a car park in front of the church. The church has played an important part in the Primitive Methodist heritage, being opened by Hugh Bourne in January 1847. The present church replaced an earlier one of 1811. The first Primitive Methodist Sunday School in the world was formed at Boylestone in 1814 and the first superintendent's farm can be seen from the church. There is a short walk across the fields to this.
Contact Rev Prof Stella Mills, Minister.
Stepaside 3rd Thursday of every month, 10.30am to 12noon.
Farmers' Social Group open to all and run jointly with the Farming Life Centre, Bakewell on 4th Thursday in every month from 2pm to 3.30pm. A programme is available from the organiser.
Stop! In the Name of God As usual, we shall be remembering this in our Sunday morning worship at 10am on 14 July (Breakfast and Holy Communion).

35 Convent of the Holy Name

Morley Road, Oakwood, Derby DE21 4TB
01332 670483 / 01332 671716 (ext 6)
email guestsisterchn@gmail.com
B, Ch, D, P, Q, Wf   *website* www.comholyname.org

Rooms 6 single, 1 double, sitting room and kitchen.
Notes The Cottage guest house is in a peaceful corner of the large Convent garden. Guests are welcome to visit for rest, retreat, holiday, reflection and study, or to experience the life of a religious community. Guests can be as private and quiet as they wish, but are also welcome to join the Community for worship and to use the Convent library. Breakfast is available when required in the Cottage, and lunch and supper are with the sisters in the Convent. Vegetarian and other diets are catered for. Cell groups and small retreat groups are welcome to book the Cottage for their own needs. The Cottage is closed on Mondays.
Contact Guest Sister on 01332 670483.
The Convent welcomes day guests (individuals and groups).
Contact Assistant Provincial on 01332 671716 (ext 6) or email assistantprovincialchn@yahoo.co.uk to book events.
February
22–24 Spring retreat. Sr Pauline Margaret
March
9 Lent quiet day.
April
11 Passiontide quiet day.
July
13 Poetry quiet day. Sr Rosemary
See website for later events.

36 The Portiuncula

St Clare's Convent, Stretton Road, Clay Cross, Derbyshire S45 9AQ   01246 251870 / 01246 862621
email portiuncula@franciscansm.org
P   *website* www.franciscansm.org

Rooms 5 hermitages, all under 1 roof in a fraternal setting, based on St Francis' Rule for hermitages. The hermitages are all ground-floor level and *en suite*. 1 hermitage has disabled toilet/shower facilities.
Notes All our hermit guests are private retreatants.
Contact Sr Patricia. ⮌ *p 76*

37 Sōzein – A Churches Ministry of Healing Trust

The Old Vicarage, Church Lane, Horsley Woodhouse, Ilkeston, Derbyshire DE7 6BB   01332 780598
email neil.broadbent@sozein.org.uk
Co, D, Q, S   *website* www.sozein.org.uk

Non-residential.
Notes Study library, listening, praying, healing ministry. Sacraments available. Spiritual direction. Ecumenical. For details of courses and quiet days please ring for a leaflet or visit our website.
Contact Rev Neil Broadbent.

38 Whaley Hall Community of the King of Love

Reservoir Road, Whaley Bridge, High Peak,
Derbyshire SK23 7BL   01663 732495
email whaleyhallckl@talktalk.net
website www.whaleyhall.com

B, C, Ch, Co, E, I, P, Q, S, V, W, Wf, Y

Rooms Accommodation for up to 40 people. We have 4 rooms on the ground floor. Our bedrooms are not fitted with mobility aids. We have a conference room with Wifi, a projector, flipchart and pens. We have breakout points and a mixture of lounges and spaces to sit. Within the grounds of the hall is the Abbey church, open daily.

Notes Whaley Hall is a large retreat house situated at the gateway of the Peak District National Park with large grounds and open countryside on to the Goyt Valley. We have good walking spots close to Castleton, Buxton and the Hope Valley. Access is easy with Whaley Bridge station just 5 mins walk away and the TransPeak bus service from Nottingham to Manchester Airport.

The hall is open for events all year round; we offer retreats for vocational, diocesan, churches, religious, parish support. We welcome church groups such as music, liturgy, bell-ringing, cycling, art and theological groups. We also welcome universities and theological colleges. For more information please contact us or go to our website.

Contact Fr Jamie.

Stop! In the name of God 12–14 July The house and Abbey church will be open for pilgrims. A chance to see the restored Sir Gilbert Scott font.

DEVON

39 Buckfast Abbey

Buckfastleigh, Devon TQ11 0EE   01364 645532
email warden@buckfast.org.uk
website www.buckfast.org.uk

D, I, P, Q, W, Y

Rooms
Monastery Guest Quarters When you stay in the monastery guest quarters, you can follow the age-old rhythm of life lived according to the Rule of St Benedict, with its emphasis on balance, quietness and 'moderation in all things', under the care of the guest master. 10 rooms, most *en suite*.

Southgate Retreat Centre Available to women and couples. Southgate has its own chapel, lounge/dining room and grounds for those following personal retreats or simply wanting a change from their normal routine. Southgate also boasts a separate hall available to hire which is ideal for presentations and talks as part of your stay or a non-residential booking. 11 rooms, 4 *en suite*.

Northgate House Hotel 33 rooms, all *en suite*.

3 self-catering cottages.

Notes The tradition of monastic hospitality is as old as the history of the Benedictine way of life itself. St Benedict encourages his followers to be hospitable in the strongest of terms: 'All guests who present themselves are to be welcomed as Christ, for he himself will say: I was a stranger and you welcomed me.'

Contact Geoff Pring.
Guided group retreats are advertised on the 'What's On' pages of our website. ❏ *p 70*

40 Lee Abbey

Lee Abbey Fellowship, Lynton, Devon EX35 6JJ
01598 752621
email publicity@leeabbey.org.uk
website www.leeabbeydevon.org.uk

B, C, Ch, D, E, I, P, Q, S, W, Wf, Y

Rooms
In the main house 8 single, 10 single *en suite*. 6 double, 9 double *en suite*. 3 twin, 13 twin *en suite*. 3 triple, 3 triple *en suite*. 2 quad *en suite*. We have 2 doubles and 1 single *en suite* rooms adapted for guests with disabilities.
In the Beacon Centre 3 family bunk rooms (1 double, 3 single). 1 family *en suite* bunk room (1 double, 1 single). 4 2-person bunk rooms. 2 3-person bunk rooms. 2 4-person bunk rooms. 2 single rooms. We have 2 rooms accessing a bathroom suitable for guests with disabilities.

Notes Lee Abbey is home to a Christian Community that hosts retreats, holidays and conferences in the main house and in the Beacon Activity Centre. The 280-acre Lee Abbey Estate in Exmoor National Park includes woodlands, streams, fields and even a private beach: it's also a dark sky reserve where the stars shine brightly. Our accommodation is freshly refurbished to make you feel welcome, and the Community from 20 nations is creative and diverse, and the views are as beautiful as ever, proclaiming the glory of their Creator. Individuals, couples, families, small groups and whole churches come to be transformed and renewed by God. Visit for a personal retreat, study and reflection, a creative, walking or themed break, or a family holiday. You'll get a warm welcome, tasty meals, space inside and out to relax, teaching, worship and entertainment. And you can join in as much or as little as you like.

Contact Simon Holland, The Warden.
February–March
25–1 IGR. Michael Mitton
March
4–8 Photography walks. Rob Kitchen
11–15 Lent silent retreat. Ruth Patterson
May
13–17 Knowing God. Jane Williams
20–24 Walk and talk. Simon Farrar
July
8–12 Summer week. Malcolm Guite
Please see our website for many more programmes.

41 Lowerfield House

Lapford, Crediton, Devon EX17 6PU 01363 507030
email enquiries@lowerfieldhouse.co.uk
website www.lowerfieldhouse.co.uk/retreats

Ch, E, P, W, Wf, Y

Rooms 2 double *en suite*, 1 twin *en suite*, 1 double with private bathroom, 2 twin with private bathroom.

Notes Lowerfield House is a spacious Grade II listed Georgian house set in its own secluded grounds of 5 acres. Set on the edge of the village of Lapford, the gardens of Lowerfield House offer many secluded corners for quiet

85

private prayer as well as more spacious indoor and outdoor areas for group activities. The village offers the fellowship of 3 churches including Church of England, a Congregational Church and the Yeo Valley Christian Fellowship. Ordinarily a 3-bedroom B&B, Lowerfield House can be adapted for day use by larger groups with appropriate meals and refreshments by prior arrangement. A 1-bed self-catering flat is available for sabbaticals. The village pub offers excellent food and additional accommodation for larger groups while The Ark is an additional meeting room and café facility run by the village churches.
Contact Stephen Munday.

42 Mill House Retreats

Rocknell Manor Farm, Westleigh, Tiverton, Devon EX16 7ES 01884 829000 / 01884 829585
email janetaylor@millhouseretreats.co.uk
B, C, I, P, Q, S, V, W, Wf *website* www.millhouseretreats.co.uk

Rooms 7 single, all double or twin including one triple (individual retreatants are not expected to share).
Notes Late 16th-century listed farmhouse with smallholding, secluded 7-acre setting, within easy reach of some of Devon and Somerset's most stunning countryside and places of interest, but also the station with mainline connection to London Paddington. The house has a warmth and character of its own where guests can feel at home in its relaxed and spacious surroundings. The 2 lounges, reading room, library/meeting room, large reception hall and chapel space also provide excellent facilities for day groups of up to 25. We would especially like to welcome those who are exploring faith outside the institution of the Church or who wish to consider new directions in life. See website for full programme, including days/weekends for bread making, knitting, creative writing, finding new direction, and mothers and daughters.
Contact Rev Jane Taylor.

July
22–24 CARM retreat. Calligraphy and Prayer.

43 Retreat by the Dart

Coach House, Staverton, Totnes, Devon TQ9 6NZ 01803 762977
email info@retreatbythedart.co.uk
B, C, I, P, S, W, Wf *website* www.retreatbythedart.co.uk

Rooms 2 en suite, self-catering studio rooms (single/twin/double) with own entrance.
Notes Retreat by the Dart is a former coach house and stables, thoughtfully renovated to provide self-contained, spacious and quiet retreat spaces, in a countryside location very close to the river Dart. The garden, with lovely woodland views, offers space for quiet reading and reflection and a cabin for meditation/prayer and creative expression. Short and longer walks can be made from the house along the river and on to the Dartington Estate. There is also the option for wild swimming in the river close by. It is ideally located between Dartmoor and the South Devon coast, with Buckfast Abbey also close by. Easily accessible by road (10 mins from the A38) and by train (Totnes is a mainline station), Retreat by the Dart is a friendly, inclusive space drawing inspiration for retreats

from the natural world, creativity and open spirituality. Debbie Thorpe has extensive experience of retreats and retreat guidance and offers self-catering residential retreats and spiritual companionship.
Contact Debbie Thorpe.

44 St Rita's Centre

Ottery Moor Lane, Honiton, Devon EX14 1AP 01404 42601 / 01404 42635
email stritas@btinternet.com
D, Wf, Y *website* www.stritascentre.org.uk

Rooms 6 single (1 with disabled facilities), 7 twin, 2 family (1 five-bed and 1 seven-bed); all with *en suite* facilities. Chapel.
Notes We offer a perfect retreat centre in which to hold your school, staff or parish retreat or in-service training. We offer up-to-date residential accommodation at St Rita's Retreat Centre; we have a chapel for daily Mass and guests are welcome to join the Community in their daily recital of the divine office. We can accommodate up to 33 people for a residential retreat and offer the highest standard of service. Meals served in our dining room are prepared using local produce where possible. We would be pleased to host your school group/parish retreat; unfortunately we cannot host individual retreats.
Contact Fr José Romero (01404 42601) or Patricia Gough (01404 42635). ❏ *p 72*

45 The Society of Mary and Martha

Sheldon, Sheldon Lane, Doddiscombsleigh, Exeter, Devon EX6 7YT 01647 252752
email smm@sheldon.uk.com
B, C, D, E, P, Q, V, Wf *website* www.sheldon.uk.com

Rooms Pound House (5 twin/double, 1 single), Long Barn (8 twin, 1 single), Linhay Lodges (4 twin/double, 1 ground floor), Pig Pens (3 twin/double, all ground floor), Hen Runs (3 twin/double, all ground floor). All accommodation *en suite*. Single people are not asked to share.
Notes Good space to reflect, relax and unwind. Most resources open to everyone. Specialist resources for people in Christian ministry at times of stress, crisis, burnout or breakdown and for your routine maintenance. Self-contained space for private retreats. Self-catering and catered groups also welcome. Beautiful converted farm buildings set in 45 acres on the edge of Dartmoor. Rooms warm and *en suite*. Medieval and modern chapels. Excellent local walking – fields, footpaths and woodlands. Art Shed (new 2017). Jacuzzi and massage. Library. Good disabled access. Privacy and confidentiality rated highly. Always happy to discuss by phone to see if our resources suit your needs.
Contact The Warden. ❏ *back cover*

December 2018–January 2019
28–2 R5 New Year (read, retreat, rest, relax, recuperate).
January–February
27–3 R5 Candlemas (read, retreat, rest, relax, recuperate).
February
1–3 Volunteer work party (Candlemas).
11–15 Retreat. Finding your inner Ignatius. Margaret Whipp

February–March
24–1 12,000-mile service. Ministers and/or spouses. Service yourself as well as your car. Quietly spacious timetable, sociable meals, workshops, 1:1 time. Recharge your batteries.
March
6 Quiet day (Ash Wednesday).
11–15 Retreat. Discerning the Angel. Angela Tilby
19–21 Workshop. Enneagram Part 1. Through personality to spirit. Karen Webb
22–23 Workshop. Share the Joy. Andrea Chance
24–29 R5 (read, retreat, rest, relax, recuperate).
April
16–23 Volunteer work party (Easter).
16–23 R5 Easter (read, retreat, rest, relax, recuperate).
April–May
28–3 12,000-mile service (see February–March).
May
27–31 Retreat. Seeing the light in life. Steve Radley
June
16–21 R5 (read, retreat, rest, relax, recuperate).
July
15–19 Retreat. Grace and forgiveness. Stephen Cherry
19–24 R5 (read, retreat, rest, relax, recuperate).
July–August
24–3 Volunteer work party.
August
4–10 Holiday week for families in ministry.
11–17 Holiday week for families in ministry.
18–22 Retreat. The stories that shape us. Margaret Silf
September–October
29–4 12,000-mile service (see February–March).
October
6–11 R5 (read, retreat, rest, relax, recuperate).
14–18 Retreat. Julian of Norwich. Simon Parke
October–November
28–1 Retreat. Seeds of Contemplation. Ian Mobsby
November
10–15 12,000-mile service (see February–March).
25–29 Retreat. The Advent of Eternity. Andrew Nunn
November–December
29–1 Volunteer work party (Advent).
29–6 R5 Advent (read, retreat, rest, relax, recuperate).

46 Tinhay Retreats

Down Farm Cottage, Lifton, Devon PL16 0EL
01566 784990 / 07982 622949
email tinhayretreats@gmail.com
B, C, I, P, Q, S, V, W, Wf, Y   *website* www.tinhayretreats.com

Rooms Camping facilities for caravans/motorhome/tents.
Notes Tinhay Retreats offers retreats and spiritual direction. Set in an old farmhouse with eight acres of smallholding, this peaceful home has a lovely garden, affiliated to the Quiet Garden Movement. We aim to provide a prayerful space for individuals and small groups. We are open to people of all denominations and none. Themed retreats are available throughout the year. For further details, please ring or email. For those who enjoy camping, a quiet site is available within the grounds. Alternatively, B&B facilities are available in the village of Tinhay.
Contact Robert Weston.

DORSET

47 The Greenhouse Christian Centre

17 Burton Road, Poole, Dorset BH13 6DT
01202 764776
email info@the-greenhouse.org
website www.the-greenhouse.org
C, Ch, Co, D, E, I, P, Q, V, W, Wf, Y

Rooms Number of rooms 22 (7 ground-floor access). 4 single *en suite*. 5 single standard. 5 double *en suite*. 6 twin *en suite*. 2 twin standard. Number of beds 30. Number of bed spaces 37.
Notes Established in 1955 as a centre of healing, The Greenhouse, situated between Poole and Bournemouth, is a great location for both personal retreat time and small group getaways. With excellent transport links and close to the sea, the city and the beauty of the Dorset countryside, it offers you and your group the perfect place to be restored, equipped and refreshed for life and ministry. We offer a wide variety of comfortable spaces from large lounges to smaller quiet rooms and a chapel, and our heated outdoor pool in our beautiful garden is open April–September.
Quiet days, prayer and worship events, and healing services once a month.
Contact Kate Strand. ❏ *p 82*
For full details of our events programme, please see our website or contact us by phone for a brochure.
January
7–9 Leaders retreat.
9–11 Leaders retreat.
11–13 Christian mindfulness. David Cole
18–20 Christians bereaved by suicide. Abi May
February
15–17 Telling stories. Ali Hull & Bob Hartman
February–March
25–1 Marilyn Baker Ministries
March
18–22 CARM retreat. Painting and prayer.
April
13–17 Silent retreat.
18–22 Easter retreat.
July
12–14 Silent retreat.
19–21 God in nature. David Cole
October
4–6 Peace in a busy world. David Cole
October–November
28–1 Marilyn Baker Ministries.
November–December
29–1 Silent retreat.
December
23–27 Christmas house party.
December–January 2020
30–2 New Year house party.

48 Hilfield Friary

Hilfield, Dorchester, Dorset DT2 7BE

01300 341741
email hilfieldssf@franciscans.org.uk
C, Ch, E, P, Q, V, W, Wf, Y   *website* www.hilfieldfriary.org.uk

Rooms Full-board:
Leo House 9 rooms (1 of which is a double).
2 self-catering houses:
Bernard House 6 rooms (1 twin, 1 double, 1 *en suite*).
Juniper House 7 rooms (1 twin, 1 *en suite*).
Self-catering houses can be booked separately or together.
Notes We welcome people to come and stay with us for prayer and retreat, for study, for a break away from their usual routine and to share something of our Franciscan life together. We can offer either full-board accommodation, eating with us in the refectory, or self-catering accommodation. All guests are welcome to join us for services in the chapel but no one should feel under pressure to do so. We invite those who wish to join us in some of the basic tasks around the Friary e.g. helping with the washing up! We don't run the place as a hotel business and we make no fixed charge for staying, but we do make a suggestion about the level of donation that we need to cover our costs for your stay. We also welcome group and individual day guests.
Contact Br Clark Berge.
Events for 2019 are currently being finalised. They will appear on our website. People can register for a copy if required by contacting Suzi Herbert at the email address above.

49 Othona West Dorset

Coast Road, Burton Bradstock, Bridport, Dorset DT6 4RN

01308 897130
email bookings@othona-bb.org.uk
C, Ch, D, E, Q, W, Wf, Y   *website* www.othonawestdorset.org.uk

Rooms 3 single (1 ground-floor access), 6 twin (3 ground-floor access), 1 double, 4 family.
Notes Perhaps the most unspoilt setting of any retreat on the south coast. The resident core community members welcome you to a comfortable old house overlooking wood, meadow and deserted beach. An ideal place to de-stress and reflect on life. 'Rooted in the Christian heritage, open to the widening future', we give a positive welcome to visitors of all faiths and none. Our approach to spirituality is down-to-earth, light-of-touch, unafraid to face change. So Othona can be especially attractive to people on the progressive 'emergent' edge of faith communities. However briefly, you are part of a community, not just a guest. You can – if you wish – join in a whole rhythm of life, from lending a hand in the kitchen or garden to helping shape a chapel service. Events during school holidays are usually child-friendly. Our 2019 programme is not shown below – please consult the website.
Contact The Warden.
February
2–8 Quiet week. The tree of life. Rev Wendy Pugh & Dr Clare Gough
For programmed events beyond February please see our website.

50 The Pilsdon Community

Pilsdon Manor, Pilsdon, Bridport, Dorset DT6 5NZ

01308 868308
fax 01308 868161
email pilsdon@pilsdon.org.uk
P, Q, W   *website* www.pilsdon.org.uk

Rooms 2 singles (ground-floor access).
Notes IGRs are available in the context of community life. We are an ecumenical community with an Anglican foundation living out a sustainable lifestyle on 12 acres of land. About 30 people live together, many of whom are struggling with issues of addiction or poor mental health, together with wayfarers and volunteers. We have a sacramental lifestyle with regular Eucharistic worship and 4 daily offices. We pursue a holiness involving a balance of prayer, manual work, hospitality and recreation. Come and share our life.
Contact The Warden.

DURHAM

See Co Durham.

ESSEX

51 The Bowling Green

8 The Downs, Great Dunmow, Essex CM6 1DT

01371 872662
P, Q, S   *email* rose.drew@btinternet.com

Non-residential.
Notes The Bowling Green was an 18th-century inn, now a very peaceful home set in a lovely garden, affiliated to The Quiet Garden Trust. There is a garden room with catering facilities, and a chapel. We aim to provide a prayerful space for small groups and for individuals of any denomination to experience silence and solitude. The ministry of healing, and spiritual direction, are available. Themed retreats are held between 9.30am and 4pm in most months. For further details, please ring or email for a leaflet. A programme of themed retreats is being organised.
Contact Rev Canon Rosemary Drew.

52 Chelmsford Diocesan House of Retreat, Pleshey

The Street, Pleshey, Chelmsford, Essex CM3 1HA

01245 237251
email retreathouse@chelmsford.anglican.org
website www.retreathousepleshey.com
B, C, Ch, D, I, P, Q, S, V, W, Wf

Rooms The Retreat House 27 bedrooms: 23 single, 2 double and 2 twin. In the main house, our 'all access' bedroom, with wet room, is on the ground floor. The first floor, now with lift access from the ground floor, has 12 single rooms (of which 11 are *en suite*) and the second floor, 6 single and 1 twin. On the ground floor of the house, there is a lounge, a dining room for up to 30 people, a guest library and an 'all access' toilet.
The Orangery available separately, is a meeting room for 15 people and is also on the ground floor.

The Evelyn Underhill Room is a separate building which can be hired independently and is a general meeting room comfortably seating 30 people.
The Gatehouse can be booked as a separate self-catering unit. 4 single and 1 double bedrooms, all *en suite*. There is a kitchen, with dining area, lounge and separate toilet.
Parsonage Cottage can also be booked as a self-catering unit. 1 double and 1 twin bedroom, bathroom, kitchen, lounge and dining room.
The Chapel is available to all guests and comfortably accommodates 30 people.
For more details/enquiries/rates/availability please contact the office via the details provided.
Notes We are open to residential and day groups as well as individuals, prayer or cell groups who are looking to meet, study, work, rest or pray. IGRs begin with supper on the first day and end after breakfast on the last day. Minimum stay for IGRs is 3 nights. Individuals are welcome any time of the year for private quiet days or retreats, subject to availability. Every weekday, morning prayers are held at 9am and midday prayers at 12.15pm. There is also an opportunity for a time of shared silent prayer on Fridays 12noon–1pm. These are usually held in the Chapel at The Retreat House and are open to all. For more details regarding the programme or any other enquiries, please visit our website or contact the office.
Contact Stewart McCredie, General Manager & Jo Hall, Assistant Manager. ❏ *p 72*

January
4–6 Weekend of prayer. Dawn of a new year. A weekend to pray for the House, yourself and 2019.
18–20 Weekend IGR. Rosemary Alonso
February
8–10 Friends weekend retreat. Jesus in the gospels. Dave Hopwood
20 Quiet day. Let all creation sing. Dr Ruth Valerio
March
2 Living with life-limiting illness. Rev Gill Moore & Barry Morgan
5 Lent quiet day. Joining the song of creation, exploring St Francis. Br Samuel
8–10 Lent weekend retreat. To be a pilgrim. Rev Dr Sally Welch
28 Quiet day. Peace and good. Rev Canon Pat Mossop
April
15–17 Holy Week retreat – the following quiet days can be booked individually:
15 Holy Week quiet day. What do we bring? Rev Elizabeth Clark
16 Holy Week quiet day. I am the resurrection and the life. The Ven Elizabeth Snowden
17 Holy Week quiet day. Praying in the light of our frontlines. Rev Dr Neil Hudson
May
4 Living with unemployment. Rev Lara Dose
6 Open day, 10am–4pm. Open to all. Supported by the Friends of Pleshey.
10–12 Music weekend retreat. Making melody. Dave & Pat Bilbrough
11 An evening with Dave & Pat Bilbrough 7.30pm Holy Trinity Church, Pleshey.
15 Quiet day. Rhythms of the soul: finding deeper communion within everyday life. Brian Draper

June
13–16 Evelyn Underhill weekend – the following can be booked separately:
13 Evelyn Underhill talk 7.30pm. Dr Micha Jazz
14–16 Evelyn Underhill retreat. Dr Micha Jazz, incorporating the following quiet day:
15 Evelyn Underhill quiet day. Dr Micha Jazz
July
11 Garden quiet day. Gospelling in the garden. Rev Hilary le Seve & Val Tyler (gardener)
15–24 IGR. For those with a desire to deepen their relationship with God. Rosemary Alonso
27 Living with mental illness. Learning to breathe. Rachel Newham
July–August
26–2 Walking week. A relaxing week of walking, reflecting, enjoying being together with each other and God. Some lunches in local pubs.
August
2–9 CARM retreat. Painting and prayer. Christine Phillips (tutor) & Margaret Stein (chaplain)
12–16 Music week. Worship works. Roger Jones
16–23 CARM retreat. Embroidery and prayer. Janet Knox (tutor) & Margaret Stein (chaplain)
September
3 Quiet day. Three views – priestly, prophetic and wise – one Creator God. Rev Dr Janet Tollington
25 Quiet day. Angel voices. Patrick Craig
October
8–10 Midweek retreat. Missionary to the Arts. Andy Kind
22 Friends quiet day. The romantic God. Bp Trevor Mwamba
November
22–24 Advent weekend retreat. The grace of waiting. Margaret Whipp
28 Advent quiet day. Being the Church in three dimensions. Rev Dr Ian Paul
December
7 Christmas sing day. Sing for joy. Stewart McCredie & Friends
24–26 Christmas house retreat. Stewart & Gill McCredie

53 St Peter's Chapel

The Chapel of St Peter-on-the-Wall, Bradwell-on-Sea, Southminster, Essex CM0 7PN

email stpeterschapel@outlook.com
P *website* www.bradwellchapel.org

Non-residential.
Notes 7th-century Saxon stone chapel in beautiful and peaceful surroundings close to the sea. Open 24 hours a day, all year, for individuals seeking solitude and peace. Available for groups (of all denominations) for quiet days and pilgrimages by prior arrangement with the chaplain. (Residential accommodation may be available at the nearby Othona Community for individuals and groups, tel 01621 776564.)
Contact Rev Brigid Main, Chaplain.
Summer Sunday evening services 6.30pm during July and August.
Annual Pilgrimage and Festival on the first Saturday in July. See website for details www.bradwellfestival.com.

89

GLOUCESTERSHIRE

54 Marist Retreat Centre

Frontstreet, Nympsfield, Stonehouse,
Gloucestershire GL10 3TZ   01453 861511
email maristconvent@btconnect.com
D, I, P, Q, S, W   *website* www.maristretreatcentre.co.uk

Rooms Ground floor: 1 single *en suite* with walk-in shower and high toilet seat, 1 double *en suite*. First floor (lift available): 2 twin *en suite*, 1 double, 3 single, 11 twin. Flat in outside building: 3 single.

Notes The Marist Retreat Centre is a homely and caring place where you can relax, slow down and enter into quiet moments. The Centre is available for individuals or groups (schools, parishes, families, support groups) of all denominations. Sisters are available as speakers for a group or to accompany an individual. We offer a special programme for primary schools. Come to rekindle the spark in your life through prayer, reflection, relaxation and spiritual guidance while exploring and enjoying culture and history in an informal setting.

Contact Directress.

55 Monastery of Our Lady and St Bernard

Brownshill, Stroud, Gloucestershire GL6 8AL
01453 883084
email brownshillbookings@bernardine.org
B, Ch, E, I, P, Q, S, V, W, Y   *website* www.brownshill.org

Rooms We have 14 rooms, 5 twin and 2 *en suite*. 8 ground-floor and 6 first-floor. Facilities include a welcoming reception area, comfortable lounge, guest library, conference room, several tea and coffee points.

Notes We are a community of RC Bernardine Cistercian nuns who follow the Rule of St Benedict. The chapel is at the heart of the monastery and the Eucharist is celebrated every morning. The Community meets 5 times daily to sing the divine office. Guests are welcome to attend. We welcome individuals, and groups of all denominations and none for retreats or quiet days, either with their own leader or guided by a Sister. For day groups we can welcome up to 30 with either a packed or cooked lunch.

Quiet days are available. Most of our retreats are led by a Sister and are open to all. There is always an element of silence and reflection included.

Please visit our website for updated programme.

Contact The Bookings Secretary.

March
8–10 Lent retreat.
19–21 Lent retreat.
November–December
29–1 Advent retreat.
December
10–12 Advent retreat.

STOP! IN THE NAME OF GOD
12–14 July 2019 – see page 68

GREATER LONDON

For Community of the Sisters of the Church (previously at Ham Common) please see Buckinghamshire.

56 Community of the Word of God

90–92 Kenworthy Road, London E9 5RA
020 8986 8511
P, Q, S   *email* communityofthewordofgod@gmail.com

Rooms Non-residential at present. Quiet sitting room and chapel, garden room (spring to autumn).

Notes Quiet space in which to pray, reflect, read, listen to music, 'be'. Spiritual direction available by request. Annual open, preached retreat using larger accommodation elsewhere.

Contact Retreat Secretary.
September
2–5 Open, preached, silent retreat at Bishop Woodford house, Ely.

57 Edgware Abbey St Mary at the Cross

Community of St Mary at the Cross, Edgware Abbey, 94A Priory Field Drive, Edgware, Middlesex HA8 9PU   020 8958 7868
email info@edgwareabbey.org.uk
D, P, Q, S, Wf   *website* www.edgwareabbey.org.uk

Rooms 3 *en suite* rooms, B&B retreat accommodation, space for parish day groups and small group meetings.

Notes Anglican Benedictine Community offering space for quiet time and spiritual renewal. Benedictine hospitality for quiet days, short-stay retreat time, spiritual accompaniment. Peaceful environment with access to gardens and abbey chapel. Visitors are welcome to join the sisters for the divine office and Eucharist.

Contact Bookings Secretary by email.

Quiet day in Advent and Lent details will be announced on our website.

58 Guild of Health and St Raphael

14 Oakleigh Park South, London
N20 9JU   07398 164477
email director@gohealth.org.uk
B, C, Q   *website* www.gohealth.org.uk

Non-residential.

Notes The Guild of Health and St Raphael has been working since 1904 to promote the church's ministry of healing, and to bring spirituality and healthcare together. It is an ecumenical Christian organisation drawing on many traditions. We support parish prayer groups and provide resources and teaching on the healing ministry. We also hold seminars, quiet days, workshops and retreats, all with an emphasis on aspects of healing. Members receive a discount on events, a quarterly magazine and a biannual journal on Christian healing. For more information about membership and events please see the website.

Contact Rev Dr Gillian Straine.

59 The Kairos Centre

**Mount Angelus Road, Roehampton, London
SW15 4JA**   020 8788 4188
email bookings.kairos@psmgs.org.uk
B, C, Ch, E, I, P, Q, S, V, Wf   *website* www.thekairoscentre.co.uk

Rooms There are 27 bedrooms comprising 18 *en suite*, 9 standard. 11 of the rooms are twin rooms giving us a total capacity when full of 38 places. The Centre also offers several meeting rooms suitable for groups of any size up to 100 people. Equipment available includes: loop system, multimedia projectors and screens, laptop, CD players, 79" touchscreen TV, DVD, flipcharts etc. The entire Kairos Centre has wheelchair access, including a lift to the 1st and 2nd floors. A large chapel on the ground floor has capacity for 120 people, a small prayerful oratory and a quiet room are open and available to all.

Notes The Kairos Retreat Centre is one of the services run by the Congregation of the Poor Servants of the Mother of God. It is an urban oasis located within 3 acres of beautifully landscaped gardens overlooking the historic Richmond Park. There is easy access to the Centre by public transport from Wimbledon, Putney, Hammersmith and Clapham Junction. All denominations are welcome to come and experience the peace of God at the Kairos Centre either for private or directed retreats. Day visitors are welcome.

Contact Michael O'Halloran.

Every Monday Taizé Prayer 7–7.45pm.
Every Wednesday Christian Meditation as an 11th Step Practice 7–8.15pm.
The option of an individually guided retreat can be taken instead of the preached retreat on the same dates in the programme below.

April
14–21 Holy Week and Easter silent retreat. Fr Tom McGuinness & Sr Magdalen Lawler
May
1–8 Preached silent retreat. Bp John Crowley
11 Quiet day. Like a watered garden: garden imagery and the spiritual journey. Sheila Farmer
12–19 Preached silent retreat. Fr Eamon Mulcahy CSSP
18 Quiet day. Ensouling Earth (contemplative art). Cari Bridgen
May–June
31–1 Silent weekend. Introduction to the Spirituality of St Ignatius.
June
3–10 Preached silent retreat. Fr Pat Collins CM
8 Quiet day. Sr Brenda Schofield SMG
10–14 CARM textile retreat. Romola Parish & Sheila Coughtrey
14–16 12-step Spirituality retreat and Christian Meditation weekend
16–23 Preached silent retreat. Fr Paul Rout OFM
22 Quiet day. Walking and exploring the Labyrinth. Sheila Farmer
July
1–8 Preached silent retreat. Fr Derek Laverty SSCC
6 Quiet day. Jesus the Light of the World (contemplative art). Cari Bridgen
9–18 Silent contemplative retreat. Fr Mariathas Selvaratnam OMI

19–26 Preached silent retreat. Fr Michael Beattie SJ
19–28 IGR. The Kairos Team
27 Quiet day. CARM textile day. Sue Ives
August
1–8 Preached silent retreat. Fr John Farrell OP
10–17 Preached silent retreat. Fr Nick Harnan MSC
August–September
1–2 30-day retreat. Spiritual Exercises.
September
6–13 Icon-writing workshop retreat. Sr Annette Lawrence DMJ
22–29 Preached silent retreat. Fr Charles Cross CP
28 Quiet day. Sr Annie Lunney SMG
October
6–13 Preached silent retreat. Fr Matthew Devereux LC
December
2–6 Preached silent Advent Triduum retreat. Bp John Crowley
7 Quiet day. A day with Mary. Sr Brenda Schofield SMG
15–19 Preached silent Advent Triduum retreat. Fr Michael Beattie SJ

60 Mount Street Jesuit Centre

114 Mount Street, London W1K 3AH
     0207 495 1673
email admin@mountstreet.info
B, Q, S   *website* www.mountstreet.info

Non-residential.
Notes Mount Street Jesuit Centre (MSJC) provides spiritual and faith formation in the spirit and tradition of St Ignatius Loyola, founder of the Jesuits. Our mission is to provide opportunities in central London for people to find a deeper meaning and purpose in their lives. Easily accessible, nearest tubes: Bond Street or Green Park; buses: 2, 10, 16, 36, 44, 73, 82, 137, 148, 414, 436.
Our programme runs through the academic year. See our full programme on the website or call for a brochure.
Contact Anne Paolino, Administrator.
Spirituality
Guided prayer Weekly prayer session every Monday 6.30–7pm.
Lunchtime lectio Weekly meditation every Tuesday, 1.40–2pm.
Monthly retreats Every month except August:
Wednesdays at the well – come to rest and be refreshed a retreat day, 3rd Wednesday of each month 11.30am–3.30pm. The invitation is to the day, but you are welcome to come for the morning or afternoon.
Ignatian retreat days 2nd Saturday of each month 11am–4pm. The invitation is to the day, but you are welcome to come for the morning or afternoon.
Spirituality courses
Beginners' guide to Ignatian spirituality 6 Wednesdays 16, 23, 30 January; 6, 13, 20 February 11.30am–1pm. Lynne Galloway & tbc
Beginners' guide to Ignatian spirituality 6 Wednesdays 1, 8, 15, 22, 29 May; 5 June 7–8.30pm. Andrew Kerr-Jarrett & tbc
Sadhana: a way to God 6 Wednesdays 12, 19, 26 June; 3, 10, 17 July 2–3.30pm. Lynne Galloway & tbc

91

Young adult ministry Series of ministries and events geared especially for young adults (aged 18–35) including: **Sunday Eucharist 7pm** Every Sunday a group of young adults who meet to pray and celebrate Eucharist together. Other events are announced on the website.
Social justice ministry London Jesuit Volunteers (LJV) connects people with voluntary placements with the poor and marginalised and provides monthly Ignatian input, peer reflection and sharing for volunteers.
Online resource offering pathways to God: www.pathwaystogod.org
Spirituality workshops or events

January
5 New beginnings. Lynne Galloway
19 The spirituality of St Paul: a model for our spiritual life? 11am–4pm. Brian Purfield
26 Work, worship and wholeness. Audrey Hamilton & David Hothersall
February
2 An extrovert's guide to Ignatian spirituality. Athena Barrett & Liz Waldy
16 Alexander Technique and mindfulness. Chris Goodchild
23 Show me the way I should go: tools for making life choices. Chris Chapman
March
2 Digital detox. Lynne Galloway
16 Mental health awareness. Malachy Keegan
23 Growing in awareness. Helen Davies & Lynne Galloway
30 Another view on why Jesus died: at-one-ment. David Cherry
April
6 Exploring Bach's *St John Passion*. Abigail Graham
27 The loving kindness of our God – who sets us free, 11am–4pm. Michael Smith SJ
May
4 Journalling as prayer. Andrew Kerr-Jarrett
18 'Who are you, Lord?' Encountering Jesus Christ in the gospels, 11am–4pm. Brian Purfield
June
1 Prayer within a busy life. Chris Chapman
15 How well do I listen? Margaret Philpot
22 Mindfulness – with body and soul. Lynne Galloway
29 Praying with art at Tate Britain. Audrey & Eamonn Hamilton
July
The following course/workshop is offered over 2 sessions. It is essential to attend both.
6 Contemplative photography: Seeing beauty in the everyday, Part 1. Tom Palmer & Raymond Martin
20 Contemplative photography: Seeing beauty in the everyday, Part 2. Tom Palmer & Raymond Martin

61 Oasis Days London

St Andrew's Church, St Andrew Street, Holborn, London EC4A 3AF   07429 612642
email martin@stmarys-harefield.org.uk
Q   *website* oasisdays.org.uk

Non-residential.

Notes Oasis Days offer quiet reflection for people who need a day to recharge their spiritual batteries and enjoy the stimulation of an excellent speaker. Oasis Days are held on the second Tuesday of each month 10.45am–3.30pm. Those leading are from across the denominational spectrum. Pre-book by telephone or email above for catering purposes or write to Rev Martin Davies, 28 Countess Close, Harefield, Uxbridge UB9 6DL. In 2019 the dates are: 8 January, 12 February, 12 March, 9 April, 14 May, 11 June, 9 July, 13 August, 10 September, 8 October, 12 November, 10 December. See website for details of speakers.
Contact Rev Martin Davies, Organiser.

62 Penlar

North Way, Pinner, Middlesex HA5 3NY
                                                07735 274630
B, C, P, Q, S, Wf   *email* contactsuewilson@gmail.com

Non-residential.
Notes Penlar is an ideal venue for non-residential groups of up to 12 people, comprising one large room, a creative room, dining room, kitchen and a quiet, secluded garden. MBTI® workshops for groups, couples and individuals are available. They are individually designed to your specific requirements and led by Sue Wilson, a Registered MBTI® Practitioner of wide experience, covering some 20 years. Quiet days are run on a monthly basis, or perhaps you would like to lead your own quiet day at Penlar?
Contact Sue Wilson.

March
23 Retreat Association Training Day. Be still and know that I am God. Learning how to prepare and lead a Quiet Day for those beginning to listen to that stillness inside themselves. Sue Wilson
September
21 Retreat Association Training Day. See above.

63 The Royal Foundation of St Katharine

2 Butcher Row, London E14 8DS   0300 111 1147
                                       email carol@rfsk.org.uk
B, C, D, I, P, Q, S, Wf   *website* www.rfsk.org.uk/retreats

Rooms 20 double, 17 single, 2 king, 3 twin, 4 family, 1 double suite. All rooms have *en suite*. We opened our new Chapelside retreat wing in early 2018; these *en suite* bedrooms are situated around an inner courtyard leading to our chapel. Please do call to book these rooms for a personal or group retreat.
Notes Situated in central London it is hard to imagine a more peaceful urban setting for a group or individual retreat. St Katharine's is an oasis in which to take time out from daily life for reflection, contemplation, or just to be. It has a rich history of hospitality and we look forward to welcoming you whether you wish to come for a day or to stay overnight. We have the rare privilege of being a few minutes' walk from the river Thames in the east of London but still just moments from Limehouse DLR station. A wonderful chance to step out of the city but not to leave it. Our beautiful chapel at the heart of St Katharine's is open

for use at all times with services held daily. We offer a variety of private rooms that can be used for personal and group retreats which include our beautiful newly opened Chapelside rooms. We also run regular quiet days throughout the year and open reflective days and a supper club each month. Please see the website for more details. During your stay with us you are warmly welcome to take a short stroll to St Katharine's Precinct and the Yurt Café. This newly-opened project is building connections with and across communities through conversation, reflection and community projects.

Feedback from a recent guest: 'A wonderful sense of deep peace from the time of arrival. Just wonderful, the ambiance, the setting and the comfort. I agree wholeheartedly with the slogan "an extraordinary urban oasis". Thank you.'

Contact Carol Rider, Lay Chaplain.

Open reflective days are on the second Monday of every month when we welcome individuals for their own quiet day.

Led quiet days we host these throughout the year, see details below.

Led residential retreats details can be found on our website.

January
26 Quiet day. Kate Monkhouse
February
16 Quiet day. Chris Chapman
April
13 Ramola Parish, CARM
May
10 Quiet day. Brian Draper
June
1 Quiet day. Richard Carter
July
13 Experiencing the labyrinth. Jan Sellers
September
14 Quiet day. Shaun Lambert
October
12 Quiet day. Will Van der Hart
November
2 Quiet day. Graham Kings
14 Quiet day. John Bell

64 St Peter's Bourne

40 Oakleigh Park South, Whetstone, London N20 9JN   020 8445 5535
email operations@stpetersbourne.com
Wf   *website* www.stpetersbourne.com

Non-residential.
Notes St Peter's Bourne is committed to providing excellent meeting and day retreat facilities for groups with a specific emphasis on peace and tranquillity. Day rates available for up to 20 guests. Fully catered or room only options. Bookings taken for all group types and specific arrangements can be made to accommodate your needs. During the summer months, a large marquee is available for outdoor events. Free Wifi available. Easy access via bus, train or car (no parking restrictions on road).
Contact Jacques Mutevelian, Operations Lead.

65 Sisters of St Andrew

99 Belmont Hill, Lewisham, London SE13 5DY
020 8852 1662
email welcome@sisters-of-st-andrew.com
B, C, D, I, P, Q, S, W, Wf   *website* www.sisters-of-st-andrew.com

Rooms 6 single with WC and washbasin, and 2 *en suite*. Disabled access within the house including a lift and path access to the surrounding gardens. Fully-equipped kitchenettes. Self-catering only. For programmed IGRs meals can be provided. Shops and amenities close by. Parking. Easily accessible from mainline stations to Blackheath/Lewisham, DLR and buses (bus stop outside the property). Proximity to A2 and A20.

Notes The Sisters of St Andrew, an Ignatian congregation, was founded in the Middle Ages to welcome pilgrims en route to Compostela in Spain. Since 1231, we continue to welcome individuals and groups for times of retreat, silence and personal reflection. Our house of welcome is a real haven, a surprisingly peaceful oasis situated halfway between Lewisham and Blackheath, close to Greenwich and Lee. The beautiful round 'Oast' House Chapel with its stained-glass windows provides a space for both personal and group prayer. Visitors are welcome to join the community prayer. There are facilities for small and larger day groups, maximum 25. Self-catering only. A well-equipped kitchen is available. Drinks are provided. Art materials, books, pictures, music and other resources are available for use in the house. The large attractive garden surrounding the house is partly landscaped and partly meadow, and also boasts a vegetable garden and a grass labyrinth. The house is situated close to Blackheath Common, Greenwich Park and smaller local parks as well as the Thames path.

The Sisters are available by request for input/facilitation/spiritual accompaniment/self-catering retreats/retreats in daily life (19th Annotation)/supervision and outreach. Please check the website regularly for an update of forthcoming events not included in the programme.

Contact The Sisters of St Andrew preferably by email or alternatively by SAE or phone.

Quiet day/Retreat day For individuals with accompaniment by one of the sisters. Booking essential.
Small residential groups For up to 6 people. Self-catering only. Booking essential.
Meditative evening prayer Including Taizé chants. Last Wednesday of each month except July/August and December, 7.30–8.30pm. Arrive at 7pm if you wish to practise the songs. No need to book.
Come away One Thursday a month 10.30am–12.30pm. For those who care for a loved one suffering from ill-health. A time to come away, pause, reflect, listen and share. Check dates on website or call. Led by Sr Regula.
Lenten journey 'No greater love', with works of the French artist Arcabas. Input, personal quiet time. Book for the whole series of 5 Wednesdays, or one or more mornings. 10am for 10.30am start to 1pm. Please book in advance. Led by Sr Marie-Christine.
Mass with the community Weekly Friday evenings 6.30–7.15pm (call to check the previous day).
All day events listed below Arrive 10am for 10.30am–4pm. Booking essential unless otherwise specified.

January

14 A Sabbath Day – 'On the seventh day God rested'. 10am for 10.30am–4pm. Come for the morning, afternoon or both. Short input, a time to pause, rest, reflect in silence. Booking essential. Sr Sigrun

February

11 A Sabbath Day – see above. Sr Sigrun

March

9 Lenten quiet day. 'Cry of the Earth, Cry of the Poor.' Sr Regula

13 Lenten journey 1. No greater love. See notes. Passion prefigured. The Incarnation. Sr Marie-Christine

20 Lenten journey 2. No greater love. See notes. Anointing in Bethany. Sr Marie-Christine

22–24 IGR. Stepping stones into silence. A silent retreat for beginners with personal accompaniment. Sisters of St Andrew

27 Lenten journey 3. No greater love. See notes. Last Supper. Sr Marie-Christine

April

3 Lenten journey 4. No greater love. See notes. Passion. Sr Marie-Christine

10 Lenten journey 5. No greater love. See notes. Death of the beloved. Sr Marie-Christine

15–17 Holy Week. Journeying in silence with Jesus in the footsteps of His Passion. Contemplate the Passion through word, music and image. Each day 2–9pm. Sisters of St Andrew

May

8 Living bread, daily bread. A creative retreat day using art material to pray the Examen. No specific skills needed. Mary Chamberlin & Sr Marie-Christine

19 Open afternoon. 2–5.30pm. Come and enjoy the urban oasis: meet each other, relax in the garden, walk the labyrinth. 4.30pm prayer in the chapel.

June

5 A Sabbath Day– see above. Sr Clare

12 Move with the Spirit into the Trinity. Exploring the Icon of the Trinity through movement and creativity 10.30 for 11am–4pm. Rev Pamela Alexander & Sr Marie-Christine

22 Making room for God – The spiritual path of St John of the Cross. A Catholic Spirituality Network day. Non-members welcome. 10.30 for 11am–4pm. Booking: 07756 864784. Chris Chapman

July

19–28 IGR. An urban oasis silent retreat with individual accompaniment. A minimum of 3 and a maximum of 8 days. Full board or self-catering. Early booking essential. Sisters of St Andrew

September

28 Day retreat with the 'Icon of Friendship'. Sr Marie-Christine

October

16 A Sabbath Day – see above. Sr Regula

18–20 IGR. Stepping stones into silence. A silent retreat for beginners with personal accompaniment. Booking essential. Sisters of St Andrew

November

9 Difficult transitions. A reflection day with inputs, personal times, sharing. Sr Marie-Christine

13 A Sabbath Day – see above. Sr Sigrun

30 Advent quiet day. Quiet pause in Advent. Sr Sigrun

December

11 Meditative evening prayer 7.30–8.30pm. See notes.

GREATER MANCHESTER

66 Katherine House FCJ

26 Singleton Road, Salford M7 4WL

0161 708 9744 / 07428 481494

email khousefcj@hotmail.com

website www.katherinehousefcj.org

Co, Q, S, Wf

Rooms Conference room accommodates 20–25, dining/meeting room accommodates 20, large garden, simple attractive oratory in the basement, coffee/tea area. Flipchart, data projector and screen are available for use by groups.

Residential accommodation (self-catering only) 9 single with own washbasin (sheets and towels are provided). 2 extra sleeping spaces available if requested. Showers and bathrooms. Well-equipped kitchen for self-catering arrangements. Simple breakfast provided.

Notes Katherine House aims to provide a hospitable meeting place for people of all faiths and none; a quiet space for prayer and reflection (for individuals and groups); a programme of events, including retreats, quiet days and short conferences; or a place where you can run your own. Katherine House is a small Christian conference centre owned and run by the Faithful Companions of Jesus (FCJ), an international Congregation of Catholic Sisters. We welcome people of all faiths and none. Spiritual direction and person-centred counselling are offered. Katherine House is approximately 3 miles from Manchester in a pleasant leafy area, north of the city.

Contact Marie Pattison, Director.

Regular day retreats, book club, film club, Bible study, holy conversations. Plus various courses and study days. Please see www.katherinehousefcj.org/programme for details or let us have your address and we would be happy to send you this season's programme.

67 Salford Prayer Guides

c/o Mary E Nono, 31 Delahays Rd, Hale, Altrincham, Cheshire WA15 8DT

0161 980 6776

07538 573621

email mary@nono.org.uk

B, C, I, Q, S

Non-residential. No premises.

Notes We are an ecumenical team working across the North West, mainly in the Greater Manchester area. Team members come from all walks of life. Lay people, religious, clergy, women and men. We are trained to accompany others in their prayer life by leading weeks of accompanied prayer, open-door retreats, quiet days, other spirituality programmes, 19th Annotation retreats and ongoing spiritual direction. We work in Churches Together settings in the main, but also in individual parishes and in our own homes. Training courses in spiritual guidance given. Other spirituality training programmes offered are as follows: teach us to pray; teach us to listen: prayer companionship experience; prayer companionship II; spiritual directors' further training/enrichment

programme. Supervision and supervision training offered. Details available on request from Mary Nono.
Contact Mary Nono.

HAMPSHIRE

68 The Community of Hopeweavers
Tardis, Beacon Road, West End, Southampton, Hampshire SO30 3BS
(bookings and enquiries) 07821 105245
(main house) 02380 473680
email contactus@hopeweavers.org.uk
B, C, Q, S, Y   *website* www.hopeweavers.co.uk

Non-residential.
Notes The Community of Hopeweavers is an Acknowledged Anglican Religious Community, based on the outskirts of Southampton. We offer space to those seeking stillness and sanctuary with Jesus Christ at the heart. Creativity has an important place as we seek God together through times of prayer using our daily office and the Eucharist, quiet days, small groups, projects and longer retreats, many of which we lead in other venues, e.g. Hilfield Friary and St Columba's Retreat House, Woking. Some become members of the Community and live to our Rule of Life. See our website for up-to-date event information and free access to the prayers we use every day.
Contact The Guardian.
    January
    19 Quiet day, hosting the Retreat Association Icon.

69 The Grail
The Hermitage, Cheriton Road, Winchester, Hampshire SO22 5HW   01962 859870
email v.wright@grailsociety.org.uk
I, P, S, W   *website* www.grailsociety.org.uk

Notes Opportunities for individual retreats may be possible, with spiritual accompaniment and healing by prior arrangement. Occasional availability for day groups of up to 10 people. Please enquire for availability.
Contact Valerie Wright.

70 The High House
Stroud, nr Petersfield, Hampshire GU32 3PN   01730 262520
P

Rooms Spacious house with oratory, library and stairlift. Indoor swimming pool and beautiful garden. Water garden. Also 2-bed ground-floor flat available for sabbaticals etc.
Notes Available for quiet days, workshops, etc (max 25 people). IGRs, theme retreats (prayer through painting).
Contact Mrs Jenny Sandys.

YOUR FIRST RETREAT?
Choosing a retreat – see page 58

71 Sisters of Bethany
7 Nelson Road, Southsea, Hampshire PO5 2AR
    02392 833498
email ssb@sistersofbethany.org.uk
D, E, P, Q   *website* www.sistersofbethany.org.uk

Rooms 6 single (2 on ground floor), 1 twin up 2 steps. Lift to all floors.
Notes C of E, but all welcome. Facilities for non-residential groups (up to 24). Facilities for wheelchair-users on ground floor. Guests are welcome to join the community for a daily Mass and in their recitation of monastic offices throughout the year and during Holy Week when the Triduum is sung. We have an extensive library, with a wide variety of books. 20-min walk from the seafront. Please notify of special diets in advance. Wifi access in 'old' house only. More details on website.
Contact Rev Mother SSB.
Open quiet days Saturdays 10am–4pm.
Open quiet afternoons Mondays 1.30–4.30pm.
Julian meetings 1st/3rd Wednesdays 2–2.45pm and 2nd/4th Thursdays 10.15–11.15am.
Deaf church first Sunday every month 2.15pm.
    December 2018–January 2019
    22–7 House closed.
    January
    18–25 Week of prayer for Christian unity.
    19 Open quiet day. Mrs Cis Delmege
    23 Unity service 2.30pm. Rev Andrew de Ville
    February
    16 Open quiet day. Rev David Simpson RN
    18 Quiet afternoon. Lynne or Trevor Cooper
    March
    9 Open quiet day. Rev Jenny Wiltshire
    April
    6 Open quiet day. Rev Dr Amanda Bloor
    8 Quiet afternoon. Revd Brian Pickett
    27 Easter carols 2.30pm.
    May
    15 Julian festival 10am–3pm.
    18 Open quiet day. Rev Simon Holland
    June
    15 Open quiet day. Sr Mary Joy SSB
    17 Quiet afternoon. Lynne or Trevor Cooper
    July
    13 Open quiet day. Sr Joanna Elizabeth SSB
    July–August
    15–12 House closed.
    September
    14 Open quiet day. Rev Tony Forrest or Rev Samantha Martell
    October
    5 Open quiet day. Rev Tony Forrest or Rev Samantha Martell
    7 Quiet afternoon. Miss Joan Mason
    November
    16 Open quiet day. Ms Angela O'Donoghue
    December
    4 Advent carols 7.30pm.
    14 Open quiet day. Mrs Jackie Brookfield
    16 Quiet afternoon. Rev Anne Cocking
    December–January 2020
    21–7 House closed.

72 Wisdom Centre

The Abbey, Romsey, Hampshire SO51 8EL

01794 830206

email reception@wisdomhouseromsey.co.uk
website www.wisdomhouseromsey.co.uk

B, C, Co, D, E, I, P, Q, S, V, Wf

Rooms *Chez Nous* cottage sits beside our stunning labyrinth. Chez Nous sleeps 4 with 3 bedrooms, a shower room (upstairs) toilet and simple kitchen facilities. A simple breakfast is supplied for guests. Accommodation is on a self-catering basis.

Notes Our hospitality is ecumenical and based on the ethos of the Daughters of Wisdom, a Roman Catholic Delegation of religious Sisters.

Contact Mel, Sue or Angela.

We have a monthly programme of Christian, interfaith and therapeutic workshops and quiet days which are open to all. Our focus is on prayer, reflection and meditation, the Wisdom of the early Church through St Benedict, Ignatius, St Francis, Thomas Merton and our founders St Louis Marie de Montfort and the Blessed Marie Louise Trichet. We also host days on Twelve Step Recovery, bereavement and mindfulness. See our website for details.

HEREFORDSHIRE

73 Belmont Abbey

Ruckhall Lane, Hereford HR2 9RZ 01432 374750

email retreats@belmontabbey.org.uk

C, E, P, Wf *website* www.belmontabbey.org.uk

Rooms 3 single, 17 twin/single *en suite.*

Notes Belmont Abbey is a Benedictine monastery. Individuals or groups are welcome to stay in the comfortable monastery guest house, Hedley Lodge, and can share in the daily round of prayer with the monastic community. Guests are welcome throughout the year for a quiet stay or to participate in an organised retreat. Parish or other groups are welcome.

Contact Br David Yates, Retreat Secretary (email preferred).

January

25–27 Sermons in stone. How the church's finest buildings express the Christian faith. Dom Brendan Thomas

February

9 The Gospel of Luke. A study day for the Sunday liturgy. Dom Jonathan Rollinson

15–17 The flowing river of tradition. How does the church change, grow and renew yet remain faithful to Christ? Abbot Paul Stonham & others

March

4–7 The shadow of the tree: our Lent retreat journeys through the Scriptures to the shadow of the cross. Dom Brendan Thomas & others

13 Lent Wednesdays. Life together (St Basil and the Cappadocians). Dom Brendan Thomas

20 Lent Wednesdays. Living amongst us (St Athanasius). Abbot Paul Stonham

27 Lent Wednesdays. The New Jerusalem (St Augustine). Dom Alistair Findlay

April

3 Lent Wednesdays. The new man (St Irenaeus and Tertullian). Dom Andrew Berry

10 Lent Wednesdays. The living word (St Jerome). Dom David Yates

18–22 The Belmont Easter retreat. Join us to celebrate the greatest Christian feast. The Belmont Community

26–28 God in the unexpected. Renewing our spiritual lives through the understanding that God reveals himself in the ordinary things of life. Abbot Paul Stonham

May

10–12 Plainsong and prayer. A Gregorian chant workshop, singing and praying these ancient melodies. Beginners welcome. Abbot Paul Stonham

June

2 Beyond Pentecost. What really happened in the Church in its early days? John Huntriss

22–24 The Catholic novel. Faith, fiction and the Catholic imagination. The Belmont Community

29 Day of recollection for extraordinary ministers of Holy Communion.

July

5–7 Love was his meaning. A weekend with Julian of Norwich, one of the most wonderful Christian voices. Dom Brendan Thomas

20 Journey into Egypt. An armchair pilgrimage to biblical and Christian Egypt. Dom Brendan Thomas

26–28 The Northern Lights. A retreat with Bede, Cuthbert and Aidan and the Saints of the North. Dom Alistair Findlay

August

12–15 The Saints through artists' eyes. Story and symbol, life and afterlife, in some great paintings. Dom Brendan Thomas

15 A day with our Lady. Praying with the Blessed Virgin Mary on the feast of the Assumption.

19–24 Beginners Icon workshop. The Icon of St Paul. Dom Alex Echeandía

26–31 Intermediate Workshop I. The Icon of St Cecilia. Dom Alex Echeandía

September

2–7 Intermediate Workshop II. An Icon of the Annunciation. Dom Alex Echeandía

14 'Lord, teach us to pray.' The 'Our Father' as the heart of Christian prayer. Dom Alistair Findlay

20–22 The monastery in the world. St Benedict in his time, and his message for today. Richard Newman & Dom Brendan Thomas

October

4–6 Piero's Tuscan Gospel. The pure, still beauty of Piero della Francesca's art and the spirit of the Renaissance. Dom Brendan Thomas

18–20 Nurturing the soul. What keeps us from going stale in our Christian lives? Archbishop Kevin McDonald, former Archbishop of Southwark, & Abbot Paul Stonham

26 The Church's best-kept secret. Why don't we know more about the Church's social teaching? Dom Andrew Berry

November
8–10 God's jesters. The ways of foolishness in the Scriptures and the saints. Dom Brendan Thomas
22–24 The Book of Revelation and the liturgy. Dom Alistair Findlay
December
2–5 The coming of our God. Finding meaning in Advent and Christmas. Abbot Paul Stonham & Dom Brendan Thomas
7 Advent day of recollection. Dom David Yates

74 Knight's Retreat

New Mill, Eaton Bishop, Hereford,
Herefordshire HR2 9QS
07925 516 362 / 01981 251 324
email renewal@knights-retreat.co.uk
B, Co, P, Q, S, W, Wf, Y   *website* www.knights-retreat.co.uk

Rooms 1 double and 2 twin (+cot if required); all *en suite* with function room with piano, grounds with stream and woods. Old-world hospitality and prayer offered in ancient former water mill. Suppers by arrangement.
Notes A peaceful well of refreshment for body and soul, somewhere informal and friendly to relax, restore and recover. Warm welcome offered to church groups, individual believers or peace-seeking members of the wider community who want to unwind and escape for a while in a quiet rural setting with private grounds to wander, pray or to walk and unwind. Ideal location for quiet days/awaydays. Footpaths and quiet roads for walking and cycling start from the front gate. Retreat from the world in blissful solitude in a haven of calm.
Contact Roger or Wendy for special rates for groups (max 6) and/or longer visits.

75 Travelling Light

House of Shalom, 3 Westview, Whitchurch,
Ross-on-Wye, Herefordshire HR9 6DB
01600 890376
email travellinglight@supanet.com
B, C, D, Q, W   *website* www.travelling-light.org.uk

Non-residential.
Notes Travelling Light runs both day and residential retreats. We hold Refocus and Reflective Quiet retreats in South Herefordshire and the Monmouth area. These are day retreats held in church premises situated in the beautiful Wye Valley. Our retreats are an opportunity to spend time away from normal routine, to slow down, find space to reflect, take stock and experience the love of God. Prayer ministry is available. Our team consists of Christians with a wide experience of faith and life. Some are members of the Northumbria Community.
Refocus retreats These themed days include teaching, sharing, creativity and times of quiet and meditation. They provide an opportunity to be alone and together with God.
Reflective quiet retreats These are times for quiet space, and are based around the prayers of the Northumbria Community.
There is no charge for the day retreats but we do appreciate a donation towards the ministry costs.

Residential retreats We run occasional residential retreats. Please see our website for further details.
Contact Robin and Carole Moulton.
Please visit our website for further information and programme updates, or phone or email for further details. Booking is essential for all retreats, preferably by email, as places are limited. All day retreats are 10am–4pm and are within easy travelling distance of Ross-on-Wye and Monmouth. If you have any queries or require further information, please do not hesitate to contact us. The 2019 programme explores the overall theme of Growth with God.
February
23 Refocus retreat at Wyesham Christian Fellowship, Monmouth. Freedom to grow.
March
20 Reflective quiet retreat at St Dubricius Church, Whitchurch.
April
13 Refocus retreat at Wyesham Christian Fellowship, Monmouth. Shoots of growth.
May
8 Reflective quiet retreat at St Dubricius Church, Whitchurch.
June
8 Refocus retreat at Wyesham Christian Fellowship, Monmouth. Seasons of growth.
September
21 Refocus retreat at Wyesham Christian Fellowship, Monmouth. Gifts for growth.
October
16 Reflective quiet retreat at St Dubricius Church, Whitchurch.
November
16 Refocus retreat at Wyesham Christian Fellowship, Monmouth. Fruits of growth.

HERTFORDSHIRE

76 Watton at Stone Methodist Church and Day Retreat Centre

High Street, Watton at Stone, Hertford
SG14 3SY   01920 831165
email wattonatstonemethodistchurch@yahoo.co.uk
D, W   *website* www.haebea.org/churches/watton-at-stone-methodist.html

Non-residential.
Notes Available for day groups of up to 50 people to run self-led retreats, quiet days and meetings. The church has modern flexible seating and benefits from an audiovisual system, data projector and microphones, an organ and CD player. The hall is ideal for meals/refreshments and breakout areas. There is a fully-equipped modern kitchen with dishwasher, large cooker and microwave. Ideal for self-catering and a welcome pack of tea, coffee, milk and sugar is provided. There is disabled access and 2 toilets, 1 of which can accommodate a wheelchair plus baby-changing facilities. It is a fully refurbished church and hall located in the middle of the village, with 2 public houses, café and village store nearby, and close to the village railway station. Kings Cross/Moorgate is around 50 mins.

97

The A10 and A1 are within easy reach, and there is a car park for 15 cars. In the grounds there is a meditation garden and there are country walks around the village and along the river Beane.
Contact Graham Guinn.

ISLE OF WIGHT

77 Haven Hall

5 Howard Road, Shanklin, Isle of Wight PO37 6HD   07914 796494
email david@havenhall.uk
Co, D, P, Pe, S, W, Wf   *website* www.havenhall.uk

Rooms 14 *en suite* double rooms with beds which can be either kingsize or unzipped to form 2 twin beds. 6 of the *en suite* rooms have living rooms and kitchens and are self-contained holiday rental apartments, suitable for private quiet retreats. All rooms have sea views. The owner, David, is a trained Anglican Spiritual Director and available for daily spiritual direction if required. His wife Arielle is a NLP trainer and Executive Coach and is also available for NLP counselling. Haven Hall can accommodate 28 people for a group retreat or workshop. There are 2 large rooms for workshops. All rooms including bedrooms are fully air-conditioned and heated. There is 1 room which is suitable for wheelchair access plus Haven Hall itself is wheelchair-accessible.
Notes Haven Hall is a very luxurious, 5-star hotel suitable for individual private retreats in one of our 6 self-catering flats, or for a group retreat of up to 28 participants. The property is on 2 acres by the sea with stunning gardens and views and very quiet. Haven Hall has a swimming pool which is heated for 3 months of the summer plus a grass tennis court. The beach is a 10-min walk along the cliff path and there are lots of walking trails nearby. Please see our website for photos and more information.
Contact David Barratt

78 St Cecilia's Abbey

Appley Rise, Ryde, Isle of Wight PO33 1LH
01983 562602
email garth@stceciliasabbey.org.uk
E, P, S   *website* www.stceciliasabbey.org.uk

Rooms 3 twin, which can be used as singles, 1 single annexe. Self-catering.
Notes Private retreats only for women and married couples. Open to retreatants who are seeking a time of prayer, silence and reflection with God, and who wish to attend daily Mass and share in some of the monastic liturgy. Mass and the divine office are in the Abbey church, sung in Gregorian chant. There is an atmosphere of peace and prayer, and an opportunity to speak with one of the sisters. RC but all denominations welcome.
Contact The Guestmistress.

**PRAY WITH THE
RETREAT ASSOCIATION ICON**
– see page 78

KENT

79 Burrswood Health and Wellbeing

Groombridge, Tunbridge Wells, Kent TN3 9PY
01892 865988
email reservations@burrswood.org.uk
C, Ch, Co, D, E, Q, S, V, W, Wf   *website* www.burrswood.org.uk

Rooms A wide variety of single, twin and double rooms. The majority are *en suite*. We have ground-floor rooms and adapted rooms should you require them.
Notes Whether you're exploring the beautiful local countryside and history, visiting family or attending a course at Burrswood, we have comfortable and individually styled rooms to accommodate you. Single or twin rooms. *en suite*/private bathrooms. All rooms have television, radio, Wifi and hospitality trays. Full/half board or B&B. Meals served in the main dining room overlooking our sumptuous gardens.
Contact Reservations Team.

80 The Friars

Aylesford, Kent ME20 7BX   01622 717272
fax 01622 715575
email retreat@thefriars.org.uk
C, D, E, I, P, Q, V, W, Wf   *website* www.thefriars.org.uk

Rooms 24 single, 30 twin, 6 family.
Notes The Friars is home to a community of Carmelite friars close to the county town of Maidstone, Kent. It is a place of pilgrimage and prayer and is open to all. Visitors are welcome individually or in groups and all are welcome to join the daily community services. Parish groups can also reserve a chapel for their own service. A full programme of retreats is offered throughout the year. RC.
Contact The reception office for a retreat programme.
Rachel's Vineyard A weekend residential retreat for people hurting after an abortion. For dates and to book please contact Pam, 07851 331816. Rachel's Vineyard Team, www.rachelsvineyard.org.uk.

January
26 Rejoice and be glad. Exploring what it means to be holy in today's world. Chris Chapman
February
23 Blessed are those who hunger and thirst for justice. How can we create a just and fair society? Pat Gaffney
March
Six Lent talks, starting on Ash Wednesday, with 6.30pm evening prayer, 7pm soup, 7.30pm talk, discussion and reflection.
6 Jesus in the wilderness. Kevin Alban
13 The Transfiguration. Michael Cox
20 Barren fig tree. Paul de Groot
27 Prodigal Son. Francis Kemsley
April
3 Woman taken in adultery. Sheila Grimwood
10 Palm Sunday. Maggie Cascioli
18–21 Easter Triduum. A chance to make our own the events of Holy Week. Sheila Grimwood, Maggie Cascioli & Paul de Groot

May
18 Quiet day. Prayer and reflection in a peaceful atmosphere. Pastoral Team
June
8 Thy Kingdom Come. Journeying in prayer from Ascension to Pentecost. Ged Walsh
July
13 Our Lady of Mount Carmel. A day of prayer, reflection and preparation for the coming feast. Carmelite Family.
August
19–23 IGR. Summer stillness. Francis Kemsley & Felicity Young
September
14 Walking with God. A pilgrimage from Chilham to Canterbury. Concludes with evensong in the Cathedral. Maggie Cascioli & Paul de Groot
27–29 Saint Thérèse weekend. An opportunity to celebrate Saint Thérèse with the Society of the Little Flower. Canon John Udris
October
11–13 Grief in loss, hope in Christ. This retreat is for anyone who has experienced a bereavement. Elizabeth Partridge & Francis Kemsley
19 A day with Teresa. How can Teresa accompany you in your journey today? Sheila Grimwood
November
9 The Wisdom of Carmel. A look at how the great figures in Carmel help us on the spiritual journey. Kevin Alban
December
6–8 Advent retreat. How the coming of God into our world gives us hope. Francis Kemsley

81 The Living Well

Canterbury Diocesan Centre for Healing and Wholeness, Vicarage Lane, Nonington, Dover, Kent CT15 4JT 01304 842847
email contact@the-living-well.org.uk
D, P, Pe, Q, W   *website* www.the-living-well.org.uk

Non-residential.
Notes The Centre offers a full programme of non-residential healing and quiet days. The facilities are also available for small parish groups and personal quiet days. Alternatively The Living Well Team can provide days outside the centre within parishes throughout Kent. Please contact us for further details.
Services of healing and wholeness Every Tuesday and Thursday 10.30am. Everyone welcome.
Deeper healing days One-to-one prayer ministry. Many of us continue to recycle or repeat hurts we have received over the years. A deeper healing day enables us to be listened to and prayed with in order to bring release and peace through prayer. It is not counselling but is an opportunity to listen to ourselves and God in a safe and welcoming place where confidentiality will be respected. 10am–4pm. Places limited. 19 January; 6 February; 1, 27 March; 8 April; 13 May; 1 June; 22 July; 9 August; 2 September; 11 October; 4 November; 6 December.
Quiet days Different themes including worship, some input and silence. Enjoy the space in the house and garden 10am–4pm. 13 February; 15 April; 12 June; 29 November.

Clergy oasis days Morning prayer at 9.30am, Holy Communion at 12.30pm. Space to be with God for ordained ministers. Places limited. 1 April; 28 June; 13 September; 18 November.
Please see our website and programme for more information on all our days.
Contact Rev Canon Sarah Chapman, Chaplain.

82 The Quiet View

146 The Street, Kingston, Canterbury, Kent CT4 6JQ 01227 830070
email lizziehopthrow@gmail.com
B, D, E, P, Q, S, V, Y   *website* www.quietview.co.uk

Non-residential.
Notes The Quiet View is a centre for contemplative spirituality and we invite you to experience peace of heart in the Garden of Kent. Rooted in Christianity we also welcome people of all faiths or none. In an area of outstanding natural beauty, the 2-acre garden is surrounded by rolling countryside. It has been designed to provide secluded quiet, natural 'rooms' for stillness and reflection. Individual and group retreats welcome – visits by appointment only. The Quiet View is affiliated to the Quiet Garden Trust. We also have a large yurt with a log-burning stove, a fully-equipped kitchen, worship resources and educational equipment. There is a permanent labyrinth in the garden and a fabric labyrinth for use in the yurt. Spiritual accompaniment and teaching on the labyrinth is available. Book a space to follow your own programme or join in our events (see our website).
Taizé style prayers 1st Fridays at 7pm in the yurt.
Contact Rev Lizzie Hopthrow.

83 Monastery of Our Lady of Hyning

Warton, Carnforth, Lancashire LA5 9SE 01524 732684
email hyningbookings@yahoo.co.uk
C, Ch, E, P, Wf   *website* www.hyning.org

Rooms 9 single, 11 twin, 1 double.
Notes Our Bernardine Cistercian monastery is situated on the Lancashire/Cumbria border, a designated area of outstanding natural beauty. Through hospitality we welcome individuals and groups who would like to share the peace and prayerfulness of our monastic guest house. Guests are welcome to join the community for daily Mass and the sung divine office. By request, sisters may be available to accompany retreatants or just to listen. At certain times we offer retreats and opportunities for catechetics. Some sisters are also involved in artistic work, including the writing of Icons. Chaplain in residence. Guests are free to use the church, library, bookshop, small gift shop, the sitting room with its tea and coffee-making facilities and meeting room. Most of our spacious garden is open to guests. Art studio available for guests by arrangement. See website for further details.
Contact The Bookings Secretary.

March
8–10 Lent retreat. Led by a sister.
11–15 Icon writing workshop. Beginners. Limited places. Led by a sister.
26 Card-making day.
April
15–23 Easter guests.
May
20–24 Icon writing workshop. Advanced/intermediate. Limited places.
June
4 Card-making day.
July
8–12 Prayer, nature and gardening.
September
23–27 Icon writing workshop. Beginners. Limited places. Led by a sister.
October
8 Christmas card-making day.
14–18 Prayer, nature and gardening.
November
15–17 Spiritual scrapbooking weekend. Led by a sister.
November–December
29–1 Advent retreat. Led by a sister.
December
23–31 Christmas guests.

84 Whalley Abbey

The Sands, Whalley, Lancashire BB7 9SS

01254 828400
email office@whalleyabbey.org
B, C, D, I, P, Q, S, W, Wf   *website* www.whalleyabbey.co.uk

Rooms 9 twin, 6 single, 2 double.
Notes Belonging to the Church of England Diocese of Blackburn, the retreat centre is located on the banks of the river Calder in the beautiful grounds of the Abbey ruins on a site made holy by the prayers of generations of monks, and provides high quality, welcoming hospitality.
Contact Christine Nelson.

January
14–16 Retreat. 'At the gate of the year' (Minnie Haskins). We reflect upon the New Year and of God's promise to walk beside us. Rev Jonathan Carmyllie
24 Quiet day 9.30am–3.30pm. 'Stand at the crossroads and look' (Jeremiah 6:16). Thoughts, questions and silence to tune into Jesus at the crossroads. Rt Rev Dr Jill Duff
February
11–13 Retreat. Setting God's people free. Living as a disciple of Jesus in everyday life. Archdeacon Mark Ireland
21 Quiet day 10am–4pm. Inhabiting forgotten values, hope, simplicity and service. Canon Peter Howell-Jones
March
11–13 Retreat. 'Kindle a flame of sacred love' (Charles Wesley). Explore what His presence amongst us means and calls forth from us as we travel through Lent. Canon Patricia Impey

21 Quiet day 10am–4pm. 'Choose life' (Deuteronomy 30:19). Reflections on how we make choices in daily life, drawing on the experience of Jesus, Moses and our own. Rev Fiona Jenkins
April
8–10 Retreat. A passionate faith. The passion of Christ, and our passion for Him. Archdeacon Michael Everitt
May
23 Quiet day 10am–4pm. 'Unless the Lord builds the house' (Psalm 127:1). Reflections on mission and context, including building a school in the Amazon. Archdeacon Michael Everitt
June
10–12 Retreat. Jesus didn't have a junk drawer. Take some time to focus on the three divine qualities of spirituality, simplicity and serenity. Ann Nutt
20 Quiet day 10am–4pm. 'super-Whalley-Alban-Abbots-Solas-are-the-focus'. Interact with the grounds, buildings and ruins of Whalley Abbey and some of the spiritual riches of 1000 years of history. Rev Dr Tom Woolford
July
25 Quiet day 10am–4pm. 'For I greet him the days I meet him' (Gerard Manley Hopkins). Rt Rev Philip North, Bishop of Burnley
August
12–14 Retreat. Walking and prayer. Walk several miles each day and use the beauty of God's creation to inspire us in prayer. Archdeacon Mark Ireland
22 Quiet day 10am–4pm. Discipleship, a call to follow the liberating Christ, exploring Luke 5:1–11 and The Farewell Discourses of John's Gospel. Donna Worthington
September
9–11 Retreat. Life after death – living well after bereavement. NB: if your bereavement is recent (less than a year) this retreat may not be helpful to you. Mandy Stanton
19 Quiet day 10am–4pm. Our common life together. Canon Peter Howell-Jones
October
24 Quiet day 10am–4pm. A tale of three Holy Lands: reflecting on biblical sites in the light of contemporary political complexities. Archdeacon Mark Ireland
November
11–13 Preaching course for licensed clergy who want to brush up on their preaching skills in the company of others. Bishop Philip North, Bishop of Burnley
21 Quiet day 10am–4pm. 'Thy Kingdom come'. What living out the Lord's Prayer means for us today. Archdeacon Michael Everitt
December
2–4 Retreat. Will Jesus really return? Explore the Advent theme and its implications in Matthew chapters 24 and 25. Rt Rev Bishop Julian Henderson, Bishop of Blackburn
19 Quiet day 10am–4pm. 'Let all mortal flesh keep silence.' Opportunity to reflect on the mystery and splendour of Emmanuel and to keep a holy silence. Rev Jonathan Carmyllie

LEICESTERSHIRE

85 Launde Abbey

East Norton, Leicestershire LE7 9XB 01572 717254
fax 01572 717454
email suzanne@launde.org.uk
B, C, D, E, P, Q, S, W, Wf   website www.laundeabbey.org.uk

Rooms 39 *en suite* bedrooms.
Notes The Warden is available to give spiritual direction on a one-to-one basis, subject to availability. Please book in advance if possible. Individuals and groups welcomed residentially and for day retreats. The House keeps a daily rhythm of prayer with morning prayer, midday prayer, evening prayer and Eucharist said daily. The Abbey has won awards from East Midlands Tourism for the care of those staying.
Contact Ven David Newman, Warden.

January
11–13 Epiphany retreat. Rev Chris Webb
14–18 Quilting and textiles sewing retreat. Rev Claire Goode
28–31 Sermon on the Mount: a spirituality for today. Rt Rev Mike Harrison
February
12–15 Soulfulness retreat: finding richer communion with God, ourselves and the world around us. Brian Draper
18–22 Living with loss. Abi & John May
21–22 Transforming church conflict. Launde Clergy Team
March
18–21 Lent retreat. David Runcorn
April
15–18 Holy Week retreat. Rev Chris Webb & Rev Cathy Davies
23–26 Easter retreat. Ven David Newman & Rev Canon Helen Newman
May
6–10 A Julian of Norwich retreat. Simon Parke
28–31 Labyrinth retreat. Barbara Wallace
May–June
31–2 Photography retreat: seeing the light in life. Stephen Radley
June
10–14 Gardening retreat/holiday. Launde Community
July
19–21 Beginners' retreat. Rev Canon Helen Newman & Rev Cathy Davies
25–28 A retreat with Rowan Williams. Rowan Williams
August
12–15 Environment retreat. Andrew Hall
19–23 Gardening retreat/holiday. Launde Community
September
2–5 Charismatic and contemplative. Ven David Newman & Rev Louise Corke
9–12 To be a pilgrim: a practical and spiritual exploration of pilgrimage. Rev Sally Welch
11–15 School for spirituality. Rev Chris Webb & Launde Clergy Team
October
21–24 Contemplative prayer retreat. Launde Clergy Team

October–November
28–1 Gardening retreat/holiday. Launde Community
November
8–10 Growing into retirement. Launde Clergy Team & Leicester Diocesan Mission and Ministry Team
25–28 Advent retreat. Ven David Newman & Rev Canon Helen Newman
December
6–8 Advent joy and transformation: praying with Handel's *Messiah*. Euan Tait
9–12 Still before Christmas. Launde Clergy Team

86 Rosmini Centre House of Prayer

433 Fosse Way, Ratcliffe on the Wreake,
Leicester LE7 4SJ   01509 813078
email djtobinic@gmail.com
D, P, Q, S   website www.rosminicentre.co.uk

Non-residential.
Notes The Rosmini Centre House of Prayer, which is in the care of the Institute of Charity (Rosminians), is situated just off the A46 in spacious grounds in the heart of Leicestershire. It is centred around what were previously a farm and a pre-war private airfield. Within a new plantation of poplar trees are a Rosary Walk and a Way of the Cross. All areas are wheelchair-accessible. It welcomes those looking for somewhere to spend quiet time alone, perhaps seeking some spiritual guidance, as well as those attracted by the varied programme of events. It may also provide an answer for groups seeking a venue for their own events. As well as the chapel, which seats 35, there is Hutton Hall seating 35–40 with kitchen, toilet and projection facilities; another hall (a refurbished hangar) that can seat up to 70; a small room seating about 8 in the former stables, plus the very well stocked Watson Library with space for small group discussions. There is a small bookshop, specialising in the writings of Blessed Antonio Rosmini.
Healing Masses usually the second Friday of each month 7pm.
Evening Prayer and Adoration each Wednesday 6pm.
Contemplative Prayer 2nd and 4th Tuesdays 2–3pm.
Divine Mercy Chaplet and Lectio Divina most last Saturdays of the month 3pm.
On two Saturday mornings of most months a variety of talks, lectures and/or discussions are organised. Also, an Advent and a Lent retreat are offered at the Centre. We aim to keep our website updated with the details of individual events, but please contact the Centre for a printed programme, which will be available from January. For catering and other purposes, it is very helpful if you can tell us you are coming to any of the events. For this and any other purpose, including hiring of rooms, please contact us.
Contact Fr David Tobin IC.

WHERE THERE'S A WILL...

Have you thought about the Retreat Association in your will? Contact us for information and advice.

email: info@retreats.org.uk or phone: 01494 569056

LINCOLNSHIRE

87 The Community of St Francis, Metheringham

San Damiano, 38 Drury Street, Metheringham, Lincolnshire LN4 3EZ   01526 321115
email metheringhamcsf@franciscans.org.uk
B, D, I, P, Q, S, V, Wf   *website* www.franciscans.org.uk

Rooms 1 single ground-floor study bedroom. Day visitors (individuals and groups): 2 rooms available – the library (max 8 people) and the chapel (max 24 people).
The Hermitage a log cabin set in the wooded grounds available as a prayer space for an individual quiet day – suitable for use all year round. The day rooms and guest room are all on ground level.
Notes In the heart of the Diocese of Lincoln, the Sisters of the Community of St Francis, an Anglican community of vowed religious sisters, welcome visitors to share their life and to use the facilities of the house, offering hospitality in various ways. The sisters at Metheringham welcome groups or individual guests, men or women, who are looking for retreat, space for rest, study, sabbatical or a quiet holiday in a friendly rural setting. The sisters may be available to spend time with groups/individuals for leading retreats, quiet days, spiritual direction, prayer guidance or simply to offer a listening ear. The community is normally open to guests between Wednesday morning and Sunday evening. Private retreats with some guidance (beginners welcome) and also IGRs by arrangement. The house is set in beautiful grounds, with good access to local walks. Visitors are welcome to join the sisters in the chapel for their daily services.
Contact The Sisters.

88 Edenham Regional House

Church Lane, Edenham, Bourne, Lincolnshire PE10 0LS   01778 591358
email edenhamoffice@gmail.com
website www.edenhamregionalhouse.org
B, C, D, I, P, Q, S, V, W, Wf

Rooms 2 single, 2 twin, all *en suite*; a separate sitting room, kitchen and dining area is provided for residents. Can be used as self-catering flat. 1 ground-floor twin-bedded *en suite* room suitable for wheelchair-users. Available for quiet days and day conferences: a large drawing room (seats 40 in a circle), the stable chapel (seats 25), the parish church, the summerhouse (seats 10 in a circle) and dining rooms.
Notes The Regional House offers hospitality in the context of an Anglican vicarage and family home. There are opportunities to partake in community activities and worship for those who would like to. The retreat accommodation is separate, quiet and very private.
Contact The Warden.
For a full programme of events see the website. We offer monthly days of reflection and IGRs at any time. Some of our retreats use the liturgy of the Book of Common Prayer.

89 Epworth Old Rectory

1 Rectory Street, Epworth, North Lincolnshire DN9 1HX   01427 872268
email curator@epwortholdrectory.org.uk
C, Q   *website* www.epwortholdrectory.org.uk

Non-residential.
Rooms We offer quiet days rather than longer-term retreats. There is no accommodation at Epworth Old Rectory; however, accommodation is available elsewhere in the town of Epworth. Details are on our website.
Notes Epworth Old Rectory is the childhood home of John and Charles Wesley and their 7 sisters. It was on this site that John Wesley was rescued at the age of 5 when the previous rectory burned to the ground, causing his mother to describe him as 'a brand plucked from the burning'. Here the Wesleys received their earliest education and inspiration from their remarkable parents Susanna and Samuel Wesley. Quiet days here enable participants to be inspired by the stories of the family and to reflect on how these stories inspire their faith and the church of today. There is also a very peaceful physic garden which is affiliated to the Quiet Garden Movement.
Contact Gillian Crawley.
Please see the website for details of our event programme.

LONDON

See Greater London.

MANCHESTER

See Greater Manchester.

MERSEYSIDE

90 Cenacle Retreat House, Liverpool

Tithebarn Grove, Lance Lane, Liverpool L15 6TW   0151 722 2271
email winniecenacle@mail.com
I, Q, S   *website* www.cenacleengland.org.uk

Rooms 7 *en suite* rooms. Conference room, chapel and dining room all accommodate 25 persons.
Notes Individually guided retreats as requested and for any length, including the full Exercises of St Ignatius. Available for quiet days.
Contact Sr Jean Page (jean.page4@btinternet.com) or Sr Winifred Morley.

91 St Joseph's Prayer Centre

Blundell Avenue, Freshfield, Formby, Liverpool
L37 1PH   01704 875850
email theprayercentre.stj@gmail.com
website www.stjosephsprayercentre.com
Co, D, I, P, Q, S, V, W, Wf, Y

Rooms 20 (not *en suite*), 2 ground floor (*en suite*). 2 main meeting rooms, 1 suitable for groups up to 18, and a larger room can accommodate up to 50 people. The Oasis is a quiet space for individuals or small groups. There is a prayer room and large chapel also available.
Notes The Prayer Centre is an ideal setting for individual and group retreats. The National Trust pine forests (red squirrel reserve) surround us and there are many woodland walks. The sea is only a 10-min walk away. Please see website for our programme of events.
Contact Sr Nora Coughlan.

NORFOLK

92 The Shrine of Our Lady of Walsingham (Anglican)

The Milner Wing, Common Place, Walsingham,
Norfolk NR22 6BP   01328 820239
email accom@olw-shrine.org.uk
website www.walsinghamanglican.org.uk
Ch, D, E, I, P, Q, V, Wf, Y

Rooms 78 single, 45 twin, 5 double, 12 triple. 1 conference room with audiovisual equipment and flipchart, 1 large meeting room and several small meeting rooms available.
Notes Walsingham has been a place of pilgrimage since 1061 when Lady Richeldis received a vision from the Virgin Mary to build a replica of the Holy House of Nazareth. Destroyed at the Reformation, and restored in 1931, the Anglican Shrine Church contains the Holy House and an image of Mary and her Son. The Shrine is open daily and a full pilgrimage programme is offered from Easter to 31 October for groups and individuals (modified programme at other times). Special events throughout the year include: the national pilgrimage; youth, young adult, children, families, healing and renewal pilgrimages; Advent and priests' retreats. Details of these and the pilgrimage programme are on the website. The Shrine welcomes individuals seeking quiet time away and independently-led retreats, quiet days and conferences, offering self-contained accommodation if required. The refectory caters for up to 200 and the fully-licensed café bar is open daily, serving light lunches, home-made cakes etc. '... one of the most important spiritual centres in northern Europe' (Archbishop of Canterbury 2013).
Contact Hospitality Department.

LOOKING FOR A SPIRITUAL DIRECTOR?

The Retreat Association can help you find one.
Call 01494 569056, email info@retreats.org.uk
or visit our website www.retreats.org.uk

93 Walsingham Retreats

Dowry House, 47–49 High Street, Walsingham,
Norfolk NR22 6BZ   01328 801018
email dowryhouse@walsingham.org.uk
website www.dowryhouse.org.uk and www.walsingham.org.uk
B, E, I, P, Q, S, V, W, Wf

Rooms 17 rooms. 8 single – 2 *en suite* on the ground floor near the chapel, 2 sharing a bathroom, 2 sharing a shower room and an extra 2 with toilet and sink. 9 twin – 4 large *en suite*, 4 on the top floor and 1 with toilet and sink. All the twin rooms can be used as singles.
Notes Walsingham's National Catholic Shrine of Our Lady runs the historic Dowry House, built around 1470 in the heart of the village in 'England's Nazareth'. A residential religious community provides hospitality, spiritual accompaniment, sung divine office and teaching on the spirituality of Walsingham. Pilgrims looking for a time of retreat, an IGR, formation, silence and prayer are all welcomed there. Eucharistic adoration is available in the main chapel and the grounds and cloister provide beautiful outdoor prayer spaces. Retreats and seminars organised by the Shrine of Our Lady will run throughout the year. Residential visitors are welcome to come on their own or as part of a group. Day groups are also welcome. Dowry House is directly opposite the main gate of the Abbey Grounds, where the Holy House of Walsingham originally stood.
Budget retreats are also offered by the Shrine at Elmham House, another facility offering over 100 beds with varying types of accommodation
Contact Sr Camilla Oberding COLW.

94 Wigwam Retreat Centre

Diana Princess of Wales International Study Centre, Riddlesworth, Diss, Norfolk IP22 2SZ
                          020 8491 0222
email pwtcfl@aol.com
B, C, Co, D, I, P, Q, W, Y   *website* www.wigwamretreats.co.uk

Rooms Various accommodation options are available – see website.
Notes Based on Christian beliefs and values, we offer quiet contemplative retreats. We are set in lovely countryside close to the ancient pathways of Peddars Way and Angles Way. Modern camping facilities available. An 11-circuit labyrinth in a Victorian walled garden is available. Please see our website for our programme of guided retreats.
Contact Les Crossland.

RETREAT ASSOCIATION
SUMMER EVENT
3 July 2019 – see page 80
Guest speakers:
Father Anastasios Salapatas, Greek Orthodox
& **Father Stephen Platt**, Russian Orthodox

NORTHUMBERLAND

95 Even Sparrows Retreats

The Open Gate Retreat House, Holy Island,
Berwick-upon-Tweed, Northumberland
TD15 2SD   (retreat centre) 01289 389222
(retreat organiser) 07594 592684
email evensparrows@gmail.com
website www.evensparrows.co.uk

Rooms 3 twin, 2 double (all *en suite*), 2 single (shared bathroom).
Notes Unique retreats which involve quiet Christian worship, biblical reflection and guided birdwatching walks. Each retreat shares the simple message that God loves us, alongside the rest of creation. Our time will be spent on and around Holy Island looking at various birds, but the specifics of each programme will depend on local bird news and migration. Autumn in particular can be truly spectacular with large numbers of birds arriving from the European continent.
Contact Mark Winter, Retreats Organiser.

May–June
31–3 Look at the birds. Timed for late spring migration.
September
6–9 Look at the birds. Timed for early autumn migration.
20–23 Look at the birds. Timed for early autumn migration.
October
11–14 Look at the birds. Timed for autumn migration.
25–28 Look at the birds. Timed for late autumn migration.

96 The Friary of Saint Francis

Alnmouth, Alnwick, Northumberland
NE66 3NJ   01665 830213
email alnmouthssf@franciscans.org.uk
D, Q, S   *website* www.franciscans.org.uk

Rooms 6 single.
Contact The Guest Brother SSF.

97 Marygate House, Holy Island

Northumberland TD15 2SD   01289 389246
email marygate.house@gmail.com
B, P, V, W   *website* www.marygatehouse.org.uk

Rooms Marygate House welcomes both groups and individuals and can accommodate up to 18 people in 6 rooms with shared bathroom and toilet facilities.
Notes Our ministry of welcome is extended to everyone, for religious, cultural and educational purposes. We are a residential centre and offer full board in our Georgian house located on the Holy Island of Lindisfarne, providing retreats and space.
Contact Sam or Don Quilty.

98 The Open Gate

Marygate, Holy Island, Berwick-upon-Tweed,
Northumberland TD15 2SD   01289 389222
email opengate@aidanandhilda.org.uk
C, I, P, W, Wf   *website* www.aidanandhilda.org.uk

Rooms 2 small singles with shared bathroom, 2 twin, 1 double, 1 larger double bedsit (all *en suite*) at the Open Gate and 1 double, 1 twin and 1 single (ground floor), all *en suite*, at a further property (400 yards away).
Notes The Open Gate is a welcoming ecumenical house of hospitality providing a warm welcome to all. We offer a wide range of group and individual retreats. Our main themes include Celtic spirituality, God in nature, aspects of prayer, pilgrimage, the saints of the north, Christian leadership and New Monasticism. The Holy Island of Lindisfarne is a tidal island just off the coast of northern England, midway between Newcastle and Edinburgh. The island is the historic northern cradle of Christianity for the English-speaking peoples, home of the saints Aidan and Cuthbert; a nature reserve and place of wild beauty; a 'thin place' where God speaks. We look forward to welcoming you.
Contact Kayleah, Jutta or Robert.

January–February
28–1 Book of (h)ours. A midweek creative retreat exploring the spirituality of the sacred book, as focus of corporate worship or as personal companion. Mary Fleeson, Tess Ward & Claire Gibbs
February
18–22 Discovering divine intimacy. Christian mindfulness and contemplation for everyone. David Cole, author and CA&H Explorer Guide
April
1–5 Walks around Holy Island. Discover hidden aspects of this amazing island in a series of light to moderate daytime walks, and reflective evening sessions. Mary Gunn & the Open Gate team
8–12 Finding the quiet. Explore how to find more inner quiet and why. Not in silence but plenty of space for silence within the week. Penny Warren, Member's Guardian of CA&H
14–21 Holy Week. Come get involved in Holy Island's rhythm of prayer, looking at how Holy Week is observed by different groups throughout the world. The Open Gate team
May
13–17 Lindisfarne landscapes. Explore the island and the relationship between art, prayer and spirituality by allowing God to speak through various art mediums. Paul Swinhoe & Maureen Simpson
17–20 Write your own psalm. A workshop exploring the key literary features and history of the Psalms, then write your own! Deirdre McGarry & Rosemary Palmeira
24–27 The Lord's Prayer. Explore the Prayer with exciting linguistic revelation. Then explore your relationship with the Lord through creative writing. Deirdre McGarry & Rosemary Palmeira
27–31 Celtic wisdom for modern life. Exploring how we can learn from our Celtic ancestors and apply their

teachings to our modern world. David Cole, author and CA&H Explorer Guide

May–June

31–3 Look at the birds. Quiet worship, biblical reflections about birds with guided birdwatching walks. For beginners and keen birdwatchers. Mark Winter of Even Sparrows

June

24–28 Telling the story. Storytelling was the main form of entertainment amongst ordinary Celtic folk. Bring a song, poem or story and hear the tales of days gone by. Fr Mike Marsh

July

8–12 Alive like the Saints. Monks carried a coffin containing St Cuthbert's body and other saints' bones. How alive in Christ are we? Abbot John Bede, Order of St Cuthbert

July–August

29–2 Fresh water from an ancient well. Sharing ways that Christian faith of the early Middle Ages can inform our walk with God in these challenging times. Kenneth McIntosh

August

12–16 Loved creation. A time to explore the Celtic Christian understanding of our unity with creation as those who are loved and called to love. Penny Warren, Members' Guardian

19–23 Contemplative slow stitching. Listen to God while quietly hand-stitching on pre-loved materials. No stitching experience required, all materials provided. Elizabeth Scott, lay minister & textile artist

26–30 Aidan and Hilda week. Celebrate the lives of Aidan, Hilda and other inspired Celtic Christians through studies, activities and reflections. Ray Simpson, author and Founding Guardian of CA&H

September

6–9 Look at the birds. Quiet worship, biblical reflections about birds with guided birdwatching walks. For beginners and keen birdwatchers. Mark Winter of Even Sparrows

16–20 Befriending silence. Silent retreat. Come experience the beauty of Lindisfarne whilst spending time in contemplation. David Cole, author and CA&H Explorer Guide

20–23 Look at the birds. Quiet worship, biblical reflections about birds with guided birdwatching walks. For beginners and keen birdwatchers. Mark Winter of Even Sparrows

27–30 Beatitudes. Explore these intriguing and enchanting declarations which are the core of Jesus' teaching. (Sign up for Parables too and receive a discount.) Deirdre McGarry & Rosemary Palmeira

October

4–7 Parables. What do they mean to you? Enter the realm of deeper understanding in the spirit through creative writing. Deirdre McGarry & Rosemary Palmeira

11–14 Look at the birds. Quiet worship, biblical reflections about birds with guided birdwatching walks. For beginners and keen birdwatchers. Mark Winter of Even Sparrows

21–25 Lindisfarne landscapes. Explore the island and the relationship between art, prayer and spirituality by allowing God to speak through various art mediums. Paul Swinhoe & Maureen Simpson

25–28 Look at the birds. Quiet worship, biblical reflections about birds with guided birdwatching walks. For beginners and keen birdwatchers. Mark Winter of Even Sparrows

November

11–15 Celtic Advent. Prepare ye a way. A new approach to celebrating the 40 days of Celtic Advent. David Cole, author and CA&H Explorer Guide

99 St Cuthbert's Centre, Holy Island

United Reformed Church, Fiddlers Green, Holy Island, Berwick-upon-Tweed, Northumberland TD15 2RZ   01289 389254

email rachel.poolman@holyisland-stcuthbert.org
website www.holyisland-stcuthbert.org

C, P, Q, S

Rooms 1 single, *en suite*, self-catering with small bedroom, lounge, shower room and kitchen facilities, plus 1 large multipurpose hall and small balcony for groups up to 45.

Notes St Cuthbert's Centre is a beautifully modernised former Presbyterian chapel and a place of welcome and stillness on Holy Island. The Centre is operated by the United Reformed Church, and offers hospitality to those who drop in during a visit to the Island, to individual retreatants in the self-contained Bothy, and to church and other groups who wish to share our space. All are welcome to join us for weekday morning prayer. Please refer to our website for up-to-date information.

Contact Rev Rachel Poolman, Warden.

100 Shepherds Dene Retreat House

Slaley Road, Riding Mill, Northumberland NE44 6AF   01434 682212

email info@shepherdsdene.co.uk
website www.shepherdsdene.co.uk

B, C, D, I, P, Q, S, V, W, Wf

Rooms 1 double *en suite*, 2 twin *en suite*, 5 single *en suite*, 1 with 3 single beds, 8 standard twin, 3 standard single.

Notes Warm and welcoming 1906 arts-and-crafts-style country house in 27 acres of beautiful grounds. Located in the Tyne Valley between Newcastle and Hexham and easily reached by road and rail. Church of England retreat house. Great, home-cooked food, peaceful atmosphere and warm hospitality.

Contact Jane Easterby, Warden.

January–February

28–1 Silent IGR. 1-1 every morning. Rev Canon Claire Maclaren & Rev Canon Stephen Herbert

February

5–7 Knitting and crochet retreat. Rev Elizabeth Brown

February–March

25–1 Clergy and readers reading week.

March

8 Lent quiet day. Rev Catherine Pickford

11–15 Silent Lent retreat. Journeying into the heart of God. Rt Rev Christine Hardman, Bp of Newcastle & Rev Canon Pete Askew, Bp's Chaplain

15 Lent quiet day. Rev Lesley Chapman

22 Lent quiet day. Rev Glen McKnight
29 Lent quiet day. Rev Canon Vince Fenton
29–31 Calming relaxation and wellbeing weekend. Fiona Cox
April
5 Lent quiet day. Rev Dr Sue Wilson
12 Lent quiet day. Rev Jeremy Chadd
May
1 Spring ramble. Rev Jeremy Chadd
5–7 Pray with the birds. Birdwatching with Mark Winter
27–30 Knitting and crochet retreat. Rev Elizabeth Brown
June
14–16 Exploring the second half of life. Rev Canon Peter Kenney
17–20 In the steps of St Cuthbert through photography and art. Rt Rev David Thompson & Rev Steve Radley
23–26 Silent retreat for clergy spouses. A chance to pray, rest and reflect together.
June–July
30–4 Cross stitch week. Barbara Thompson. Contact barbatwoodlands@hotmail.co.uk for details.
July
15–17 Revisiting the miracles. John Bell, Iona Community
21–25 Art week with professional artists. Alan Reed
August
5–12 A week in the country. Houses and gardens of the North East. Rev Dr Sue Wilson & Warden, Jane Easterby
25–30 Northern Saints pilgrimage. Rev John & Gina McManners
23–26 Rest and relax. Fiona Cox & Barbara Stewart
September
25 Autumn ramble. Rev Jeremy Chadd
October
16 Quiet day. Time Wisdom. Very Rev Michael Sadgrove
16–18 Knitting and crochet retreat. Rev Elizabeth Brown
October–November
28–1 Let the rivers flow: ways to thrive when things feel dry. Very Rev Geoff Miller, Dean of Newcastle Cathedral

NOTTINGHAMSHIRE

101 Sacrista Prebend Retreat House
4 Westgate, Southwell, Nottinghamshire
NG25 0JH   01636 816833
email sacrista_prebend@btinternet.com
B, C, D, P, Q, V, Wf *website* www.sacristaprebend.wordpress.com

Rooms 2 twin rooms (1 *en suite*, 1 shared facilities), 1 single room with shared facilities, 1 ground-floor room with adjacent facilities.
Notes This quiet house and garden opposite Southwell Minster offers space for personal retreat, quiet days, meetings and courses. No catering is provided, but overnight guests may use the house kitchen to prepare their own meals.
Contact Rev Canon Tony Evans.

February
9 Rest, reverence, obedience, delight. We'll learn about John Owen; explore rest, reverence and delight as ways of loving God; and have a nod at obedience. Rev Canon Valerie Rampton
March
12 Roots and fruits: trust, vulnerability and gift in the Christian life. Being 'rooted and grounded in love', abiding in Jesus and being pruned to bear his fruit. Canon Angela Ashwin
May
11 All the world's a stage: a study day in faith and Shakespeare. Examining how Shakespeare reconstitutes key Christian ideas through dramatic presentation. Rev Canon Dr Alison Milbank
May
17 The face of Jesus in art. On this reflective day we will explore ways in which Jesus has been depicted in art from the earliest times up until today. Rev Matthew Askey
June
8 This creative day has been organised in partnership with the Creative Arts Retreat Movement. Rev Annabel Barber
15 Techno-fasting. What can we learn from the ancient Christian spiritual disciplines that will help us to disconnect from technology and reconnect with ourselves and God? Matt Arnold
22 Quiet day. 'For such a time as this'. We will reflect on the story of Esther and explore how we, as his people, might reach the very heart of God. Rev Canon Sylvia Griffiths
July
6 Imagining the Divine. We will explore biblical imagery for God and how it helps us relate to a God we cannot see. Rev Iain McKillop
September
7 'I've never… been on a Quiet Day.' A day just for you and others who don't know what to expect or what to do. Sally Smith
21 Joy in creation. Today we'll be looking at the poetry of Thomas Traherne, as well as other poets, e.g. Gerard Manley Hopkins and Mary Oliver. Penny Young
October
12 Quiet day. Explore what The Jesus Prayer is, how we pray it and how it can assist us in our life with God. Rev Canon Dr Jim Wellington
November
30 'Heaven in Ordinarie'. A traditional quiet day with short addresses and silence, drawing upon the poems of George Herbert, to explore the meaning of Advent. Very Rev Dr John Moses, formerly Dean of St Paul's

WOULD YOU LIKE TO SUPPORT THE WORK OF THE RETREAT ASSOCIATION?
See our website:
www.retreats.org.uk/donate.php
for ways in which you can support us.

OXFORDSHIRE

102 The Abbey

The Green, Sutton Courtenay, Abingdon, Oxfordshire OX14 4AF   01235 847401
email admin@theabbey.uk.com
C, Ch, Co, D, E, Q, S, V, W, Wf   *website* www.theabbey.uk.com

Rooms 7 single, 6 twin. Individuals or groups.
Notes The Abbey is home to an open and inclusive spiritual community contributing to the transformation of consciousness in the world. It offers a sacred space and a relaxing environment that supports spiritual growth, personal development and group transformational learning. The Abbey community welcomes individual visitors and offers facilities for day and residential events that are used by groups from the public, private and voluntary sectors. We offer a programme of retreats, talks and other events on spirituality, healing, creativity, reflection on social issues, environmental concerns and interfaith dialogue. Please see the website for details. For sat nav/GPS use OX14 4AE.
Meditation 3 times a day. Monthly 3-day rest and renewal retreat.
Contact For details email the Administrator or see the website.

103 Carmelite Priory

Chilswell House, Boars Hill, Oxford OX1 5HB
01865 735133 / 01865 730183
email retreats@carmelite.org.uk
B, D, E, I, P, Q, S, W, Wf *website* www.carmeliteprioryoxford.com

Rooms The Centre has 27 rooms of which 13 are twin. The chapel, dining room, conference rooms and the majority of the bedrooms are on the ground floor, with no steps. The conference rooms comprise of a seminar room equipped with hearing loop and AV system, a large meeting room overlooking Boars Hill and a boardroom. We hope that everyone who comes to stay with us for a while will experience an unforgettable encounter with God and others.
Notes The Carmelite Priory is set in 17 acres of beautiful and peaceful surroundings overlooking Oxford. The Retreat Centre is run by a small community of Discalced (Teresian) Carmelite friars who live their lives in allegiance to Jesus Christ focusing on prayer, retreat ministry and teaching in the tradition of St Teresa of Avila and St John of the Cross. As a team of friars and laypeople working together, we welcome guests of all faiths, nations and social groups, as well as those with no faith who desire to search their own way to the wholeness and the meaning of life. We offer preached and guided retreats, based mostly on Carmelite spirituality and the contemplative tradition. We are also available for private groups and individuals on private retreats.
Contact Ruth Preston. ❏ *p 1*
Cherith days 'so Elijah did what the Lord had told him. He went to the brook of Cherith, east of the Jordan, and stayed there.'
Carmelite day Talk followed by prayers and time for recollection. Soup lunch – please book.

December 2018–January 2019
31–3 3-day IGR.

January
5 Spiritual enrichment lecture series. Praying the Psalms. Vincent O'Hara OCD
19 Spiritual enrichment lecture series. Painting as prayer: the experience of the sacred in art. Guillem Ramos-Poqui PhD

February
2 Spiritual enrichment lecture series. Contemplative awareness. Living the divine presence. Angela Rogerson
4–8 Midweek IGR.
8–10 How insights from Carmelite spirituality can be applied in real life situations. Liam Finnerty OCD
16 Spiritual enrichment lecture series. A learning hidden deep in the heart. Reflections from *The Third Spiritual Alphabet*, Guide of St Teresa. Julienne McLean

March
1–3 An introduction to what we mean by Carmelite spirituality and an exploration of some of its key characteristics. Matt Blake OCD
2 Spiritual enrichment lecture series. Praying in the company of Mary. Anne Harriss OCDS
4–8 Midweek IGR.
16 Spiritual enrichment lecture series. Carmelite prayer, mindfulness and mental prayer. Prof Peter Tyler
22–24 The road less travelled. Lent offers us an opportunity to embrace Jesus' agenda for happiness. Philip McParland
25–29 Midweek IGR.
25–29 Cherith days. See above.
29–31 Growing in our following of Jesus Christ, enriched and guided by the poetry and teaching of St John of the Cross. Matt Blake OCD

April
6 Spiritual enrichment lecture series. Centering prayer. Margaret McNulty
8–12 Midweek IGR.
8–12 Cherith days. See above.
12–14 (Palm Sunday) Reflections in preparation for Holy Week. Liam Finnerty OCD
13 Spiritual enrichment lecture series. The three ways of the spiritual life and prayer – the fiery nights. Heather Ward OCDS
17–21 Easter retreat at the Carmelite Priory. 'He is Risen!' Matthew 28:6. Carmelite Community.

May
4 Spiritual enrichment lecture series. The living flame of love – encountering the mystery. Ian Matthew OCD
6–9 Cherith days. See above.
17–19 The prophet of prayer, contemplation and zeal for the word of God: Elijah and influence in the Carmelite tradition. Matt Blake OCD
18 Spiritual enrichment lecture series. Feelings, supernatural communications and prayer. Gillian Coxhead
29 Carmelite day. See above.

May–June
31–2 (Ascension) A 'man of letters': Blessed John Henry Newman and his apostleship of the pen. Fr Michael Miners OCDS

June

1 Spiritual enrichment lecture series. Discerning growth/regression in prayer. Julienne McLean

7–9 (Pentecost) Reflections on the presence and action of the Holy Spirit in the life of believers today. Liam Finnerty OCD

15 Spiritual enrichment lecture series. 'Lord, teach us to pray': the perfect prayer. Tony Parsons OCD

21–23 Called to holiness: God has given you a task to fulfil. A weekend of discernment for 20- to 35-year-olds. John McGowan OCD

26 Carmelite day. See above.

29 Spiritual enrichment lecture series. Transformed by prayer. Michael McGoldrick OCD

July

1–5 Cherith days. See above.

1–7 6-day IGR.

5–7 'Come be my light': St Teresa of Calcutta as a 'saint of darkness'. Fr Michael Miners, OCDS

15–16 Vigil retreat. Our Lady of Mount Carmel. Thaddeus Ekuma OCD

21–24 3-day IGR.

25 Carmelite day. See above.

August

5–8 Short course. The wisdom of St John of the Cross: entering its depths and exploring ways of sharing it. Matt Blake OCD

16–18 The second act. 'We cannot live the afternoon of life according to the morning programme' Carl Jung.

September

2–6 Cherith days. See above.

2–8 6-day IGR.

25 Carmelite day. See above.

October

4–6 The way of humility and wonder: the spirituality of Therese of Lisieux and GK Chesterton. Rev Canon John Udris

14–15 Vigil retreat. St Teresa of Jesus. Liam Finnerty OCD

18–20 'The door of entry into this castle is prayer and meditation.' Retreat drawing on the wisdom of St Teresa's *The Interior Castle*. Matt Blake OCD

November

4–8 Midweek IGR.

4–8 Cherith days. See above.

13 Carmelite day. See above.

15–17 'The vast solitude in which God will make himself heard'. Exploring the wisdom of St Teresa's *The Interior Castle*. Matt Blake OCD

November–December

29–1 'His name will be called Wonderful, Counsellor, Mighty God, Everlasting Father, Prince of Peace', Isaiah 9:6. Reflections in preparation for Christmas. Thaddeus Ekuma OCD

December

6–8 St Teresa of Avila's love for Fr Jerome Gratian. John McGowan OCD

9–13 Midweek IGR.

13–15 Our transformation in relationship with the God of love and beauty: the Spiritual Canticle of St John of the Cross.

16–22 Midweek IGR.

20–22 Christmas preparation weekend retreat. The mystery of Christmas. Liam Finnerty OCD

104 Charney Manor

Charney Bassett, Wantage, Oxfordshire
OX12 0EJ   01235 868206
email sales@charneymanor.com
B, D, Wf   website www.charneymanor.com

Rooms Charney Manor offers simple, comfortable accommodation in single and twin *en suite* bedrooms for up to 35 residential guests. We also offer individuals an option to have a few days of relaxation on a B&B or fully-catered basis. A self-catering cottage within the grounds of Charney Manor (which sleeps up to 8 people) can be booked through our preferred booking agent. Further details of all our facilities can be found on the website.

Notes Charney Manor, owned and managed by the Religious Society of Friends (Quakers), provides the ideal venue for religious, educational and other groups to use for day conferences, awaydays, meetings, and residential retreats. There are 2 large conference rooms, the beautiful and historic Solar and the Barn. The latter has wheelchair access. Charney Manor also offers our own varied programme of spiritual and educational events throughout the year.

Contact Nicola Cooper, Retreat Administrator.

February

15–17 The drawing room. Kel Portman

March

22–24 Writing with the spirit. Kim Hope

April

12–14 Enquirers retreat. Finding out about Quakers. Quaker Quest team

April–May

30–3 Experiencing Shakespeare. John Lampen & colleague

June

12–14 Experiment with light. Facilitators from the Experiment with Light Network

July

23–25 Poetry: where words walk on the edge of silence. Philip Gross

August

23–25 Working with those who support asylum seekers. Sanctuary Everywhere programme.

September

6–8 Enquirers retreat. Finding out about Quakers. Quaker Quest team

October

23–25 The Holy Mountain: deep nonviolence and sustainability. Laurie Michaelis

November

1–3 Membership retreat. Finding out about Quakers. Quaker Quest team

22–24 Sinking down the seed. Alex Wildwood

FOR A LIST OF COURSES IN SPIRITUAL DIRECTION

email: info@retreats.org.uk
or phone: 01494 569056

105 Community of St Mary the Virgin

Guest Wing, St Mary's Convent, Denchworth
Road, Wantage, Oxon OX12 9AU　01235 763141
email guestwing@csmv.co.uk
B, C, D, I, P, Q, S, W, Wf　*website* www.csmv.co.uk

Rooms 20 bedrooms, including 2 twin, 1 bedroom with
study area, 1 small flat with *en suite* facilities, 1 ground-
floor bedroom with *en suite* facilities for the less able.
Notes St Mary's Convent is undergoing a complete
refurbishment of its Guest Wing. In 2020 there will be new
conference facilities, available to both overnight and day
guests, as well as 20 *en suite* bedrooms and refurbished
space for study, discussion, prayer and reflection. The
Convent is surrounded by beautiful secluded gardens.
During the period of refurbishment in the second part of
2019, overnight guests will be able to stay in White Lodge,
a large and peaceful Edwardian house set in the Convent
grounds. In the main Convent building, the wonderful
Song Room will host day groups of up to 18. Retreat guests
are able to join the Sisters for daily office and Eucharist in
St Mary Magdalene's Chapel, and to use the Grade II* listed
St Mary's Chapel for prayer and reflection. All guests will be
offered light lunches and supper will be provided for those
staying overnight.
Contact Guest Wing Reception. ❏ *inside front cover*

106 Newman's College at Littlemore Oxford

International Centre of Newman Friends, c/o
The Spiritual Family The Work, Ambrose
Cottage, 9 College Lane, Littlemore, Oxford
OX4 4LQ　01865 779743
email littlemore@newman-friends.org
P, Wf　*website* www.newmanfriendsinternational.org

Rooms 3 self-catering cottages, each accommodating 2–3
people, breakfast can be provided.
Notes Blessed John Henry Newman said about the
'College', his home at Littlemore from 1842 to 1846: 'As I
made Littlemore a place of retreat for myself, so I offered it
to others.' The Spiritual Family The Work is the guardian of
the College today. The Sisters offer rooms for private
retreats to those who wish to pray and study at this place
as Newman did. The guests pray in the chapel where
Newman was received into full communion with the
Catholic Church; they may participate in the daily prayer
life of the community (divine office, adoration of the
Blessed Sacrament, Mass in the chapel or parish church)
and use the specialised Newman library. Groups of up to
18 are welcome for day retreats. RC.
Contact The Guest Sister.

March
1–3　Quarantore. 40 hours of prayer before the Blessed
　　　Sacrament, with an opportunity for the sacrament
　　　of reconciliation.
October
8　John Henry Newman night walk pilgrimage from
　　Oxford to Littlemore.

107 Ripon College Cuddesdon

Cuddesdon, Near Oxford, Oxfordshire
OX44 9EX　01865 877400 / 01865 877479
email info@rcc.ac.uk
B, C, D, I, P, Pe, Q, S, W, Wf　*website* www.rcc.ac.uk/retreats

Rooms 38 singles (22 *en suite*), 4 doubles (2 *en suite*),
2 self-contained double/family flats. A range of
conference/ meeting rooms to accommodate 2–80 people,
historic dining hall, award-winning new chapel, peaceful
grounds in beautiful rural village location only
7 miles from Oxford city centre.
Notes A leading theological college training people for
ministry in the Anglican Church. In term-time guests live
alongside our residential community and are welcome to
participate in as many aspects of College life as they wish:
worship, meals and study opportunities. At all times, the
historic buildings, peaceful location and extensive grounds
offer an excellent venue for retreats, sabbaticals, meetings
and conferences. Guided retreats are also offered during
the summer vacation. All welcome.
Non-guided retreats The College offers a quiet setting
for a break from the rigours of day-to-day life. In term time,
you can join in the life of the College, or come in the
vacations for a quiet place for rest and reflection.
Contact Gill Keeble-Childs, Events Manager.

July
14–20　Summer School in Biblical and Theological Studies:
　　　　the relationship between Science and Faith.
　　　　Lectures, excursions and daily worship exploring
　　　　areas of debate within science and religion.
August
12–16　Creativity and prayer. Explore your creative skills
　　　　whilst enjoying shared worship and good
　　　　company in a tranquil setting.

108 St Katharine's, Parmoor

SRPF, St Katharine's, Parmoor, Henley on
Thames, Oxfordshire RG9 6NN　01494 881037
email office@srpf.org.uk
P, Q, W, Wf　*website* www.srpf.org.uk

Rooms 13 *en suite* in St Katharine's: a mixture of single,
double and twin, accommodating 24 people. Also 9 rooms
in St Joseph's annexe: 6 single (4 on the ground floor), 3 twin
plus a small lounge/common room. On the ground floor of
St Katharine's there is a large function room seating up to
120, dining room seating up to 60, 2 sitting rooms, library (2
rooms) and a large entrance hall with baby grand piano.
Notes An oasis of peace set in the rural tranquillity of the
Chilterns. In the spirit of true ecumenism we welcome
those of all denominations, faiths and beliefs, for quiet days
and residential retreats. The house is suitable for a variety of
uses including retreats, seminars, workshops, meetings,
church social functions and private functions. We have a
peaceful walled garden which supplies the house with
fresh fruits and vegetables throughout the year. Our
catering team provides excellent fresh food cooked on the
premises which enables us to cater for most dietary
requirements. Situated 7 miles from High Wycombe and
Henley-on-Thames and 5 miles from Marlow.
Contact The Warden.

109

109 St Stephen's House

16 Marston Street, Oxford
OX4 1JX 01865 613504 / 01865 613500
email assistantbursar@ssho.ox.ac.uk
P, Wf website www.ssho.ox.ac.uk

Rooms 44 single (18 *en suite*), 5 twin/double,
4 twin/double *en suite*. The Bishop's Room (*en suite*
twin/double with kitchen) and the self-contained double
en suite Edward King Suite with lounge and kitchen.
Church with fine organ and separate chapel. Dining room
for 60, 2 large seminar rooms equipped with a computer,
digital projector, interactive white board, DVD/video
player, connection to the Internet/Wifi, and 1 smaller
seminar room. Cloistered garden provides an oasis of calm
within a short walk of Oxford city centre.
Notes The former monastery home of the Cowley Fathers,
now a thriving theological college and permanent private
hall in the University of Oxford, offers its facilities for parish
retreats, sabbaticals, study periods, conferences and
choral/music concerts. Private retreatants in ordained
ministry welcome. Limited secure parking available.
Contact The Conference and Event Manager.

110 Stanton House

Pound Lane, Stanton St John, Oxford
OX33 1HF 01865 358807
email office@stantonhouse.org.uk
P, Wf website www.stantonhouse.org.uk

Rooms 4 singles (one with ground-floor access, *en suite*),
2 twin, 4 double (2 *en suite*), 2 sitting rooms and prayer
room. Available for individual retreat guests, small resident
groups and day groups up to 20.
Notes Stanton House is an independent evangelical
retreat house set in beautiful spacious grounds near
Oxford, allowing space and peace for time with God.
Comfortable accommodation in a family atmosphere with
home cooking. Guests may plan their time to suit their
needs, with team members available for prayer on request,
and short evening devotions.
Contact Please telephone or email for more information
and bookings.

**PRAY
WITH THE
RETREAT
ASSOCIATION
ICON**
– see page 78

SHROPSHIRE

111 Little Detton

Cleobury Mortimer, Kidderminster, Shropshire
DY14 8LW 01299 513211 / 07825 030607
email revsue55@yahoo.co.uk
C, D, P, Pe, Q, S, W, Wf, Y website www.littledetton.co.uk

Rooms Large dining room/lounge. Ground-floor bedroom
with *en suite*, double/family room with *en suite*,
double/family room with shared shower room, single with
shared shower room.
Notes Set in glorious Shropshire countryside we open
Little Detton, our own home, seeking to share God's
blessing with others. Beautiful views, restful garden and
smallholding with Shetland cattle, Jacob sheep, Oxford
sandy and black pigs, ducks, chickens, turkeys and bees,
plus our two dogs.
Home-cooked food using, where possible, ingredients
produced by ourselves. We raise our animals and work the
land as respectfully as we can with no chemicals and using
traditional vintage equipment. During the year various
activities can be open for visitors to join by arrangement. We
can also offer various crafts including rustic woodwork,
blacksmithing, silk painting, jewellery/bead work, felting, and
art materials are available. Pets welcome by arrangement.
Contact Sue Barrett.

SOMERSET

112 The Ammerdown Centre

Ammerdown Park, Radstock, Nr Bath, Somerset
BA3 5SW 01761 433709
email centre@ammerdown.org
B, C, Ch, D, I, P, Q, S, V, Wf, Y website www.ammerdown.org

Rooms 40 *en suite* bedrooms: 16 single (2 ground floor),
16 twin (1 self-catering unit), 7 double, 1 family room. 3 of
the bedrooms (1 single, 2 twin) are specially equipped for
users with disabilities. Lift. Exquisite chapel. Separate
contemplation and meditation room. Beautiful outdoor
labyrinth. Library and bookstall. Licensed bar. Free Wifi
throughout the building. 4 conference/meeting rooms for
up to 85 people. Loop system in all the meeting rooms and
in the chapel. Ample free parking.
Notes Ecumenical centre open to all, regardless of faith
tradition or background. Set in idyllic peaceful countryside
11 miles from Bath and 20 miles from Bristol. Daily prayer
services in the chapel. Excellent food cooked freshly on the
premises (special diets catered for). Ideal for private
retreats and personal breaks or to take part in one of
Ammerdown's many courses and guided retreats on offer
throughout the year (see listing below – please check
website or ring office before booking, as changes can take
place). Outside groups also welcome for residential or day
events, with special rates available to charities and church
groups. Open at Christmas for our Christmas houseparty.
Private guests are always warmly welcome at the
Ammerdown Centre, whether they are looking for a short
relaxing break or seeking time out for reflection.

Short courses
Come and paint in the beautiful grounds of Ammerdown Park! A 10-week course of 2-hour sessions.
7, 14, 21, 28 January; 4, 11, 25 February; 4, 11, 18 March.
Helena Softley's singing workshops informal and great fun! A 6-week course of 1.5-hour sessions.
8, 15, 22, 29 January; 5, 12 February. 1, 8, 15, 22 October; 5, 12 November.
Seeing the world through the camera lens Capturing the everyday drama of the rhythm of life. Digital photography course over 3 days. 30 March; 27 April; 1 June.
Helena Softley's Movement for Wellbeing and Joy workshops Learn simple dance movements to all styles of music, and experience the power of dance and self-expression. 9, 16, 23, 30 April; 19, 26 November; 3, 10, 17 December.
Personal skills for peaceful communities This course examines over 6 weeks what individuals can do to create constructive conversations and action about divisive issues. 9, 16, 23, 30 May; 13, 20 June.
Contact Administrator (centre@ammerdown.org).

January
4–6 It's not what you think: meditation and yoga as Christian practices. Meditation takes us beyond thought so that we begin to see things as they really are.
4–6 Workshop. The art of memoir writing. A safe, supportive and confidential space where you will learn ways to create your own memoir.
12 Explore a multi-sensory experience centred around an interactive Candala (an illuminated art form designed to light up our world) of grace incorporating 108 clay beads.
18–20 Course. Art therapy and anger. Taking participants through some of the art therapy processes that can help with anger and anger management.
19 Quiet day. A day to be still and reflect on times of transition in our ordinary lives: new beginnings, joys and sorrows, death and dying.
22 Talk. Jesus in the Bible and Qu'ran.
23 Talk. Holocaust, remembering and the dangers of forgetting.
26 Living in the present, and the presence, of the God who is the 'I Am', not the 'I was' or 'I will be'.

February
1–3 Course. Alive: living fully, living happily, living fearlessly. Discover how you are more important than you think you are. Learn to recognise and use your intuition.
1–3 Course. In search of the unknowable. Working with three practices: The Law of Three enables us to see and appreciate the dynamic flow of creation.
8–10 Course on Elijah, an extraordinary miracle-working prophet. We will look at his life and consider the miracles he performed and much more.
9 Quiet day, focused on three of the 'I Am' sayings of Jesus. Take time out from our busy lives to pray, reflect and meditate.
12 Talk. Being fair to the Pharisees, and other matters requiring care, as Christians prepare to celebrate Easter.
24 Doors are open to welcome us to different places

of worship in Bristol, including the Baha'i, Muslim, Jewish, Buddhist, Christian, Sikh and Hindu faiths.
24 Learn to Morris Dance! This taster day offers a chance to try out dances, with their distinctive styles, from different parts of our country.

March
1 Workshop. The next step on our human journey. Explore how world changes are guiding us to shift to a new level of consciousness.
6 Embracing difference. Using respectful curiosity to engage with others through developing cultural confidence and competence. A day enriching your understanding of cultural confidence and competence.
18–20 An opportunity to learn traditional silversmithing techniques such as saw piercing, soldering and polishing so you can develop your own ideas into beautiful pieces of jewellery.
18–22 Chinese brush painting – China's rural life. Covering the essentials for those new to the art form and demonstrations of painting subjects.
25–27 Discover the Enneagram. Through information, discussion, brief video clips and guided imaging, participants come away with a living experience.
27 Practising hospitality in a hostile environment.
27 Batik: go with the flow. Immerse yourself in the delightful flowing art medium of this ancient Asian and African art.
31 An introduction to mindfulness for anyone facing difficult challenges in their life, hoping to improve their wellbeing.

April
2–4 Retreat. Why is it so hard to forgive – or feel forgiven? Explore the psychological processes involved in forgiveness, which are different from what many suppose.
5 Transitions quiet day. See 19 January.
5–7 Workshop. Transcendental cinema. Explore how watching certain types of films can offer experiences which speak to our deeper selves.
6 Cubism: looking at Picasso. Starting with a talk and demonstration about Picasso's work, you will then create your own version of a simple cubist drawing.
9 'Just like Andy Warhol!' This course takes you through the process of translating your designs into hand-cut stencils and printing them onto fabric or paper.
15–17 The cross of Christ today. Six meditations/reflections on the cross which is the central symbol associated with Jesus Christ and his followers.
18–21 Easter retreat. An opportunity to meditate on and participate in chosen themes and ceremonies from the Holy Week liturgy. Fr Daniel O'Leary
27 Course. Candala of friendship. See 12 January.

May
4 Course exploring ways to develop skills and abilities in changes you face, drawing on the wisdom that you have acquired throughout your life's experience.
4–5 Course. Listening and gathering: holding space with spirit. Inviting you to explore the personal aspects and spiritual source of such practice.

5–10 Spring break. This week is especially designed for senior citizens looking for a break in lovely surroundings and good company.

6–10 Jane Austen's Georgian miscellany 2. Explore the realities of the Georgians' daily lives through a glimpse into their families, houses, sports, pastimes, education and professions.

11 Workshop. Beyond tea and biscuits: extending hospitality. Looking at the theology of hospitality with focus on biblical, historical and contemporary examples of its practice.

11 Multi-media or mixing it up! A play day offering a chance to combine some of the wonderful range of artistic media available today.

11 Life drawing. Enjoy a day of fun exercises to get you back into or begin the practice of drawing from life.

17 Meet our Muslim neighbours. Hear about the importance of fasting during the month of Ramadan; observe the breaking of the fast and the Magrib prayer.

20–23 Redwork embroidery. A very relaxing and rewarding technique covering a variety of hand embroidery stitches, with added embellishments.

22 Talk. Remembering the future: the challenge of reconciliation.

25 'I Am' sayings quiet day. See 9 February.

26–31 Retreat. The laughter of mercy: Mozart's *Marriage of Figaro*. Builds on Ammerdown's creative tradition of exploring spirituality in fresh and unusual ways.

May–June

31–2 Willow weaving. Enjoy a weekend of basket-making as you submerge yourself in the art of weaving a willow basket.

31–2 Workshop. Developing the sensitive within: trusting your intuition. Explore how intuition is constantly calling us to relate to the world in a profoundly meaningful way.

June

7–9 Finding stillness and strength. This interactive weekend will include sacred texts, poetry, music, meditation, prayer, guided reflections and discussion with times of silence.

7–9 The river of faith. Reflect on this metaphorical journey and ask: How is the river flowing now? What form might it take in the future?

8 Course. Candala of reconciliation. See 12 January.

8 Study the structure, form and history of Gregorian chant, how it emerged as the musical language for the first 1200 years of Christianity.

10–14 Timeless guides on rocky roads. Revisit familiar gospel stories in light of real contemporary experience and challenges, exploring with fresh eyes what they mean today.

14 Printing with polystyrene. Using polystyrene we will design an image to transfer onto the foam which we will then use to make prints from.

14–16 Course. Presence: become fully aware, fully powerful, fully active. Explore the source of this power of presence and its impact on the world around you.

14–16 Women prophets. We will look at Miriam, Deborah,

Huldah and other women prophets. A prophet's role is to pass on God's teaching.

14–16 An introduction to mindfulness for anyone needing to take stock and destress. Simple meditation practices helping to tune in to what the body is saying.

17–20 Course. Artist's sketchbook: Coptic binding. Introducing Coptic binding, an ancient and highly useful binding.

18 Batik. See 27 March.

21–14 Living Theology Summer School. Reflect on the writings of Pope Francis and Scripture. Bp Crispian Hollis, retired Bp of Portsmouth & Brendan Callaghan SJ

24–26 Discover how stories in the Bible, classical, fairy tales and the primarily novels today, inspire and challenge us in our walk with God.

July

1–4 Course. Flower embroidery. Covering several interesting ways of incorporating garden flower designs into a piece of hand stitched embroidery.

2–4 Retreat. Spiritual gifts of ageing. Exploring how the natural psychological processes associated with ageing can enrich our lives – if we let them.

6 Celebrating two extraordinary women. Julian of Norwich, Christian mystic and theologian 1395; Etty Hillesum, Jewish, victim of Holocaust, 1943.

6 Life drawing. See 11 May.

8 Talk. God in Christian and Muslim thought.

10 Participatory workshop. Rethinking security. What does the word 'security' mean to you? Explore this and other fundamental questions.

24 Talk. Salaam, Shalom – the fruits of Muslim Jewish dialogue.

August

5–9 In friendship and love, the Enneagram and relationships. Expect type-based panels, exploratory exercises, meditations and a gradual opening to deep relationship.

10 What does the Bible say about LGBTQI+? Interpreting Scripture with integrity and inclusivity. Introducing participants to issues faced by LGBTQI+ individuals in the context of faith.

10 Quiet day. Transitions of life. See 19 January.

10–16 Bobbin lacemaking is fun, creative and stimulating especially when like-minded students come together to learn new skills and extend their knowledge.

12–16 Drawing and coloured pencils. Suitable for anyone with some experience, it will cover a wide range of subjects and techniques using this lovely medium.

19–21 Crewelwork. Learn how to stitch Jacobean-style motifs using hand embroidery stitches such as grid stitch, French knots, long and short, chain stitch and stem stitch.

19–21 Environmental spirituality in Judaism and Christianity. Exploration of Laudato Si, Pope Francis' magnificent encyclical on the environment in the light of Jewish and Christian spirituality.

21 Course. Learning cultural competence and confidence and exploring bias. Learner-centred and participative, encouraging self-reflection and gentle challenge.

26–30 IGR. Spend several days in silence with an experienced spiritual director, who will guide you in praying, reading, and reflecting. Sr Felicity Young

26–30 Receive guidance on reading problematic texts in the New Testament as well as dealing with prayers Jesus would have said as a faithful Jew.

September

2–6 Autumn break. This week is especially designed for senior citizens looking for a break in lovely surroundings and good company.

9–13 IGR. Spend several days in silence, accompanied in praying, reading and reflecting. Judy Holyer

9–13 Chinese brush painting: China in blue, green and gold. Explore four beautiful subjects using wonderful deep mineral colours and gold ink.

9–13 Workshop/retreat. Playing in the presence of God. Not about creating works of art but about paying attention to what happens during the creative process.

10 Life drawing. See 11 May.

14 'I Am' sayings quiet day. See 9 February.

19–21 Environmental spirituality in Judaism and Christianity. See 19–21 August.

21 'Just like Andy Warhol!' course. See 9 April.

24–27 Spiritual gifts and the Enneagram: subtypes and soul. Identify the subtleties of our subtype to confront what really holds us back from awareness of our essence.

25 Batik. See 27 March.

25 Talk. There's no place for hate! What is hate crime? How big a problem is it? What can we do about it?

September–October

29–4 Finding fulfilment. Discover the three aspects of ourselves – body, mind, and spirit – to discover what stops us being fully open and available.

October

5 An introduction to mindfulness for anyone facing difficult challenges in their life, hoping to improve their wellbeing.

8 Poetry as a vital spiritual exercise.

8–10 Human development: a spiritual journey. Explore the processes through which we become who we are now.

11–13 Lift up your voice with an accomplished choir leader. A weekend of song in the Ammerdown chapel. Jane Harris

12 Book Club day. *Small Great Things* by Jodi Picoult and Why I'm No Longer Talking to White People about Race by Reni Eddo-Lodge.

17–18 Listening and gathering course. See 4–5 May.

19 Come for a stitch day. Find out how to make a quick background for your work. Then enjoy trying out lots of different stitches.

20 Meet our Jewish neighbours. Join the celebration of the Festival of Sukkot, celebrating harvest. Make a 'sukkah', a shelter where farmers traditionally sleep and eat during harvest.

21–23 Silversmithing. See 18–20 March.

21–25 This course introduces beginners and advanced to the art of writing, covering the basics of using a broad-edge pen, colour, principles of layout and design.

24 Colograph. Make interesting and textural colograph printing blocks using objects or materials, which we will then print onto a variety of papers and surfaces.

25 Colograph. See above.

28–31 Workshop. The art of memoir writing. Providing a safe, supportive and confidential space where you will learn ways to create your own memoir.

November

4–7 Appliqué embroidery. We will use several different designs, incorporating fabric appliqué with hand embroidery covering many aspects of this lovely technique.

9 Candala of peace. See 12 January.

15–17 Workshop. A hand embroidery class for students to finish off some of those UFOs – UnFinished Objects!

22–24 Quiet weekend. Transitions of life. Be still and reflect on times of transition in our ordinary lives: new beginnings, joys and sorrows, death and dying.

27 Talk. Things that make for peace. Some reflections on conflict resolution and peacemaking.

November–December

29–1 Advent retreat. Reflections on the beauty, challenges and pain of all life and of our own in particular.

December

7 Transitions quiet day. See 19 January.

22–27 Our Christmas house party is always popular. People love spending Christmas at Ammerdown, and we do our utmost to make sure they have a good time.

113 House of Prayer

2 Parkfields, High Street, Butleigh, nr Glastonbury, Somerset BA6 8SZ 01458 851561
B, Co, D, I, P, Q, S, W *email* elizabethrees_ocv@hotmail.com

Rooms 3.

Notes House of Prayer in village 3 miles south of Glastonbury. IGRs (30-day, 8-day or less), spiritual direction, counselling and supervision.

Contact Sr Elizabeth Rees OCV.

114 St Nicholas Wayfarer's Church

Kilton, Somerset TA5 1ST 01278 733 504
B, D, I, P, Pe, Q, S, V *website* www.stnicholayfarerschurch.co.uk

Non-residential.

Notes St Nicholas was decommissioned as an Anglican country church in 2004. Now fully renovated with disabled facilities it has become a drop-in prayer and daytime retreat centre. Set in a very rural area overlooking the estuary and the Welsh mountains. Easily accessible, 1 mile north of the A39, it offers quiet space, beautiful views, half/full-day retreat opportunities for the individual, pairs or groups (max 12). Affiliated to the Quiet Garden Movement. We specialise in lectio divina (praying the Scriptures) and can offer spiritual direction.

Contact Sr Annette Stapleton OCV LCSi MA (Theology).

STAFFORDSHIRE

115 Reflections / Hermitage

Little Hayes, Beaudesert Park, Cannock Wood,
Rugeley, Staffordshire WS15 4JJ   01543 674474
email polhill@reflectiongardens.org.uk
I, P, Q, S, W   *website* www.reflectiongardens.org.uk

Rooms Self-catering Hermitage, sleeps 1.
Notes The Reflections gardens, based on Ignatian Exercises, link themes of environmental concern and the Christian spiritual journey. The Hermitage is a free-standing unit in the grounds for self-catering retreatants. Extensive woodlands of Cannock Chase adjoin the house. We welcome visitors to the gardens by appointment from February to November, both individuals and groups. IGR available. Please phone or email to arrange a suitable time.
Contact Rev Christine Polhill or John Polhill.
We do not have a set programme. Visitors are welcome at any time (by prior arrangement) between February and November. We will lead or support quiet days for groups by arrangement.

116 St Chad's House, Leek

3 Southfields, Leek, Staffordshire ST13 5LR
01538 382483
email stchadsleek@gmail.com
website www. leekparish.org.uk/churches/st-chads-house
B, C, P, Q, Wf

Rooms 1 double *en suite* room with connecting sitting room on 1st floor for individual retreats. Chapel, library, lounge and dining room (capacity 12) for day guests.
Notes St Chad's House is a three-storey terraced house on a private road and looks out over a quiet wooded valley. It is a 5-min walk from the town centre but feels very quiet and secluded. The house offers a programme of quiet days and events on prayer and contemplation for day guests. It can be booked for church groups for awaydays, church quiet days, etc with or without catering. An attractive *en suite* double bedroom and sitting room are available for individual retreatants. Overnight retreats are offered on a bed and breakfast basis (other meals can sometimes be provided). The house is overseen by the Anglican parish and has a focus on Celtic Christianity in the resources that are used. The house has a well-stocked library of Christian books with a section on Celtic Christianity. Leek is on the edge of the Peak District with many lovely places to walk within a short drive. Leek town has plenty of places to eat.
Contact Mike Fitzsimmons, Warden.

**GIVE SOMEONE
THE GIFT OF A
RETREAT!**

– see page 64 for details

117 Shallowford House

Shallowford, Stone, Staffordshire ST15 0NZ
01785 760233
email info@shallowfordhouse.org
C, D, I, P, Q, S, V, Wf, Y   *website* www.shallowfordhouse.org

Rooms Ground floor: 2 twin *en suite* wheelchair-accessible, 2 twin *en suite*. First floor: 9 single *en suite*, 1 single own bathroom, 6 twin *en suite*, 4 double *en suite*, 1 triple *en suite*.
Notes Serving the Christian community from the heart of the country, Shallowford House is set within an established wooded area and secluded gardens in the beautiful Staffordshire countryside. The house has a comfortable lounge, well-stocked library and at its heart a beautiful chapel and prayer room. The wildlife meadow with various ponds, labyrinth and plenty of benches all allow the retreatant space to take in God's creation. There is a variety of retreats and quiet days through the year for individuals or groups. It is also an ideal venue for your church or group retreat or awayday.
Contact Simon Hudson, Director.
Visit our website for up-to-date details of all that we offer.
Quiet Mondays 7 January, 4 February, 11 March (Lent), 1 April, 13 May, 3 June, 1 July, 12 August, 2 September, 7 October, 4 November, 2 December (Advent).
May–June
31–2 Silent retreat.
July
15–19 Creative retreat. Mary and Martha.
August
12–14 Summer retreat.
October
9–11 Autumn quiet retreat.
November
11–13 Pre-Advent retreat.
22 Christmas craft day.
December
6 Advent quiet day.

SUFFOLK

118 Clare Priory

Ashen Road, Clare, Suffolk CO10 8NX
01787 277326
fax 01787 278688
email clarepriory@clarepriory.net
B, D, I, P, Q, S, V, W, Wf, Y   *website* www.clarepriory.org.uk

Rooms 5 single *en suite* on ground floor, 1 single *en suite* on 1st floor, 1 double *en suite* on 1st floor, four 2–4 bedded rooms with adjacent bathrooms on 2nd floor.
Notes Please see the website for our programme of events. You are welcome to come at any time for spiritual guidance, to join in the daily routine of the Augustinian community and to enjoy the peace and prayerfulness of Clare Priory. Please see www.clarepriory.org.uk for our 2018 programme.
Contact Kathy Reddick.

119 HOME Retreat Centre, Monks Eleigh

Monks Eleigh United Reformed Church,
Brent Eleigh Road, Monks Eleigh, Suffolk
IP7 7AU   01473 310169
            email homeretreat.m.e@gmail.com
I, P, Q, W   *website* www.hadleighurc.org.uk

Non-residential.
Bright, comfortable and spacious hall, with comfortable seating for up to 40 people. Fully-equipped kitchen. Accessible toilet. Large TV monitor with HDMI setting for laptops. B&Bs available in the vicinity.
Notes Set in the heart of this beautiful village, with inn, community shop, post office and craft centre. Also available close by for guests is 'The Quiet Garden', a 5-acre woodland area. HOME welcomes people of all faiths and denominations for quiet days, self-led retreats and meetings.
Contact Mr Ronnie Howson.

120 Quiet Waters Christian Retreat House

Flixton Road, Bungay, Suffolk NR35 1PD
                            01986 893201
             email mail@quietwaters.org.uk
C, Ch, D, E, P, Q, S, V, Wf   *website* www.quietwaters.org.uk

Rooms 9 bedrooms comprising 5 twin, 2 double and 2 single. (1 double and 1 single are *en suite*, 1 double and 1 twin have ground-floor access.)
Notes Quiet Waters is an interdenominational retreat house that has been providing a place of retreat for individuals and groups for over 40 years. Set in 2 acres of grounds bordering the River Waveney, this 9-bedroomed Georgian house offers an informal, homely atmosphere and serves home-cooked food. We provide a safe environment in which to seek God, unwind and be refreshed. Although we are not a silent retreat house, there is plenty of opportunity to find peace and quiet or have fellowship with other Christians. The house keeps a daily rhythm of prayer in the peaceful chapel. Guided retreats are available on request and the team offers a 'listening ear' and prayer (we do not offer counselling). Quiet Waters operates as a faith venture. Whilst we have suggested donations for individuals we only ask that you pay what you can afford. (Groups up to a maximum of 15 people over 7 rooms are charged a set fee.)
Our particular call is to 3 main groups of people: tired, hurt, weary and wounded Christians; those wishing to 'seek the Lord' (traditional retreats), either individuals or groups; those involved in Church and parachurch activity in need of rest and refreshment. Our events are posted on our Facebook page which can be accessed from our website. Do feel free to email or phone us for further information.
Contact The Quiet Waters Team.

121 Ringsfield Hall

Hall Road, Beccles, Suffolk
NR34 8JR   01502 713020
             email info@ringsfield-hall.co.uk
C, Ch, D, E, P, V, W, Wf, Y   *website* www.ringsfield-hall.co.uk

Rooms 1-bed Hermitage for single retreats with small kitchenette and toilet/washroom.
For group retreats, 14 bedrooms in the Hall: a single, dormitories of 8, 10, 10 and 5; 2 double rooms; 3 twins; and a variety of family-sized rooms.
Notes We're non-denominational, and like to offer warm, welcoming space for anyone and everyone. If staying at the Hermitage, we leave you to it, but staff are on hand to help as required. If staying at the Hall as a group, this can be on a self-catered basis or with full board – either way, we hope you'll find we offer warm hospitality.
Contact Simon Paylor.

122 Claridge House

Dormans Road, Lingfield, Surrey RH7 6QH
                            01342 832150
    email welcome@claridgehousequaker.org.uk
C, Ch, D, I, P, Q, Wf   *website* www.claridgehousequaker.org.uk

Rooms We have 2 single bedrooms in our ground-floor annexe sharing an accessible shower room. In the main house on the ground floor we have rooms that are accessible for disabled, including 1 *en suite* twin room and 1 single room with an *en suite* bathroom/wetroom. Upstairs on the first floor there are 8 bedrooms – 1 double, 4 twin rooms and 2 single rooms, all *en suite*, and a double room with a charming Victorian bathroom across the corridor.
Notes Claridge House is a Victorian Quaker property set between the villages of Lingfield and Dormansland. In keeping with the simple and peaceful environment, there are no TVs; however high quality Wifi is available for guests' use throughout the house. Alcohol and smoking are prohibited on the premises. We are unable to accommodate children and pets.
Contact Lilianna Illes, Manager. ❏ *inside back cover*
Claridge House offers a variety of retreats and courses ranging from yoga, meditation, writing courses, massage retreats and more.

123 House of Prayer

35 Seymour Rd, East Molesey, Surrey KT8 0PB
                           020 8941 2313
             email admin@christian-retreat.org
B, C, I, P, Q, S   *website* www.christian-retreat.org

Rooms 8 rooms (5 *en suite*).
Notes The House of Prayer provides a breathing space in the hubbub of life, a prayerful space for solitude and silence. The House is ecumenical and is run by the Sisters of the Christian Retreat, a Roman Catholic congregation.
Contact The Administrator. ❏ *p 80*

January
11–13 Weekend silent IGR. House of Prayer team
20–25 Finding fulfilment. Life is only real when I am.
Jill Benet, Jacqueline Evans & Antonio Benet
26 I am the 'Thou' of God. Jill Benet
February
10–17 8-day retreat. Intensive centering prayer. Jill Benet
23 Thomas Merton: master of contemplation. Peter
Tyler
March
1–4 Exploring the welcome prayer practice. Jill Benet &
Jacqueline Evans
8–10 Weekend silent IGR. House of Prayer team
23 Lent quiet morning. Finding the treasure.
Sr Melanie Kingston
30 Finding meaning in the margins. Chris Bemrose &
Mike Mullins
April
5–7 Lent retreat. The grace of emptiness. House of
Prayer team
27 Richard Rohr – theology and spirituality.
Lynne Scholefield
May
11 The mystic for today 1. Sr Melanie Kingston
25 Flourishing through prayer. New developments in
positive psychology. Patrick Coyne
27–31 The wisdom of love in the Song of Songs.
Stefan Gillow Reynolds
June
7–9 Centering prayer immersion weekend to deepen
our practice. Jill Benet
11–13 Midweek silent IGR. House of Prayer team
22–23 Creative weekend. Touching the soul.
Sr Melanie Kingston & Sr Anne Dunne
July
6 The mystic for today 2. Sr Melanie Kingston
12–19 6-day silent IGR. House of Prayer team
September
6–8 Weekend silent IGR. House of Prayer team
15–20 Immersion retreat. Gift of life: life and living, death
and dying. Jill Benet
28 Visions of the living light (Hildegard von Bingen).
Julie Hopkins
October
5 The still of the moment. Helen Overell
19 The mystic for today 3. Sr Melanie Kingston
22–24 Midweek silent IGR. House of Prayer team
26 Born to fly. Margaret Silf
October–November
27–3 8-day intensive retreat. Centering prayer. Jill Benet
November
8–10 Weekend silent IGR. House of Prayer team
22–24 The psychology of centering prayer. Jill Benet
30 Light without and light within. Antonia Lynn
December
6–8 Advent retreat. House of Prayer team

124 Ladywell Retreat and Spirituality Centre

Ashstead Lane, Godalming, Surrey GU7 1ST
01483 419269
fax 01483 426244
email retreat@lady-well.org.uk
P, Q, Wf   *website* www.ladywellretreat.org.uk

Rooms Non-residential.
Notes Ladywell Retreat and Spirituality Centre is an oasis
of peace in the stunning Surrey countryside, within easy
reach of London. Find space and freedom to explore your
own deep desires, values and beliefs in a reflective
atmosphere. Ladywell, where the Retreat and Spirituality
Centre is located, is the Motherhouse of an international
Catholic religious congregation – the Franciscan
Missionaries of the Divine Motherhood. People of all faiths
and none are welcome to come as individuals or in groups,
to use our facilities. Ladywell is an ideal place for reflective
days of prayer. The administrator will be very happy to
discuss your specific needs with you. Ladywell has
spacious grounds and lovely woodland walks. Ladywell is
about to undergo a major renovation programme and
therefore our programme for 2019 and 2020 will be greatly
curtailed. However, we will continue with our days of
prayer monthly. We will remain available for day events
such as personal days of prayer or for groups to hold day
events.
Contact Retreat Administrator.
Days of prayer Days to ponder, pray and be still, with the
opportunity for spiritual input.
January
23 Day of prayer. Fr David Myers
February
13 Day of prayer. Fr Anthony Maggs
March
12 Day of prayer. Fr Victor Darlington
April
3 Day of prayer. Fr Gerard Flynn
May
9 Day of prayer. Fr Kevin Dring
June
11 Day of prayer. Fr Jeremy Garratt
July
11 Day of prayer. Fr Adrian Graffy
August
20 Day of prayer. Speaker tbc
September
11 Day of prayer. Fr Victor Darlington
October
8 Day of prayer. Fr David Parmiter
November
7 Day of prayer. Speaker tbc
December
3 Day of prayer. Speaker tbc

INTRODUCING RETREATS & PRAYER PACK
A pack including resources for prayer and a short film about the value of retreats
www.retreats.org.uk/resources.php

---

125 St Columba's House

Maybury Hill, Woking, Surrey GU22 8AB

01483 766498

email admin@stcolumbashouse.org.uk

B, C, Ch, D, E, P, Q, S, Wf *website* www.stcolumbashouse.org.uk

Rooms 26 bedrooms. 21 single and 1 twin (all *en suite*) in the main house. Redwood House which is situated in the grounds has 3 twin/double (all *en suite*) plus 1 twin with adjacent shower room. All have internet connections. The main house is fully accessible for wheelchairs with a lift to the 1st floor and 2 bedrooms with accessible showers and alarm systems. Redwood House is accessible for wheelchairs in its 2 downstairs meeting rooms. Our 10 meeting rooms, all with free Wifi, accommodate between 3 and 50 people. St Columba's Chapel can seat up to 80 and has a hearing loop, sound system, Clavinova piano and a selection of worship resources. St Peter's Oratory seats 20. Fairtrade refreshments are available throughout the day and home-cooked food is served in the Refectory. Redwood House is also available on a self-catering basis, including for cell groups, small meetings and holiday lets.

Notes St Columba's House is a contemporary Christian retreat and conference centre within easy reach of London. We are open to residential and day groups as well as individuals who are looking for a peaceful environment in which to meet, study, work, rest or pray. Alongside our house programme we plan bespoke events as requested. St Columba's House is an Anglican foundation. We offer hospitality to all, regardless of faith, but ask that the Christian ethos of the house is respected by guests.

Contact Rachel Moore, Chaplain or Elaine Derrick and Jules Winton, the Front-of-House Administrators. ❑ *p 4*

January
16 Sixty minutes of mindfulness: a Christian perspective. Suzette Jones
17 Christian book group. *The Book of Revelation for Dummies*. Giles Hutchinson
23 Spiritual spa day for women. Tricia Phillips
28 Quiet Monday with Holy Communion: looking at Scripture. St Columba's House

February
6   Sixty minutes of mindfulness: a Christian perspective. Suzette Jones
7   Workshop. Weaving a sacred circle. Alison Eve & Rachel Moore
13 Quiet day. Celtic Christianity. David Cole

March
13 Quiet day. Sacred in the city. Margaret Silf
20 Sixty minutes of mindfulness: a Christian perspective. Suzette Jones
21 Christian book group. *Gateway to Hope: An Exploration of Failure*. Giles Hutchinson
22–24 Time with Jesus. Wholeness Through Christ Team
25 Quiet Monday with Holy Communion: looking at prayer. St Columba's House

April
10 Sixty minutes of mindfulness: a Christian perspective. Suzette Jones
26 Guided day. A Journey to Wholeness. Maggie Hilditch
27 Exhibition open day. A Journey to Wholeness.

April–May
27–31 Exhibition of paintings. Hope – A Journey to Wholeness.

May
13 Quiet Monday with Holy Communion: the labyrinth. St Columba's House
16 Christian book group. *Unbelievable?* Giles Hutchinson with guest Justin Brierley
29 Sixty minutes of mindfulness: a Christian perspective. Suzette Jones

June
26 Quiet day. Come away with me and rest. Rachel Moore

July
15 Quiet Monday with Holy Communion: looking at song. St Columba's House
17 Guided day. Letting go and moving on. Tricia Phillips

August
9–11 Time with Jesus. Wholeness Through Christ Team
30 Sanctuary space day. The Community of Hopeweavers

September
7   Heritage open day. St Columba's House
19 Christian book group. *Parable and Paradox*. Giles Hutchinson
26 The Lord's Prayer: seven sonnets, seven meditations. Malcolm Guite

October
14 Quiet Monday with Holy Communion: creativity. St Columba's House
22 Praise for all seasons: reach for your harp. Mark Rudall & Rachel Moore

November
1   All Saints creative quiet day. The Community of Hopeweavers
12 Praise for all seasons: turn up the volume. Mark Rudall & Rachel Moore
21 Christian book group. *Paul: A Biography*. Giles Hutchinson
26 Praise for all seasons: the takeaway. Mark Rudall & Rachel Moore
27 A Celtic Advent quiet day. David Cole

December
7   Advent service. Cloth for the cradle.

Check the website throughout the year for the most up-to-date information (dates may be subject to change) and for other events including Encounter with Jesus days, led by a team from Wholeness Through Christ.

126 Wychcroft, Diocese of Southwark Retreat & Resource Centre

Wychcroft House, South Park Lane, Bletchingley, Redhill, Surrey RH1 4NE

01883 743041

email wychcroft@southwark.anglican.org

D, Wf *website* www.wychcroft.org

Rooms 23 bedrooms: 10 single, 12 twin, 1 triple. All have washbasins, mirror and shaver socket. Separate showers and bath facilities provided.

117

Notes Wychcroft is the Diocese of Southwark Retreat and Resource Centre. It is widely used for the training within the diocese. Wychcroft also serves as a centre for parish house parties, conferencing, retreats and study groups. Situated 22 miles south of London in the picturesque Surrey countryside, Wychcroft exists particularly to resource the mission of God, providing opportunities and space for nurture and prayer. With its large lounge, small common room, separate chapel and dining room/conference room, the building provides a flexible space. Free Wifi is available, along with visual and audio equipment. The Centre Manager, along with the house team, provides a warm welcome with flexible unobtrusive service together with freshly prepared food.
Contact Richard Ellis, Centre Manager.

SUSSEX

EAST SUSSEX

127 Penhurst Retreat Centre

The Manor House, Penhurst, Battle, East Sussex
TN33 9QP   01424 892088
                                  email info@penhurst.org.uk
B, C, D, E, I, P, Q, S, W, Wf   *website* www.penhurst.org.uk

Rooms 9 bedrooms. Main house: 4 twin *en suite*, 1 double *en suite*, 1 single *en suite*, 1 single with designated bathroom. Annexe: 1 twin *en suite* (ground-floor access), 1 twin *en suite* (ground floor, adapted for wheelchair-users). All rooms available for single accommodation.
Notes 17th-century manor house adjacent to a small parish church, providing a haven of tranquillity. Set in an area of outstanding natural beauty, this is an ecumenical centre offering a warm welcome to all. The house is available for individual or small group retreats and catered quiet days throughout the year. There is also a programme of led and accompanied retreats. This centre has a particular heart for UK and overseas mission. There are dedicated retreats/workshops for those with mission connections and a 10% discount is offered to associates of agencies/churches that are members of Global Connections. There is a small art room in the grounds.
3- and 4-night silent retreats An opportunity to take time out with God, to receive his love by prayerfully pondering the Scriptures. See programme for leaders to each retreat.
Contact The Penhurst Office.

February
18–21 Emmaus Road. Encountering Jesus on our journey. An opportunity to come aside and be with Jesus, as we each consider our journey with Him. Jack & Sandra Telfer

March
6–8 Broken but blessed. Journeying from pain to peace with unlikely guides. How we can be transformed through our pain to become a blessing to others. Rebekah Domer

8–10 Open post-abortion healing retreat. An opportunity for those affected by abortion to explore the emotions involved. Jenny Baines & Judy McGibbon

15–17 Divorce recovery workshop. Aims to make some sense of divorce and helps you find ways of moving forward at whatever stage you find yourself. Mandy Callf & Sue Clipsham

18–20 Retreat. Breathing space for the body, mind, soul and spirit. An opportunity to allow God to breathe into our breathing space. Chris & Sue Monckton-Rickett

22–24 Enneagram. God-shaped people. Becky Widdows

27 Making a joyful noise/singing for pleasure. A day to join together raising funds for Penhurst whilst singing a rich variety of songs. Laurie & Brigid Main

April
23–26 Women in leadership. Unique opportunity for women in leadership to examine their relationship with God and others in a restful, spiritual environment with one-to-one accompaniment. Jenny Butter

April–May
29–3 Silent IGR. David & Becky Widdows

May
6–10 Come and engage with Jesus and find healing for difficult questions, disappointment and hidden pain. With an opportunity for one-to-one prayer ministry. Jen Rees Larcombe, Beauty from Ashes

11 Discernment: making decisions and seeking guidance. Are we judging or discerning? Do we make decisions based on head, heart, gut instinct? Peter Parr & Heather Jane Ozanne

13–17 Silent IGR. A journey into silence, an individually guided retreat with a difference. Peter Doodes & Fiona Bower

17–19 Music and spirituality theology. Richard King & Lee Hassell

May–June
31–2 Rediscovering Sabbath. Come and explore the deeper meaning of entering into God's Sabbath rest as a spiritual discipline that can radically change your life. Christine Strohmeier

June
21 A day for people who want to engage with Jesus and find healing for difficult questions, disappointment and hidden pain. Jen Rees Larcombe, Beauty From Ashes

24 Boundaries. A day with teaching on boundaries and space to spend time with God, to be built up and affirmed. Mandy Callf

June–July
29–7 Silent IGR of 8, 6 or 4 nights. Maureen Stringer

July
12–14 Time for Marriage weekend. No matter how long you have been married, you will benefit from spending some time on the relationship you want to last a lifetime. TFM team

23–24 Live like the kingdom is near. What does this mean and how is it an essential mindset to grow as a disciple of Jesus? Bp Richard Jackson

August
5–9 Retreat. Creative space. Provides mainly undirected free personal space, a chance to be as well as

create. Bring any creative ideas you wish to explore. Jill Hoffman

19–22 Silent IGR. Dawn Pointing

September

2–6 Photography retreat. Light of life. Choose to see beauty in the present moment, through the photographic process of 'drawing with light'. Steve Radley

7 Flourishing. Explore the shift in spirituality from heaven-focused to one which leads to an appreciation of the interconnectedness of all life and deeper engagement with humanity. Peter Parr & Heather Jane Ozanne

16–19 Silent IGR. Judy Cannan

23–27 Retreat for people who want to engage with Jesus and find healing for difficult questions, disappointment and hidden pain. Jen Rees Larcombe, Beauty From Ashes

September–October

30–4 Seeing the song of nature. A week about light in a composition and capturing it in watercolours. Experience 'seeing the song of nature'. Viv Walkington

October

9–13 Finding your purpose. Becoming energised. Come and understand further who God has created you to be and how and where you can use these gifts to serve Him. Jenny Butter

14–18 A journey into silence, an IGR with a difference. Peter Doodes & Fiona Bower

21 Pilgrimage workshop. A quiet day to draw aside and reflect on where we are on our pilgrimage through life, both the outer and the inner journey. Mandy Callf

25–27 Living with loss following bereavement. This is a gentle retreat for people of all ages (over 18) who have suffered loss through bereavement. Abi May

November

4–8 Silent IGR. Dilys Threshie

WEST SUSSEX

128 Chichester Cathedral

4 Canon Lane, Chichester, West Sussex PO19 1PX
01243 813586
email bookings@chichestercathedral.org.uk
B, D, I, P, Q, Wf *website* www.chichestercathedral.org.uk

Rooms 4 large double/twin, 3 standard double, 1 single with disabled access.
4 Canon Lane offers 2 conference rooms, a dining room, a garden room, an oratory for individual prayer and 8 superb *en suite* bedrooms. There is also a beautiful walled garden.
Notes 4 Canon Lane is located in the heart of the Georgian city of Chichester, within the picturesque grounds of the Cathedral's close. A former archdeaconry, it has been restored to its former glory, offering the perfect setting for awaydays, meetings, quiet days, residential weekends and conferences for up to 40 people.
Contact Maria Gordon, Bookings Administrator.

129 Monastery of the Holy Trinity

Crawley Down, Crawley, West Sussex RH10 4LH
01342 712074
Ch, Q, S, Wf *email* brother.andrew@cswg.org.uk

Rooms 6 single. C of E.
Notes C of E contemplative mixed community.
Contact Brother Andrew, Guestmaster.

130 The Open Cloister, Worth Abbey

Paddockhurst Road, Turners Hill, Crawley, West Sussex RH10 4SB
01342 710318
fax 01342 710311
email toc@worth.org.uk
B, D, E, P, Q, S, W, Wf, Y *website* www.worth.co.uk

Rooms
St Bruno's House Residential accommodation for The Open Cloister: rooms (some *en suite*) 14 twin and 2 family rooms for 4. Enquiries welcome from groups of up to 36 guests and individual guests.
Compass House Non-residential day centre, meeting room for up to 35 guests. Self-catering with kitchen and toilet facilities.
Monastery Guest House (men only) 3 single rooms, 2 twin.
Abbey Church complex Non-residential. Use of Abbey Church (seating c850), bookshop, Unity Room (seating 80) and some ancillary rooms for liturgy, days of recollection etc.
Bermondsey Huts A base for camping for up to 80 in summer (May–October) only. Bunk room for 8 and leaders' room for 3. Washing facilities, kitchen, day room and an acre for camping in sight of the Abbey Church. Ideal for extended families and large self-catering groups seeking inexpensive accommodation.
Notes Worth Abbey is home to a community rooted in 1500 years of Benedictine monastic wisdom. The monks express the gospel through a community life of prayer and service. They continue the Benedictine tradition of hospitality and education, running a school, a parish and a retreat house. Currently, they support the Lay Community of St Benedict and sponsor Compass. The BBC TV series *The Monastery* and *The Big Silence* were filmed here.
The Open Cloister Our vision is to offer a retreat focused on the search for God in prayer and community. We invite men and women of all Christian denominations and none to explore today's world through the eyes of faith. Suitable for beginners and young people. For details see our website or contact the Booking Secretary 01342 710318; toc@worth.org.uk.
Quiet days Normally on the second Friday of each month (excluding August). Sharing the monastic rhythm of prayer led by the monastic team.
Retreats for young people For almost 40 years, Worth has hosted student and young adult groups. To find out more or to book a retreat, either for a chaplaincy or as an individual, please contact The Open Cloister.
Compass Support for Catholic men and women discerning a possible call to the religious life. www.compass-points.org.uk, enquiries@compass-points.org.uk

Please refer to our website for full details of our retreat programme which will be regularly updated throughout 2019, during which we will be particularly concentrating our focus towards teenagers and young adults at weekends. ❏ *p 3*

131 The Priory, Storrington

School Lane, Storrington, Pulborough, West Sussex RH20 4LN   01903 742150
email storrington@chemin-neuf.org
B, C, D, I, P, Q, S, V, W, Wf, Y   *website* www.chemin-neuf.org.uk

Rooms 19 rooms accommodating 36 people.

Notes The Chemin Neuf Community is an international Roman Catholic community with an ecumenical vocation and with members from many different Christian denominations. It was founded in France in 1973 and stems from the charismatic renewal and Ignatian spirituality. The community offers a friendly welcome at The Priory on the edge of the South Downs. IGRs on request according to availability. Unless specified otherwise, all retreats are led by members of Chemin Neuf. The community has a special mission (Cana) to couples and families. For 1 week in summer (see our house in Cornwall, Sclerder Abbey) and weekends through the year couples can enjoy time together to pray, share and reflect while their children follow their own programme. The Priory with its chapel is also available for day events accommodating up to 70 people.

Contact Sr Iwona.

February
23–24 Cana weekend for couples and children. Come for a 'top up' after the Cana week or to experience a taster of the week.
27 Quiet day 10am–4pm. Silent time with guided prayer. Accompaniment available if required.
March
10–15 Spiritual Exercises of St Ignatius. Guided silent retreat to know Christ more intimately in order to love and serve him better and to recognise God's call.
27 Quiet day (see 27 February).
30–31 Weekend for 14–18s. Suitable for confirmation retreat.
May
18–19 Cana weekend (see 23–24 February).
June
5 Quiet day (see 27 February).
July–August
28–2 Summer camp for 14–18s. An opportunity to share fun, outings, fellowship within a Christian community setting.
November
tbc Cana weekend.
December
tbc Quiet day.

132 TS Resolute/CYE Retreats

Christian Youth Enterprises, Jubilee Building, Chidham, Chichester, West Sussex PO18 8TE
01243 573375
email admin@cye.org.uk
B, D, Q, S, W, Wf   *website* www.cye.org.uk

Rooms 14 cabins, all *en suite*. 1 limited mobility cabin on the main deck with wheelchair access. Cabins mostly sleep 4 in bunk beds but for retreat purposes will be single occupancy unless otherwise requested. The cabins are all bright and comfortable, with portholes and underfloor heating.

Notes TS Resolute is a newly-converted residential ship situated in an area of outstanding natural beauty in Chichester Harbour. All rooms on the main deck enjoy panoramic views out to historic Bosham and the South Downs beyond, and down into the wider Bosham Channel. The ship is firmly anchored to the sea wall and rises and falls gently on the tide.
We are a community of Christians living and working at CYE Sailing Centre, and our winter season affords us the opportunity to invite retreat guests to share our stunning location. Our programme has recently expanded to include the occasional guided retreat and labyrinth workshop as well as our regular silent, self-guided events. All our events include the offer to meet with an experienced spiritual director.

Contact Christine McLeish, Retreats Manager.

January
5 New Year's quiet day.
March
1–3 Lent retreat.
October
25–27 Reflective walking weekend.
November
30 Advent Eve quiet day.
January 2020
4 New Year's quiet day.

RETREAT ASSOCIATION
SUMMER EVENT

3 July 2019 – see page 80

Reflecting on the **Retreat Association Icon**
& **How Icons speak to us**
in our contemporary world

Guest speakers:
Father Anastasios Salapatas, Greek Orthodox
& **Father Stephen Platt**, Russian Orthodox

WEST MIDLANDS

133 St Mary's Convent

98 Hunters Road, Handsworth, Birmingham
B19 1EB   0121 554 3271 / 07752 146323
email spirituality@mercyhandsworth.org.uk
B, I, P, Q, S, Wf   *website* www.mercyhandsworth.co.uk

Rooms 12 single rooms, 1 single and 1 family self-catering flat. Conference room up to 30 people and meeting room up to 15 people with all IT facilities. Full catering with special dietary requirements provided. Wheelchair and lift access is limited. Lawns, grounds and car parking facilities.
Notes This Pugin convent in Handsworth was established in 1841; a central hub for the Sisters of Mercy in the UK and beyond. The retreat centre has undergone extensive refurbishment and is now open to the public offering private and guided retreats. The building has a heritage trail, with many interesting exhibits, and it is also a place of outreach for the local community. Come for a day, a few days or a week and find peace and tranquillity in the quiet corridors and rooms of this beautiful building. Spend time in the chapel or walk in the gardens and enjoy time on your own. You will never know that you are in the centre of the city.
Contact The Guest Sister.
Please see website for our programme of events.

134 Woodbrooke

1046 Bristol Road, Selly Oak, Birmingham
B29 6LJ   0121 472 5172
fax 0121 472 5173
email marketing@woodbrooke.org.uk
B, C, D, E, I, P, Q, S, V, W, Wf, Y *website* www.woodbrooke.org.uk

Rooms 55 single rooms (44 *en suite*), 9 twin rooms (7 *en suite*), 5 double rooms (4 *en suite*), 2 family rooms (*en suite*). Only 61 rooms available for booking at any one time.
Notes 'I had deep and moving experiences within the exercises and techniques. I experienced a new depth to silence and stillness ... and I had fun! Thank you.'
Set in 10 acres of beautiful organically managed gardens and woods, Woodbrooke is a perfect place for a retreat. We want every visitor to leave refreshed, renewed and inspired, which is supported by the care we give to all guests; the sense of community alongside the space and freedom to be alone; the historic Grade II listed former home of George Cadbury; and the values of peace, simplicity, truth and equality make for a truly unique experience.
Some of our retreats draw from specific spiritual traditions. Others offer quiet time set aside with no specific spiritual or religious input, perhaps with a creative or seasonal theme. Many, however, have a 'Quaker' quality. Exploration and experience are central to the Quaker way, so we aim to ground our spiritual journeying in the real stuff of our lives.
There is more information about Woodbrooke's retreats on our website, where you can also find details of short courses. Please do call us for a chat about any questions that you may have.
Contact Marc Harbourne-Bessant, Reservations Manager.

January
11–13 Clearing the way. Jennifer Kavanagh & Penny Foston
February
2–7 IGR. Resting in presence. Gill Pennington
11–15 IGR. Time set aside. Timothy Ashworth & Frances-Henley Lock
February–March
11–24 Deepening the life of Spirit. An online retreat exploring prayer and spiritual practice. Julia Ryberg
March
1–3 A drop of stillness. Lesley Collington
4–8 Icon painting as a spiritual practice. Basia Mindewicz
April–May
1–12 An online retreat for young adult friends. Martin Layton
April
15–17 Introduction to life writing for transformation. Farrukh Akhtar
May
20–24 Gathering of fools. A deep retreat exclusively for people who have done a fool course with Angela Halvorsen Bogo
29 Online retreat. Seeking sanctuary and stillness. Gill Pennington
June
3–5 Quaker retreat. Look not out but within. Eleanor Jackson
7–9 Singing retreat. Mark Russ
28–30 The wisdom of the Psalms. Spiritual guidance for everyday life. Deborah Shaw
29 Online retreat. Seeking sanctuary and stillness. Gill Pennington
July
15–17 Awakening of the sacred feminine. Lynne Sedgmore & Gill Pennington
19–21 Earth over retreat. Time to knead. Maud Granger
August
16–18 Centering prayer and Christian meditation. Richard Eddleston
25–30 Mindfully together. Monastic & support team
September–October
16–27 Online retreat. European Quaker voices. Julia Ryberg
September
21–22 Quiet day. Experiment with light. Gill Pennington
23–25 Walk with a smile into the dark. Jennifer Kavanagh & Annique Seddon
October
22 Online retreat. Seeking sanctuary and stillness. Gill Pennington
October–November
27–1 IGR. Resting in presence. Gill Pennington
November
19 Online retreat. Seeking sanctuary and stillness. Gill Pennington

WILTSHIRE

135 Sarum College

19 The Close, Salisbury, Wiltshire SP1 2EE

01722 424800

email courses@sarum.ac.uk

C, D, I, S, Wf

website www.sarum.ac.uk

Rooms Sarum College has 40 *en suite* bedrooms, many are newly refurbished. The Wren bedrooms at the front of the college have uninterrupted views of the Cathedral, several others have lovely views overlooking the rooftops of the Close and spire. Rooms are single, double and twin; all have tea and coffee-making facilities. The lift gives access to all the floors, and there is a common room which has been recently refurbished which has easy chairs and a licensed bar for guest use. The college has 6 seminar rooms, a conference hall, chapel, excellent theological library, specialist theological bookshop, common room, bar and dining room.

Notes Sarum College is a Christian education, training and conference centre in the beautiful setting of Salisbury's Cathedral Close. We provide an ideal space for reading, reflection, prayer and study and welcome residential conferences as well as individual guests or groups.
In addition to self-directed reflection, prayer and study, you can tailor your stay by adding mentored reflection, or opting for a guided study leave or sabbatical. Our Renewing Ministry programme includes sessions with a ministry consultant or spiritual director. We also run individually guided retreats and a number of days of spiritual reflection throughout the year led by Pat Clegg. If none of these options seem to fit with what you think you need, get in touch and talk to us.

Contact Alison Ogden.

Theology quest and questions (Spring term) Tuesdays from 8 January. Weekly evening lectures opening the study of Christian theology to those who want to know what they believe, why they believe it, and whether they should keep on believing it.

Postgraduate study taster day Saturdays 23 March, 8 June, 7 July. To explore flexible study programmes in theology, ministry and related subjects. Opportunity to sample teaching sessions and have informal discussions with tutors.

January

19 Glory. Introduction to approaches to the suffering that seems to fill both human and non-human worlds, including recent debates about 'natural evil'.

21–24 The nature of contemporary spirituality. An introduction to contemporary approaches to the study of spirituality through theological, philosophical, psychological, political and aesthetic methodologies.

21–24 Reflective practice. An introduction to contemporary models of reflective practice in the educational, theological, and business worlds.

25 Lunchtime concert 2018–19 series: Serena Kay & Joanna Miller-Shepherd.

26 Nevertheless she persisted: theology, faith and feminism. Explore contemporary issues in feminist

theology through performance poetry, art, story-sharing and conversation.

29 Wisdom for mission from the Church Fathers. We draw especially on the Cappadocian Fathers of the 4th century to look at orthodoxy, action and contemplation.

30 Song of disciples. A theological and devotional perspective on songs from the Bible which express some discipleship journey themes.

31 New monasticism: boundary-crossing communities. Explore the recent emergence of communities who live historic monastic ideals in radically new ways.

February

8–9 Michael Perham symposium. Speakers with first-hand experience of Michael Perham's ministry.

11 Spiritual directors forum. Listening in Spirit? How do we experience the work of the Spirit in our lives and our listening?

11–14 Biblical study break. The Bible and the emotions: faith and feeling in early Christianity. Engage with the Bible to gain a deeper understanding of both migrants and host communities.

16 Awkward reverence: exploring the poetry of Philip Larkin. How might a person of faith approach Larkin's work?

18–21 Relocating religion: cultural and spiritual realignments. Diverse perspectives on the shifting place of contemporary religion.

22 Lunchtime concert 2018–19 series: Bill Benham & David Price.

28 Rural ministry – learning from chaplaincy. Fresh perspectives from chaplains on mission and ministry in rural contexts.

March

1–3 Tragedy and congregations. This weekend is for ministers, lay leaders and those with an interest in practical theology.

4–7 Western Christian mysticism. An overview of the historical development of the Western Christian mystical tradition with analysis of key historical figures and movements.

4–7 Christian initiation. Examine key historical periods which provide a context for contemporary rites and the theologies which lie behind them.

8 'Weeping at the grave we make our song'? Funeral ministry and the Church of England. Funerals are changing. This is for all those interested in learning more about funeral ministry.

12 Film as religion. Can we watch film faithfully? A richly illustrated day with group discussion. Colin Heber-Percy

16 Creativity, culture and Christian mission. A day for practitioners to explore how the creative arts can inform Christian engagement with culture today.

19 Leading in a second chair. A chance to explore leadership challenges for those who do not appear at the top of an organization.

22 Lunchtime concert 2018–19 series: Duo Brikcius.

26 Eaten up: food, God and us. Food is essential yet contested at every level – from our individual relationship to its wider political significances. Alison Webster

27 John of the Cross: the much misunderstood mystic. A day to explore the writings, life, piety and art of this man through lectures, prayer, art and music.

28–29 A history of sin. This course will examine various scriptural understandings of sin and then explore how these are developed in early Christian traditions of prayer. Angela Tilby

April

1–4 Re-imagining church in a changing culture. Go beyond the headlines to the continuing decline in church membership to critique the contemporary church.

1–4 Art, belief and spirituality (MACS optional module). Examine the relationship between Christian spirituality and art from historical, cultural and theological perspectives.

5 The legacy of African-American spirituals for congregational song. Music theology and spirituality in African-American spirituals.

15–18 Holy Week at Sarum. An opportunity to contemplate Jesus' journey to the cross by engaging with the artist of 'stopping Places' who leads the retreat, Mary Flitcroft.

29 Spiritual directors forum. Vocation, identity and affirmation. How do spiritual directors root our role in our own sense of self, spirituality and vocation as well as accountability and professionalism?

May

2 How the letter to the Ephesians can enable your church to grow. Explore how the vision of the letter to the Ephesians can bring direction, energy and vitality to our local churches.

8 Preaching, poetry and prophetic speech. How poetic processes and forms are integral to preaching practice, and the prophetic possibilities of poetic preaching.

9 Pastoral liturgy day. A fresh approach to the art of leading worship. Course for those involved in leading worship to recover the value of this ministry and its role in the local church.

13 Death and life. Christian resources to enable people of all ages to face the reality of their own mortality and engage with the hope of resurrection.

13–16 Mass culture: theological engagement and spiritual practice. This module considers the phenomenon of mass culture as that which approximates to the actual 'lived culture' of millions of people today.

13–16 Music in Christian worship. Explore the variety of musical styles in Christian worship from diverse perspectives.

15 Stained glass. Follow the journey of a stained-glass window from inspiration and design through its different processes to installation.

17 The Desert Fathers and Mothers. This is for all interested in the history of spirituality, early monasticism and spiritual direction.

18 Faith in fiction: Anglican women novelists. A study of the work of Rose Macaulay and PD James whose novels were a vehicle to explore faith.

20–23 Biblical study break. The world of Jesus: archaeology, geography and texts. We will explore the world of Jesus through archaeology, geography and New Testament texts.

June

4 Music in worship. Music and the Christian faith: a day with JS Bach. How Bach interprets the core beliefs of Christianity through music.

5 New thinking in pastoral and practical theology. This day will explore key thinkers and the way pastoral and practical theology has developed over the last 30 years.

6 Richard Hooker, Apostle of Anglicanism. How the life of Anglicanism's leading apologist is relevant to the dilemmas and conflicts of Anglican identity today.

10 Servant leadership.

11 The Bible on film. Examine the range of interpretations of the Jesus story as portrayed in film and reflect on the way film depicts biblical stories and themes.

17–20 Change and conflict (MACAL module).

17–20 Liturgy and spirituality (co-validated MACS and MACL). Examine the ways in which liturgy and spirituality relate, both conceptually and with reference to debates.

25 Strategies for mission from a Celtic Saint. We will investigate some underlying themes of Beuno's ministry and the strategic insights for mission in the church today.

26 What is our story of old age? Listening and learning from the experience of ageing. Reflections upon the experience of ageing, drawing from key thinkers in this area.

July

2 A day with Julian of Norwich and Margery Kempe. Two mystics speaking from the depths of their spiritual experience to offer unconventional wisdom.

September

16–17 Francis and the Sultan. A conference on the meeting during the Fifth Crusade of St Francis of Assisi and Sultan Malik al-Kamil, as inspiration for Christian-Muslim dialogue today.

27 Pastoral liturgy day. Finding our voice in Advent. This day will explore the range of liturgical opportunities for marking the season of Advent.

September–October

30–3 Foundations and forms of Christian spirituality. An introduction to the nature of spirituality in the Christian tradition until the end of the 18th century.

30–3 Christian faith and leadership. Explore and analyse how theology and spirituality underpin and challenge an understanding of leadership within and outside faith-based contexts.

October

4 Sarum singing break 2019. A musical retreat for anyone who enjoys singing liturgical church music.

4 Lunchtime concert 2019–20 series. Concert 1: Diana Brekalo (solo piano).

7 Theology and human culture. Engage with the 'texts' and practices of human culture and explore the relationship between theology and culture through creative and critical perspectives.

7–10 Approaches to liturgical studies. This module will

introduce students to the sources and methods used by scholars in the evaluation and interpretation of liturgical forms.

11 Reflective Journalling. Explore how journalling helps to reflect on the shape of our living in the context of our work and world.

17 Preaching the Old Testament. An overview of the issues and questions that need to be addressed when preaching from the Old Testament.

18 Arts and crafts study day with Peter Burman.

30 Sense and stigma in the gospels: depictions of sensory-disabled characters. A quest to refigure characters with sensory disabilities featured in the gospels.

November

1 Lunchtime concert 2019–20 series. Concert 2: Gillian Wormley (soprano) & Din Ghani (lute).

4–7 Biblical study break. Digging into Isaiah. Careful reading and exploration of these 27 lyrical, carefully-edited chapters, much quoted in the New Testament.

9 Sing Gregorian chant 2019. This day offers the chance to experience and sing Gregorian chant in a friendly context.

13 Leading by story. The social sciences have taken a 'narrative turn' which offers new ways for thinking about how we work together.

15 Seeking the Trinity in modern art. Drawing from Christian theology, explore a wide range of well-known modern and contemporary artists to gain a deeper insight into their work.

19 Inspiring music in worship. Engaging with the rural Church. How to nurture the musical and liturgical life of small congregations with limited resources.

19 Poetry and spiritual practice. 'Teach us how to pray.' Poetry and prayer. This day will explore the role of poets as instructors in the art of prayer as an affective experience.

20 Gospel of Matthew. Matthew invites us once again to understand and make up our own minds about his convictions concerning Jesus, his perspectives on ethics, ethnicity and gender.

25 Working Together. Biblical examples of ministry and working together are critiqued to better understand the various forms of authorised ministry and the role of the laity.

25–28 Sexuality and spirituality. An academic examination of the interface between sexuality and spirituality considering the historical, theological and psychological context.

29 Dementia: who cares for the carers? We will hear carers' stories and reflect on their needs for practical and spiritual support.

December

2–5 Text, interpretation and imagination. We will explore how these texts inform, and are informed by, human creativity.

2–5 Liturgy and mission. An introduction to the relationship between mission and liturgy.

6 Lunchtime concert 2019–20 series. Concert 3: Miriam Wakeling (cello) & Chris Guild (piano)

WORCESTERSHIRE

136 Barnes Close, Community for Reconciliation

Barnes Close, Chadwich, Bromsgrove,
Worcestershire B61 0RA   01562 710231
email cfrenquiry@aol.com
D, E, P, Q, Wf, Y   *website* www.cfrbarnesclose.co.uk

Rooms 2 twin *en suite* (ground floor), 1 single *en suite* (ground floor), 2 twin *en suite*, 3 twin, 1 double, 1 single *en suite*, 1 triple, 2 quadruple *en suite*.
Notes Group and individual retreats. Led or private. Ecumenical. Reflection days run 10am–4pm.
Contact Ian Ring, Community Coordinator.
Reflection days 2nd Thursday of the month except August 10am–4pm. An opportunity to open the Bible, to be still and let God speak.

March

19–21 Lent retreat. An opportunity to take time out and reflect.

April

18–23 Easter at Barnes Close. An opportunity to reflect on the Easter story, walk, rest and relax with friends old and new.

June

17–21 Members week. Walking with CfR, walking with each other, walking with God.

September

5–11 Time away. A leisurely holiday week, with evening entertainment.

17–19 Healing and wholeness retreat. An opportunity to explore the nature of the healing ministry in the local church.

November

26–28 Advent retreat. An opportunity to spend time with God preparing for Advent and Christmas.

137 Holland House

Main Street, Cropthorne, Pershore,
Worcestershire WR10 3NB   01386 860330
email accounts@hollandhouse.org
C, D, I, P, Q, V, Wf, Y   *website* www.hollandhouse.org

Rooms 19 single, 6 twin, 1 twin *en suite*, 1 twin accessible room. Library, drawing room, chapel, conference room with large screen, laptop and Wifi. The Den is a small house in the grounds that can be hired as meeting rooms or self-contained flat (restricted availability).
Notes Holland House is a Christian house that works 'in harmony with Creation', to provide delicious food and drink either sourced locally or mindful of ecology. We welcome both churchgoers and those still looking for a spiritual home. We have a proud history of supporting the Christian LGBT community and now partner Worcester Interfaith Forum to promote understanding and goodwill across faith traditions. This is an Open House offering unconditional hospitality to all.
Contact Rev Ian Spencer, Warden.

January
24 Richard Rohr meditation.
31 Yoga for Christians.
February
18–22 CARM retreat. Poetry.
20 Praying differently.
March
6 Richard Rohr meditation.
12–13 Yoga for Christians in Lent.
15 Friendly lunch.
18–22 Enneagram with Simon Parke.
April
10 Praying differently.
15–18 CARM retreat. Painting.
May
9 Richard Rohr meditation.
23 Yoga for Christians.
June
13 Praying differently.
July
12 CARM retreat. Colours of God.
18 Richard Rohr meditation.
25 Yoga for Christians.
September
2–6 CARM retreat. Calligraphy.
11 Richard Rohr meditation.
24 Yoga for Christians.
October
18–20 John Bell.
22 Praying differently.
November
7 Richard Rohr meditation.
19 Yoga for Christians.

138 House of the Open Door

**Childswickham House, Childswickham,
Buckland Road, Broadway, Worcestershire
WR12 7HH** 01386 852084
email hod@houseoftheopendoor.org
D, P, Q, W, Wf, Y   *website* www.houseoftheopendoor.org

Rooms 10 rooms in 2 buildings.
The Retreat House 5 upstairs rooms accommodating
2 (minimum) to 4 guests, 2 rooms downstairs: a double
and a quadruple. No en suites (2 bathrooms upstairs,
accessible shower/toilet downstairs), sitting room, scullery
with fridge and microwave, tea/coffee in all rooms.
The Cottage Twin downstairs, triple and quadruple
upstairs, sitting room, kitchen downstairs for
self-catering with cooker, fridge, microwave, tea/coffee in
all rooms, bathroom upstairs, shower/toilet downstairs.
Rooms can be booked as singles by arrangement.
Notes Childswickham House is the home of House of the
Open Door, a lay ecumenical community and retreat
centre. We are in a quiet village location on the edge of the
Cotswolds. Our facilities are set around a courtyard going
into 2 acres of garden. Our chapel, the hub of our
communal prayer life, is available for use by guests. Our
ethos is that we are 'a house of prayer for all nations', and
our aim is to provide a place where Christians can be

blessed and refreshed in body and soul. Contact us for
details of our programme or visit our website.
Contact Bookings Secretary (please contact by email or
phone).

139 The Retreat

**Stoke Bliss, Tenbury Wells, Worcestershire
WR15 8RY** 01885 410431
email mdk46@phonecoop.coop
website www.sites.google.com/site/holidaysattheretreat
C, P, Pe, W, Y

Rooms Ground floor: entrance porch, twin bedroom,
separate bathroom. First floor: small, fully-equipped
kitchen, large lounge/dining with double futon sofa bed.
Self-catering. Food can be ready for you including organic
vegetables if required. Sorry not suitable for wheelchairs,
but pets and children welcome.
Notes I have lived at The Retreat since 1984 and have
welcomed people for holidays and respite since 1995.
Parking for 2 cars. Set in countryside 5 miles from shops at
Bromyard and Tenbury Wells. Walks from the door, plenty
of places to sit in the wildlife garden and reflect. No TV and
mobile phone connection unreliable. Plenty of books of all
types, jigsaws, games etc. Log burner to keep you cosy in
winter. Cathedral cities of Hereford and Worcester 20 miles
away. Quiet Garden at St Mary's Kyre. No formal
programme but you are welcome to share times of quiet
reflection with me. Visitors are welcome to request time for
a meditative artistic experience: pilgrimage tree trail, clay,
pastels or woolfelt work.
Contact Maggie Kingston.

140 The Society of St Francis

**St Mary at the Cross, Glasshampton, Shrawley,
Worcester WR6 6TQ** 01299 896345
email glasshamptonssf@franciscans.org.uk
P, Q   *website* www.franciscans.org.uk

Rooms 3 single, 2 twin.
Notes Glasshampton Monastery is an Anglican retreat
house open to people of all denominations seeking a time
of prayer and quiet in a rural setting. Guests are welcome
to join the brothers for the 5 daily services in chapel, and
for silent meals in the refectory. Rooms are also available
for individual day guests, or for a group of up to 12 people
for quiet days. Day groups are asked to bring their own
lunch. The monastery is closed to guests between Monday
mornings and Tuesday afternoons.
Contact The Guestbrother SSF.

GIVE SOMEONE THE GIFT OF A RETREAT!

– see page 64 for details

YORKSHIRE

NORTH YORKSHIRE

141 Holy Rood House

Centre for Health and Pastoral Care, with The Centre for the Study of Theology and Health
10 Sowerby Road, Sowerby, Thirsk,
North Yorkshire YO7 1HX   01845 522580
email enquiries@holyroodhouse.org.uk
C, Ch, Co, E, P, S, V, Y   *website* www.holyroodhouse.org.uk

Rooms Residential 24 (single, twin, double); non-residential 35+ Thorpe House, for training and conferences. Chair lift and ramp. *en suite* available and new Access and Carer's Suite.
Notes Our new Access and Carer's Suite, and new Chapel to Garden Access, are both available for our guests to benefit from.
Holy Rood House is a therapeutic retreat centre close to the bustling Herriot market town of Thirsk, and continues to provide safe space with an inclusive and welcoming ethos. Together we work and pray towards justice and peace, creating inclusive and healing liturgies and offering retreats, spiritual direction, pastoral accompaniment and professional counselling, complementary therapies and creative arts for all ages. The small residential community welcome guests to their home.
The Centre for the Study of Theology and Health continues to provide opportunities for research and reflection on the interface between psychology, the arts, theology and spirituality, and all aspects of health and wellbeing. Resources include a specialist library, art gallery, conference space, and residential and non-residential courses and workshops. See website for full programme. The programme also includes women's and men's spirituality weekends, research seminars, annual summer school, and the hymns for healing project (exploring the theology of hymns and songs in relation to health and healing) which has just published its own book of hymns. See website or contact us for full details.
Contact Rev Elizabeth Baxter, Executive Director.

December 2018–January 2019
31–3 New Year house party.
January
26 Winter Quiet Garden retreat. Helen Warwick
February
1–3 Retreat. The freedom of years: ageing in perspective. Harriet & Donald Mowat
23 Northern conference of Holy Rood House and The Guild of Health and St Raphael.
March
1–3 Community Companions spring retreat.
29–31 Retreat. Lenten longings. Rev Elizabeth Baxter & Rev Dr Gillian Straine
April
17–23 Holy Week and Easter retreat. Helen Warwick
24–30 Self-catering for holidays: individuals, families, groups.

May
3–5 Men's spirituality retreat.
11 Spring Quiet Garden retreat.
17–19 Retreat. Exploring healing through chronic illness. Helen Warwick
June
8–9 Celebration weekend.
21–23 Women's spirituality solstice retreat. Wisdom dances in delight. Rev Dr Jan Berry
July
tbc Summer school.
22 Summer Quiet Garden retreat. Helen Warwick
August
17–31 Self-catering for holidays: individuals, families, groups.
September
6–8 Men's spirituality retreat.
27–29 Community Companions autumn retreat.
October
18–20 Women's spirituality retreat. Creative weaving and the holy weaver. Helen Warwick
November–December
29–1 Advent retreat. Holy Rood Community
December
23–27 Christmas house party.
December–January 2020
31–3 New Year house party.

142 Parcevall Hall

Skyreholme, Appletreewick, Skipton,
North Yorkshire BD23 6DG   01756 720213
email admin@parcevallhall.org.uk
B, C, Ch, D, E, P, Q, S, W, Wf, Y   *website* parcevallhall.org.uk

Rooms 1 family *en suite*, 1 double *en suite*, 2 twin *en suite*, 6 standard twin, 7 standard single.
Notes Parcevall Hall is the retreat house of the Anglican Diocese of Leeds, welcoming private bookings from individuals and groups, secular and religious. We offer guests warm hospitality: good, home-cooked food, comfortable bedrooms, peace and tranquillity. The Hall is a charming and homely Grade II* building surrounded by 24 acres of gardens and woodland. We're within half a mile of the Dales Way, and the pretty Dales towns of Skipton, Grassington and Pateley Bridge are a short drive away. Parcevall Hall runs a yearly programme of events which can be viewed on our website. These include literature and art appreciation, led walking breaks, Lent, Easter and Advent retreats, singing, music and crafts events, and new for this year two days of birdwatching in the spring with ornithologist Chris Bradshaw.
Private bookings are welcome. Single guests tell us they feel relaxed and comfortable here; we don't charge a single supplement and you won't be asked to share your room.
Contact The Warden. Please contact by phone or email.

January
28 Open quiet day I. Do I have to believe that? 10am–4pm. No booking required, please bring your own lunch. Canon Adrian Botwright
February
4–7 Clergy reading week. Rev Canon Stephen Treasure

March
5–8 Lent retreat days and residential stays.
13 Friends of Parcevall Hall Eucharist and lunch.
15–17 Heart and soul singing retreat I. Keely Hodgson
19–21 Recorder players' workshop I. Terry Smurthwaite
22–24 Literature appreciation I. Poetry from Wales.
Hugh Parry
April
1–4 Springtime walking in Wharfedale.
18–22 Easter retreat days and residential stays. Please visit
our website for details.
23–25 Art appreciation I. Landscapes of wonder.
Tim Stimson
29 Open quiet day II. Do I have to witness? 10am–
4pm. No booking required, please bring your own
lunch. Fr Derek Mills
April–May
29–2 Fellowship of Contemplative Prayer retreat II.
May
13–15 Beginner's birdwatching and the dawn chorus.
Chris Bradshaw
21 Friends of Parcevall Hall Eucharist and annual
dinner.
24–26 Recorder players' workshop II. Mary Tyers
June
6 Study day. 'The Word Heart Deep'. Religious poetry
of the English Reformation. Joyce Simpson
10–14 Anglican Association Retreat (part silent). 'simple
Prayer' – biblical references on our personal
experience of God. Rev Canon Andrew Hawes
July
2–4 Friends of Parcevall Hall annual gathering and
AGM.
August
1–4 Summer walking in Wharfedale.
5 Open quiet day III. Do I have to do that? 10am–
4pm. No booking required, please bring your own
lunch. Canon Adrian Botwright
6–8 Art appreciation III. Klimt and the Golden Age of
Vienna. Tim Stimson
16–18 Recorder players' workshop III. Margaret Shearing
August–September
30–1 Literature appreciation II. Shakespeare's extras.
Hugh Parry
September
18–20 Knitting, crochet and felting retreat. Rev Elizabeth
Brown
October
3 Friends of Parcevall Hall Eucharist and lunch.
7–10 Autumn rambling in Wharfedale.
11–13 Heart and soul singing retreat II. Keely Hodgson
14 Open quiet day IV. Do I have to say that? 10am–
4pm. No booking required, please bring your own
lunch. Canon Adrian Botwright
15–17 Recorder players' workshop IV. Sandra Foxall
25–27 Fellowship of Contemplative Prayer retreat II.
December
5 Friends of Parcevall Hall Eucharist and Christmas
lunch.
6–8 Recorder players' workshop V. Ruth Burbidge
10–13 Advent retreat. Canon Adrian Botwright
18–20 Quietly contemplating Christmas.
23–27 Christmas house party and retreat.

143 St Oswald's Pastoral Centre
Woodlands Drive, Sleights, Whitby,
North Yorkshire YO21 1RY   01947 810496
email stoswalds@stoswalds.net
website www.stoswaldspastoralcentre.org.uk
C, E, I, P, Pe, S, V, W

Rooms 11 singles and 4 twin plus 2 single *en suite* self-
catering apartments.
Notes The house is run by a resident religious community
with regular services. It is a secluded, quiet house with
beautiful gardens in the midst of good walking country
and 3 miles from the picturesque town of Whitby.
Contact The Sister in Charge.
January
5–12 IGR. Sr Janet Elizabeth OHP, Coral Spencer TOHP &
Rev Gillian Cornish
February
11–15 Spring cleaning week. Come and help the sisters
spring clean. We may well also be helping the St
Hilda's Priory sisters move their convent up the
garden!
March
22–24 Lent retreat. tbc
April
13–20 Holy Week and Easter. Rev Judith Trickett & Sisters
OHP
May
20–24 Walking retreat. On the Way 1. Come and enjoy the
beautiful countryside of North East Yorkshire. The
walks are 5–7 miles and not too difficult.
June
24–28 Be inspired! Creative week. Have fun, have a go
with words and crafts, and don't worry about the
results. Sisters OHP, Sue Thomason & Steph Bradley
July
6–13 IGR. Sr Janet Elizabeth OHP, Coral Spencer TOHP,
Rev Glenda Webb, Rev John Hall Matthews tbc
August
10–17 Holiday week. Time for a quiet holiday at
St Oswald's. Come and enjoy being in North
Yorkshire, relaxing in the garden or enjoying the
countryside.
September
2–6 Walking retreat. On the Way 2. A second chance to
enjoy the beautiful countryside of North Yorkshire,
just as summer is drawing to its close.
27–29 Transition. Change is always difficult to manage,
this weekend helps us understand and deal with all
the changes that life can throw at us. Rev Pete
Askew

FOR A PACK
ON PLANNING AND ORGANISING
A QUIET DAY
send £6.00 to the Retreat Association, PO Box 1130,
Princes Risborough, Buckinghamshire HP22 9RP

144 Scargill House

Kettlewell, Skipton, North Yorkshire BD23 5HU

01756 760500

email admin@scargillmovement.org

B, C, D, E, I, P, Q, S, V, W, Wf, Y *website* www.scargillmovement.org

Rooms 2 ground-floor accessible with wet room, 4 double with shared bathroom, 4 double, 4 twin *en suite*, 2 linking *en suite* family rooms, 1 triple with shared bathroom, twin and single rooms with shared bathroom, possibility of some additional single and bunk bed rooms if required.

Notes Our aim is to welcome each guest as unique and special, as if we're welcoming Jesus. We are a group of people of all ages, nations, backgrounds and denominations whose aim is to love and serve everyone God sends us.

Contact Michyla Hickling.

January

14–18 Getting crafty. An opportunity to relax and create! Bring along your unfinished, or never started, projects to do in the company of others.

21–25 IGR. Our team of experienced spiritual directors will accompany you through your silent retreat, offering a daily one-to-one session for up to an hour.

25–27 Renew, refresh, restore. Just when you thought you couldn't go on, along comes a weekend at Scargill just for you! Drop everything for a rest and a treat.

February

1–3 Time for God. Always wanted to do a retreat but never quite got round to it? Here's your chance to come on a retreat for beginners!

8–10 Loving God, neighbour AND self – Christianity, mindfulness and self-compassion. Explore how we can grow richly in our love for God, our neighbours and ourselves.

11–15 Enneagram 3 course – God-shaped people. We look at sub-types and continue exploring the Enneagram within the Christian tradition. For those with a good understanding of their Enneagram space.

22–24 Renew, refresh, restore. See 25–27 January.

March

11–15 Lent retreat.

April

15–18 Holy Week.

18–22 Easter weekend.

April–May

29–3 The free-running mind. Growing into our mindful identity in Christ. Shaun Lambert

May

3–5 Vocations weekend. Everyone is called. Derek Walmsley

6–10 Enneagram 2 – God-shaped people. Margi Walker & Diane Stone

June

24–28 Light in the shadow of bereavement.

July

15–19 Enneagram 1 – God-shaped people. Margi Walker & Diane Stone

September

23–27 CARM Retreat. Embroidery and prayer. Claire Watts & Sue Ives

23–27 Quiet Garden week. Matt Freer

October

7–11 IGR. Margi Walker & Team

14–18 Revisiting the Psalms. John Bell

November

18–22 Enneagram. Margi Walker & Diane Stone

November–December

29–1 Advent craft retreat. Diane Stone

December

2–6 Advent retreat week.

145 Summerscales Quiet Garden

11 Regent Road, Skipton, North Yorkshire BD23 1AT

01756 794885

Q, S *email* cheney@uwclub.net

Non-residential.

Notes We aim to provide a ministry of hospitality in a prayerful environment. Attractive garden. All-weather chalet with electric heater provides quiet 'prayer space' and comfortably accommodates up to 4 people. Refreshments provided. Some books and prayer material available. Toilet facilities are in the house (upstairs). Situated on local bus route. No dogs other than guide dogs. Times and dates can be flexible. No set charge but donations welcome.

Contact Katharine Cheney.

146 Wydale Hall and the Emmaus Centre

Wydale Lane, Brompton by Sawdon, Scarborough, North Yorkshire YO13 9DG

01723 859270

email admin@wydale.org

C, Ch, D, E, I, P, Q, V, W, Wf, Y *website* www.wydale.org

Rooms Wydale has 29 bedrooms (single, double, twin and family) with accommodation for up to 55 guests, including a ground-floor room for those with mobility problems. All rooms are *en suite* and have tea and coffee-making facilities. There is a beautiful chapel, a sitting room with valley views and 2 large meeting rooms. Wydale Hall can cater for 2 day conferences at the same time. The Emmaus Centre is self-catering and can sleep up to 50 people in shared dormitories.

Notes 'A prayerful community renewing the Church's mission – not just a venue.' Wydale is the Diocese of York Retreat and Conference Centre. An 18th-century house set in 14 acres of beautiful gardens which include a walled garden, prayer labyrinth, terraces and children's play area. Available for groups or private stay. Full- or part-board. Open with inspirational programme of events all year, specialising in holiday breaks at Easter and Christmas. Full events listing for 2019 available on the website.

Contact The Manager. ❏ *inside back cover*

SOUTH YORKSHIRE

147 Whirlow Spirituality Centre

Whirlow Grange Close, Whirlow, Sheffield
S11 9SY   01142 353704
email admin@whirlowspiritualitycentre.org
website www.whirlowspiritualitycentre.org
B, C, Ch, D, E, P, Q, S, V, W, Wf

Non-residential.
Notes The Chapel of the Holy Spirit seats up to 60 and overlooks our beautiful gardens. Our comfortable lounge houses a Christian Spirituality library of more than 1,500 titles, available to read or borrow. Two toilets (one accessible) and a kitchen are available. The Quiet Room is available for individual or small group retreats (2–4). Patio doors lead from the lounge to another small garden. We have parking for up to 20 vehicles.
A place to be still, find rest and meet with God, Whirlow Spirituality Centre at the Chapel of the Holy Spirit is set in a peaceful garden on the edge of the Peak District. Visitors, individuals or groups, are encouraged to explore their spirituality through prayer, reflection and resourcing from the Christian tradition. We are here for those who are or are not part of a formal group; for those of any status within those groups: all stories and identities are honoured. We will do what we can to support all travellers on their spiritual journey.
Managed in partnership and overseen by a chaplain, Whirlow is served by a team of volunteers and visiting speakers from a variety of backgrounds. Take a look at our events programme on the website, book a space for a quiet day or join one of our regular, reflective services detailed below.
Contact Rev Joy Adams, Chaplain or Anna Potts, Events Coordinator.
Space to be Every Sunday morning (8.30–8.15) 45 minutes of silent, self-directed contemplation.
Reflective communion Tuesdays (9.45–10.30) and 3rd Sundays (7–8pm).
Reflective worship including occasional Taizé worship every 1st Sunday (7–8pm).
Simple quiet days every third Tuesday of the month beginning with the Reflective Communion service, closing by 3.45pm.
Days of retreat designed and facilitated to offer maximum quiet and solitude (9.30am–4.40pm).
We who sing, pray twice opportunity to learn and sing spiritual songs and chants in 4-part harmony in a contemplative atmosphere (7.30–9.30pm). See events programme for dates.
Praying without words a monthly opportunity to practise silent prayer in community for all levels of experience, all faiths and none. Thursdays (7.30–9pm). See events programme for dates.

WEST YORKSHIRE

148 The Briery Retreat and Conference Centre

38 Victoria Avenue, Ilkley, West Yorkshire
LS29 9BW   01943 607287
email briery@btconnect.com
B, Ch, D, E, I, P, Q, S, V, W, Wf   *website* www.briery.org.uk

Rooms 1 flat with *en suite* and living area, 2 ground-floor *en suite* single rooms, 1 ground-floor disabled room with *en suite*, 12 first-floor *en suite* single rooms, 4 first-floor *en suite* twin rooms. All first-floor rooms are accessible by lift. 3 second-floor single rooms sharing 2 bathrooms. In the grounds there is a self-catering cottage with a single *en suite* room on the ground floor and 2 single rooms on the first floor sharing a bathroom. The Briery can sleep 26 as singles, with a total of 30 beds.
Notes The Briery is a place of spiritual renewal where those who come can find God in an atmosphere of love, prayer, healing and peace. We invite you to share the peace and tranquillity of our house in the Yorkshire Dales where all are welcomed with friendliness and compassion. We offer IGRs and welcome those seeking a quiet day for prayer or a private retreat. We can also accommodate groups who require peace and space for their training/study days. We run a number of parish retreats throughout the year. Ongoing spiritual direction and supervision are available.
Contact The Retreat Administrators during office hours 9am–5pm Monday–Saturday.

January
19 Prayer Guides' retreat day. Briery Team
26 Parish retreat day. Briery Team
March
20 Lenten day of reflection. A journey to Easter with Blessed John Henry Newman. Fr Dennis Cassidy
22–24 Living with a life-changing loss through bereavement, Part 1. The aim of this retreat is to better equip ourselves to deal with life-changing loss. Abi & John May
23 Lenten day of reflection. A journey to Easter with Blessed John Henry Newman. Fr Dennis Cassidy
30 RCIA for those preparing for baptism. Briery Team
May
8–15 Preached retreat. Following Jesus as disciples in today's world. What is it to be a Christian today? What/who is at the heart of the matter? Jesus. Fr John Farrell OP
18 RCIA for those newly baptised. Briery Team
June
5–12 Preached retreat. What does it mean to say that we believe Christ is risen from the dead? Fr Thomas Scanlon CP
27 Retreat day. The river of faith – where next? Margaret Silf
July
2 Parish retreat day. Briery Team
15–22 Preached retreat. The Jesus of the gospels. Meditations on the four gospels. Their portrayal and meaning for Christian discipleship today.

129

Fr Donald Senior CP

August
5–14 8-day IGR. Fr Paul Fletcher SJ & Briery Team
7–14 6-day IGR, as above.
September
6–8 Living with a life-changing loss through bereavement, Part 2. This retreat is intended for those who would like a follow-up to Part 1. Abi & John May
October
25–27 Parish retreat weekend. Briery Team
28–31 Parish retreat. Briery Team
November
1–3 Circle dancing. Hilary Webster
8–10 Parish retreat weekend. Briery Team
December
6 Advent day of recollection. A journey to Christmas with blessed John Henry Newman. Fr Dennis Cassidy
7 Advent day of recollection, as above.
13–15 Advent preached retreat. Mark's Gospel: the beginning of the Good News about Jesus Christ, the Son of God. Fr Bernard Bickers

149 Hinsley Hall

62 Headingley Lane, Leeds LS6 2BX 0113 261 8000
fax 0113 224 2406
email generalmanager@hinsley-hall.co.uk
D, Wf *website* www.hinsley-hall.co.uk

Rooms 67 people in 52 single and twin rooms mostly *en suite*.
Notes A complete refurbishment has created this conference centre in Leeds, for Christian and other groups. The centre caters for meetings, conferences, retreats, parish groups, training courses and workshops. Located 1.5 miles from the centre of Leeds in pleasant grounds with car parking and easy access by public transport.
Contact The General Manager.

150 House of the Resurrection

Stocks Bank Road, Mirfield, West Yorkshire WF14 0BN 01924 483346
email guests@mirfield.org.uk
B, C, D, E, I, P, Q, S, V, W, Wf, Y *website* www.mirfield.org.uk

Rooms 43 single and 2 twin with washbasins, 4 double and 4 single *en suite*.
Notes Retreats hosted by a C of E monastic community. Victorian house in 20 acres of grounds overlooking the Calder Valley. Worship is with the brothers in the community church; plainsong daily offices and daily Eucharist. Individual guests are welcome. Concessions are available.
Contact Mike Street, Administrator.

January–February
27–3 Winter IGR.
February
8–10 Pilgrimage weekend.
18–22 Pre-Lent clergy retreat.
25–28 Meeting God in the garden. Seasons of spiritual growth.

March
1–3 Railway retreat.
1–3 CSMV & CR joint retreat (at Wantage).
22–24 Lay Lent retreat. Prepare for the Pasch.
29–31 Pilgrimage weekend.
April
2–4 Churches in a pluralist world. The theological legacy of John Neville Figgis CR.
13–21 Holy Week experience.
May
6–9 Greek for fun.
24–26 Spring bank holiday pilgrimage weekend.
June
2–9 Spring IGR.
21–23 Labyrinth retreat.
July
1–5 Monastic experience.
August
5–7 Singing retreat. Heart and soul.
11–18 Summer IGR.
23–25 Bank holiday retreat.
August–September
30–1 Arts retreat. Defence against the dark.
September
6–8 18 to 30s retreat.
October
4–6 Film retreat. *From Here to Eternity.*
20–27 Autumn IGR.
November
1–3 All Saints pilgrimage weekend.
25–29 Pre-Advent clergy retreat.
December
6–8 Advent lay retreat.
13–15 Retreat. Hebrew for beginners.

151 Westwood Christian Centre

Westwood Edge Road, Golcar, Huddersfield HD7 4JY 01484 845042
email info@westwood-centre.org.uk
B, C, D, I, P, Q, V, W, Wf, Y *website* www.westwood-centre.org.uk

Rooms In 1993, Westwood was converted by an intrepid and visionary couple from a gradually fading church on a windswept hillside to 5 beautiful self-contained flats, each with their own distinctive character. As a non-profit organisation we aim to make our accommodation as affordable as possible.
Notes Much has been written about the benefit of the spiritual disciplines of solitude and silence, of retreating from everyday life in order to rest, re-examine, refresh and renew. Westwood provides time and space in peaceful surroundings for people to do just this. We welcome people of all faith and none, and expect to find God hiding in the most unexpected faces and places.
Contact Eleonora Rosca.

LOOKING FOR A SPIRITUAL DIRECTOR?
The Retreat Association can help you find one.
Call 01494 569056, email info@retreats.org.uk
or visit our website www.retreats.org.uk

SCOTLAND

More information about retreat centres in Scotland (all denominations) is available from the Scottish Episcopal Church, www.scotland.anglican.org

ARGYLL

152 Bishop's House, Isle of Iona

Argyll and Bute PA76 6SJ   01681 700111
           email iona@island-retreats.org
C, E, P, W, Wf   website www.island-retreats.org/iona.html

Rooms 7 single and 8 twin, all with washbasin and hospitality tray. Guests share a dining room, library, spacious lounge, prayer balcony and the St Columba Chapel at the heart of the house. Outside, there are gardens front and back, with immediate access to the coastline. Our daily worship is open to anyone and everyone.
Notes Built in 1894, Bishop's House on Iona is a welcoming and relaxed retreat house hosting groups and individuals for week-long stays and shorter breaks. We are situated close to the Abbey and also face the Sound of Iona. (You can access a beautiful small beach at the bottom of the garden.) The intimate St Columba Chapel, right at the heart of the house, holds 2 daily services. Bishop's House has a reputation for good, wholesome home cooking, and we're privileged to be described by many of our guests as their 'second home'.
Contact Robert McLellan, Manager.
As a retreat house predominantly serving groups, we have Open Weeks in 2019 which are specially reserved for individuals and couples. We also host private guests alongside groups, so it is always worth phoning or emailing at other times to see if we have a cancellation or additional availability.

153 Cuil

Dalilea, Acharacle, Argyll PH36 4JX   01581 600334
           email cuilbookings@gmail.com
P, Pe   website www.saramaitland.com/hermitage

Rooms 1 double, 1 twin, bathroom, kitchen/living room.
Notes The purpose of the house is for solitary silent retreats although couples are welcome. It is very rural, off grid (but has some solar power) and with no resident director. There is, however, telephonic support and emergency contacts are provided. Although all on one level, the house requires some physical capacity to carry wood, light fires etc. It is difficult to access via public transport without a 2-mile walk. Self-catering, very beautiful highland location and great wildlife. Retreatants may stay for any length from 1 night to 3 months.
Contact Sara Maitland. Please contact initially by email.

INTRODUCING RETREATS & PRAYER PACK
A pack including resources for prayer and a short film about the value of retreats
www.retreats.org.uk/resources.php

AYRSHIRE

154 The College of the Holy Spirit & Cathedral Guest House

College Street, Millport, Isle of Cumbrae
KA28 0HE   01475 530353
       email office@cathedraloftheisles.org
B, C, Ch, D, E, P, Q, Wf, Y   website www.cathedraloftheisles.org

Rooms 1 twin en suite, 2 double en suite, 1 family en suite (1 double & 2 singles, ground floor), 1 standard family (1 double & 1 single), 2 standard doubles, 4 standard twins (1 with accessible shower), 4 standard singles. 1 double suite (private lounge, ground floor). Suite available at reduced cost for those in full-time stipendiary ministry. Ideal for individual retreats – offered on B&B basis with good eating available close by for evening meals.
Notes The College is a combination of a Visit Scotland 3* guest house and a Christian retreat house. It is located next to the UK's smallest cathedral, the Cathedral of The Isles. Both were built at the same time in 1851 by the architect William Butterfield. The College was originally built for students of theology in the Scottish Episcopal Church. The aim of The College of the Holy Spirit (with the Cathedral) is to create a centre for spiritual development and artistic expression for individuals and groups, and to offer hospitality to guests and the local community on the Isle of Cumbrae. Art facilities available in on-site community art studio. Bursaries available.
Contact The Manager.

DUMFRIES & GALLOWAY

155 Elshieshields Tower

Lochmaben, Lockerbie, Dumfries & Galloway
DG11 1LY   01387 810280
       email ann.shukman@gmail.com
B, P, Q   website www.elshieshields.co.uk

Rooms
Bothy The self-contained Bothy is fully furnished and equipped for 1 person, with kitchenette, shower room, single bed, writing table. All linen provided. It stands in a secluded position looking out on the old orchard and has its own entrance, parking and garden area. It is particularly appreciated by people seeking time out for reflection and prayer, and by students who come to use the library in the Upper Room.
Barn The Barn is available for day groups of up to 40. Wood-burning stove. Coffee facilities. Tables, projector screen, piano.
Upper Room in the medieval tower (up 40 stone steps) contains an extensive library on spirituality and church history, with special emphasis on Russian Orthodoxy and icons.
Notes Retreatants are welcome to roam in the 20 acres of gardens and woodland going down to the Water of Ae. The little Oratory in the cottage yard is always open for quiet prayer. Regular silent prayer meetings are held in the Barn on the first Saturday of every month, 9.30 to 10.30am.

131

Please check for timings in the summer months. Elshieshields is 7 miles from Lockerbie (railway station) and 6 miles from M74, junction 18.
Contact Rev Dr Ann Shukman.

FIFE

156 A Dip into Serenity

Cragmount, Kirkton of Balmerino, Newport on Tay, Fife DD6 8SA   01382 330567 / 07770 797778
            email dipser@sky.com
Q   *website* www.dipintoserenity.com

Rooms Self-catering accommodation suitable for one person or a couple.
Notes A Dip into Serenity is a Christian spiritual retreat situated in north-east Fife in Scotland. It is intended to provide a haven of peace for those who are in need of spiritual refreshment or for those who are starting a spiritual journey. We do not 'lead' as such, we believe the Holy Spirit will do this once you have made yourself receptive through 'being still'.
The retreat is an extension built into the basement of our house which is built on a slope and offers excellent views across the river and surrounding hills. It provides comfortable but simple self-catering accommodation for single people or couples in a beautiful location. Although you will be guests in part of our private home there is a separate entrance to the retreat which offers as much privacy as you desire.
Contact Bryan Weir.

GLASGOW

157 Ignatian Spirituality Centre, Glasgow

35 Scott Street, Glasgow G3 6PE   0141 354 0077
         email admin@iscglasgow.co.uk
B, C, D, I, Q, S, V, W, Wf, Y   *website* www.iscglasgow.co.uk

Non-residential.
Notes We offer Ignatian, individually guided, silent residential retreats at other centres; see listing for dates and places. Every year we run a pilgrimage to Spain in the footsteps of Saint Ignatius Loyola. We also offer training in Ignatian Spirituality, days of prayer and regular group meetings. We have a men's group, young adults group, Taizé, First Friday, Book Club and Tuesday prayer group. The Ignatian Spirituality Centre also offers courses in the Christian Faith and Living Theology. The Centre is run by the Jesuits, a Roman Catholic religious order in Glasgow city centre, near St Aloysius Church. The team is ecumenical. We welcome people of any denomination and all who are open to the Christian faith.
Contact The Administrative Secretary.
Twenties and Thirties group meets alternate Sundays at 6.30pm, see website for details.
Men's Group a supportive group of men considering faith and life, 1st Monday of each month.

Taizé Evening of Prayer an hour of Taizé chants, prayers and silence, every 3rd Monday (except July and August) 7.30pm.
Eat, Pray, Breathe a half hour of prayer and reflection every Tuesday (except July and August) 1pm.
Book Club 1st Thursday of each month (except July and August) 2–4pm.
First Friday Retreat a morning of quiet reflection each 1st Friday of the month (except July and August) 10am–1pm.
Non-residential retreats
  February
16 Support day for volunteers and carers. Day with input, reflection, sharing and friendly support 11am–3pm.
  March
2 A visit to two of Glasgow's cathedrals. Sr Isabel Smyth
6 Lent online retreat till Easter Sunday, www.lentretreat.uk
9 Day of prayer for Lent. The Eucharist in art 10.30am–4.30pm. Geoff Wheaton SJ
16–17 Talking about mental illness. How we can support people suffering from mental illness and also their carers? Looking at stress, anxiety, depression and psychosis. Dr Gill Yellowlees
  April
6–7 The Enneagram as an aid to spiritual growth. Going deeper into the Enneagram for those who already know their Enneagram type. Fr Myles O'Reilly SJ & Mary Foley
13–14 Non-residential weekend retreat.
  May
18 Support day for volunteers and carers. Day with input, reflection, sharing and friendly support 11am–3pm.
24–26 Living theology course. A weekend course of theology study for the non-specialist.
  June
1 Day of reflection. Growth in faith 10.30am–4.30pm. Sr Gemma Simmonds CJ
Residential retreats
  April
8–15 IGR on the Island of Iona.
  June–July
26–30 30-day retreat, Loyola, Spain. See website for details.
29–8 3, 4, 6 and 8-day retreats in Drumalis, N Ireland. See website for details.
  July–August
27–3 Ignatian Spain. A pilgrimage in the footsteps of St Ignatius of Loyola.
  August–September
30–6 IGR at Minsteracres, Co Durham.

FOR A LIST OF COURSES IN SPIRITUAL DIRECTION
email: info@retreats.org.uk
or phone: 01494 569056

HIGHLANDS

158 The Coach House Kilmuir Trust

Kilmuir, North Kessock, Inverness IV1 3ZG

01463 731386

email office@coachhousekilmuir.org

B, C, D, E, I, P, S, W, Wf   *website* www.coachhousekilmuir.org

Rooms 1 twin *en suite* (ground floor and suitable for person with disabilities), 1 twin *en suite*, 3 single *en suite*, 2 singles.

Notes Retreat centre welcoming people from all faiths and none, situated in the Scottish Highlands, close to Inverness, yet nestling below beech woods with inspiring views across the waters of the Moray Firth. This haven provides a peaceful place for quiet reflection, rest and prayer. Full board provided. Facilities include a comfortable sitting room, library, beautiful octagonal sanctuary for prayer and meditation, garden with sea views, art resources, a large outdoor labyrinth. Ample opportunities for walks, including along the coast, and up through fields and woods.

Our programme includes Ignatian and individually guided silent retreats, as well as periods when individuals or small groups may arrange their own retreats. Also offered 'The Spiritual Exercises in Daily Life', spiritual accompaniment, and occasional weekend and day workshops. Please visit our website for further information regarding our full programme and centre.

Contact Ruth Flockhart, Coordinator.

March

4–12   Individual retreats. Come for 4, 6 or 8 nights' silent retreat with spiritual accompaniment available. Ignatian IGR available.

April

18–21   Easter retreat. Stretch marks. A group retreat, reflecting and meditating together on Jesus' passion, death and resurrection. Ruth Flockhart & Janet Lake

May–June

31–8   Individual retreats. Come for 4, 6 or 8 nights' silent retreat with spiritual accompaniment available. Ignatian IGR available.

July–August

30–8   8-day (9 nights) silent IGR with spiritual accompaniment. Ignatian IGR available.

August

22–26   4-night individual silent retreat. Spiritual accompaniment available. Ignatian IGR available.

22–30   8-night individual silent retreat, as above.

October

7–15   Individual retreats. Come for 4, 6 or 8 nights' silent retreat with spiritual accompaniment available. Ignatian IGR available.

November

5–13   Individual retreats. Come for 4, 6 or 8 nights' silent retreat with spiritual accompaniment available. Ignatian IGR available.

December

6–8   Advent group retreat. Ruth Flockhart & Claire Starr

MORAY

159 Pluscarden Abbey

Elgin, Moray IV30 8UA   01343 890257

fax 01343 890258

email pluscarden@gmail.com

D, E, P, S, W   *website* www.pluscardenabbey.org

Rooms Men's guest house 12 single rooms with washbasin; 1 single room on ground floor with *en suite* for disabled man. Showers and toilets on each floor.

Women's guest house 9 single rooms with washbasin; showers and toilets along the corridor. All rooms are on ground floor. NB Women's guest house is self-catering, with essential foodstuffs provided.

Notes Roman Catholic Benedictine monastery. All denominations welcome. Guests and visitors are welcome to all the services in the Abbey church. Pluscarden Abbey, whose buildings date from the 13th century, is the home of a community of contemplative Benedictine monks, set in peaceful countryside of fields, woods and hills. Guests and retreatants are received throughout the year for stays up to a fortnight, except for 5 days at Christmas and during the community retreat. Guests may read, walk, take part in manual work, and share our prayer. Booking can be arranged on our website, where there is further information about the Abbey, or by post or fax. We do not usually accept bookings by telephone.

Contact The Guestmaster (for men) or the Warden (for women).

June

11–13   Annual Pentecost lectures. A series of 4 lectures at St Scholastica's retreat, on a theological topic.

PERTH & KINROSS

160 Bield at Blackruthven

Blackruthven, Tibbermore, Perth PH1 1PY

01738 583238

email info@bieldatblackruthven.org.uk

B, C, Co, D, I, P, Q, S, V   *website* www.bieldatblackruthven.org.uk

Rooms 5 twin (1 ground-floor access), 3 double, 1 single. Day group facilities for up to 30 persons. Heated barn space available for larger events. Facilities include a separate chapel, meeting rooms, art room, walled garden, orchard labyrinth, indoor heated swimming pool, tennis court. Food served consists of as much home-grown organic produce as possible.

Self-catering Lodge House with 1 double, 1 twin and 1 single. Available for retreats, sabbaticals and holidays. Access to all facilities when the Bield is open.

Notes Situated in 30 acres of parkland and surrounded by the estate farm, the Bield offers plenty of scope for retreat, reflection, healing and relaxation. Community members are available, if desired, to listen, counsel, offer spiritual direction, pray and facilitate work in the art room. Individuals or groups may organise their own time or be assisted in designing a programme that meets their needs. For programmed retreat days and events see website. IGRs

133

and Individually Directed Retreats. People of all faiths or none are welcome but the vision and worship of the community are centred in the person of Jesus Christ. We run a varied and broad programme of retreats – please see our website for up-to-date information and programme fliers.

Contact Muriel Fegan, Bookings Secretary.
Our retreat programme includes the following:
Reflective Silence. 1, 2 or 3 days in silence (Guided Retreat).
Capacitar days and tasters.
Journey into Healing days (Gestalt work).
A Day of Blessing.
Creative Journeying. Art and spirituality retreats and tasters.
Exhibitions for reflection in the Barn Gallery.
Male Rites of Passage – see themalejourney.org.uk
Spiritual direction.

161 St Mary's Pastoral & Retreat Centre

St Mary's Monastery, Hatton Road, Kinnoull,
Perth, PH2 7BP   01738 624075
                    email info@kinnoullmonastery.co.uk
D, P, Wf   *website* www.kinnoullmonastery.co.uk

Rooms 28 single *en suite*, 4 single with shared bathroom, 2 twin with special needs bathroom.
Notes St Mary's Monastery is an international, multicultural, ecumenical place that offers its visitors the opportunity for relaxation, renewal and rest. As a Redemptorist community, we offer a full programme of courses and retreats as well as serving the local community with weekly church services. We welcome groups for retreats, meetings, conferences, Chapters as well as individuals who may wish a time of retreat, relaxation and renewal.
Contact The Administrator. ❏ *inside front cover*

February
11–15 Healing ministry. Fr Jim McManus CSSR
18–22 Spirituality of self-esteem. Fr Jim McManus CSSR
March
4–8 Silent Lenten retreat. Fr T MacCarte CSSR
April
16–21 Holy Week retreat. Fr Peter Morris CSSR
May–June
13–27 Sabbatical course.
July
8–12 'You are my Beloved ... in you I am well pleased.' (Mark 1:11). Fr Kieran Brady CSSR
15–22 Retreat for religious. Fr Jim McManus CSSR
August
11–16 Holiday in Scotland.
19–26 Retreat for religious. Fr Ciarán O'Callaghan CSSR
September
9–13 Retreat for priests and deacons. Fr Jim McManus CSSR
October–December
21–5 Sabbatical course.
December
13–15 Advent retreat. Redemptorist Community

SCOTTISH BORDERS

162 Whitchester Christian Centre
Borthaugh, Hawick, Scottish Borders
TD9 7LN   01450 377477
          email enquiries@whitchester.org.uk
          website www.whitchester.org.uk
B, C, Ch, Co, D, E, I, P, Pe, Q, S, V, W, Wf, Y

Rooms 3 single, 9 twin/double, 1 family all *en suite*.
3 ground-floor rooms suitable for people with physical disabilities.
Notes A comfortable Victorian country house situated 2 miles from Hawick, set in 3 acres of landscaped gardens and woodland offering peace and quiet for individual or group retreats, quiet days and holidays. We have a chapel, large comfortable lounge, conservatory, meeting room, library, guest kitchen, Wifi, home cooking and a very warm welcome. Regular services in chapel. Prayer ministry and counselling available.
Contact The Warden.
Please see website for details of events.

WALES

CARMARTHENSHIRE

163 Bryndolau and Kites' Nest Cottage
Cwmifor, Llandeilo, Carmarthenshire SA19 7AT
                    01558 824514
          email davidsteel@mypostoffice.co.uk
C, Ch, E, P, W, Wf   *website* www.kitesnestcottage.co.uk

Rooms Self-catering for 2 in Kites' Nest cottage.
Wholefood continental breakfast available on request.
Group day meetings of up to 14 can be catered for in the main house (Bryndolau) and a vegetarian lunch/refreshments can be provided.
Notes Peaceful accommodation on the edge of the Brecon Beacons. Stunning views from all rooms. Guests may share the surrounding 5 acres of meadow and garden. Wildlife pond, shepherd's retreat hut. Suitable for retreats, holidays and short breaks. Castles, gardens and National Trust properties nearby. National Botanic Garden of Wales, Aberglasney Gardens and coast. Watercolour tuition by arrangement. 10% discount for singles. Open all year round including Christmas and New Year.
Contact David and Ros Steel.

CONWY

164 Loreto Centre

Abbey Road, Llandudno, Conwy LL30 2EL
01492 878031
email loretocentre@yahoo.co.uk
B, C, D, E, I, P, Q, S, Wf   *website* www.loretocentre.org.uk

Rooms Please visit our website or contact us by telephone for up-to-date accommodation information.
Notes The Centre is run by Loreto Sisters (RC), offering retreats and self-catering accommodation for all denominations. A variety of ecumenical groups use us for their own programmes. Ongoing spiritual direction is also available. 1-day non-residential conferences can be accommodated with lunch etc provided. Self-catering directed retreats may be available outside the programmed times. 30-day retreats (full Spiritual Exercises) available by private arrangement.
Contact Retreat Secretary, please contact by telephone, email or through the website.

March
1–3 Fun, faith and friendship. A weekend for those in their 30s and 40s to meet others of their own age group for some socialising and faith-sharing.
April
17–21 Holy Week retreat. A chance to celebrate the liturgies of Holy Week in the context of a prayerful retreat.
May
6–13 6-day IGR.
13–20 Preached retreat. Fr Chris Thomas
June
7–9 Living theology. A summer school in Christian faith.
17–24 6-day IGR.
July
1–8 Preached retreat. Fr Richard Sloan
22–31 8-day IGR.
August
13–22 8-day IGR.
September
18–27 8-day IGR.
27–29 Artist as co-creator. A weekend using art to recover the child within and become co-creators with God. Jen & Annie Bromham IBVM
November
1–3 Silent retreat with workshops. Praying with Ignatius of Loyola and John of the Cross. Ewa Bem IBVM
11–18 6-day IGR.
11–20 8-day IGR.
December
2–6 Advent Triduum.

FOR A LIST OF LEAFLETS ON PRAYER, RETREATS AND SPIRITUAL DIRECTION SEE OUR WEBSITE
www.retreats.org.uk/leaflets.php

---

165 Noddfa Spirituality Centre

Conwy Old Road, Penmaenmawr, Conwy
LL34 6YF   01492 623473
email noddfapen@aol.com
C, D, E, I, P, W, Wf   *website* www.noddfa.org.uk

Rooms Main House 15 single, 6 twin, 4 double. Shalom 8 rooms for self-catering.
Notes For parish groups, we welcome people to a safe place to connect with God, themselves and others on their spiritual journey. Carers retreats. Use of facilities for groups organising their own retreats. Private retreats.
Contact Mary Jo McElroy.
February
8–11 Zenways retreat.
15–17 Serenity retreat.
March
21–28 IGR. Margaret Fielding, Fergus O'Donoghue & Lynne Chadwick
April
18–21 Easter Triduum.
May
20–24 CARM painting and prayer retreat.
June
3–6 Celtic retreat. Julie Hopkins
17–20 Capacitar training. Pat Cane
July
10–17 IGR. Mary Nono, Tess Rynn & Dermot Mansfield
18–25 IGR. Brian Noble, John McCluskey & Una Coogan
July–August
30–3 Catholic People's week.
August
1–4 Workshop/retreat. Diarmuid O'Murchu
23–26 Serenity retreat.
September
19–26 Retreat.
December
13–16 Zenways retreat.
See website for updates to this programme.

166 Ruach Retreat

Llys Gwynt, Old Mill Road, Dwygyfylchi, Conwy
LL34 6TB   01492 622279
email davidandzoya@ruachretreat.co.uk
B, Co, P, Q, S, W, Wf   *website* www.ruachretreat.co.uk

Rooms 1 double and 1 single. Bathroom, lounge, conservatory and spacious garden available for the sole use of retreatants. Room for day retreats/quiet days/awaydays for up to 10. Other rooms available for day visitors.
Notes David and Zoya moved to Llys Gwynt to fulfil a vision of opening their home to people of all faiths or none. It offers a small, quiet retreat opportunity for those needing space and a place to be. David and Zoya can be on hand to offer a listening ear, pastoral counselling and prayer if needed. It has room for 1 or 2 residential retreatants at any one time and space for small groups on a daily basis. Day visitors can lead themselves or be led by either David and/or Zoya.

Llys Gwynt is a mile off the A55 and 4 miles west of Conwy. It is set at the foot of the Sychnant Pass amid low hills and green pastures. It is a haven of tranquillity. There are many walks from the cottage and eating places within walking distance. Local buses go to Conwy, Llandudno and Bangor. The cottage has 1 or 2 steps between some ground-floor rooms and has stairs to the bedrooms. Residents can either share meals with David and Zoya or prepare their own. Day groups will be offered light refreshments throughout the day and a simple lunch can be prepared if needed. Hospitality is the key. We recognise the need to offer a bespoke format that works for individuals and groups.
Contact David and Zoya for further details and to chat over your needs.

167 St Augustine's Priory, House of Prayer

Cliff Road, Old Colwyn, Conwy, North Wales
LL29 9RW   01492 514223
email enquiries@houseofprayer.org.uk
B, C, D, I, P, Q, S, W, Wf, Y   *website* www.houseofprayer.org.uk

Rooms All rooms are *en suite*. 14 single, 2 twin and 1 double. 6 rooms only are accessible by lift. There are no ground-floor bedrooms. Conference/meeting room, sitting room, reading room, library, art room, 2 dining rooms, four 1–1 meeting rooms, a sacred space and a chapel. There is a tea station on each floor. Full-board with a minimum stay of 2 nights.
Notes The Priory has a pleasant garden with a labyrinth and seating areas. The sea is within 5 mins' walking distance with other accessible walks and with more beautiful scenery a short bus or car ride away. Although a predominantly RC establishment all denominations are welcome to use these facilities. We offer individually guided retreats, space for private retreats and quiet breaks for individuals or groups.
Contact The Administrator, by email or telephone. ❏ *p 82* Please see the website for the programme of retreats etc.

DENBIGHSHIRE

168 St Beuno's Jesuit Spirituality Centre

Tremeirchion, St Asaph, Denbighshire
LL17 0AS   01745 583444
email info@beunos.com
B, C, D, E, I, Q, S, W, Wf   *website* www.beunos.com

Rooms 60 single, of which 33 are *en suite*.
Notes We are a Jesuit spirituality centre with a team of priests, religious men and women and lay people. We offer the full Spiritual Exercises of St Ignatius 3 times a year and also in 'stages'. We also have a full programme of silent individually guided retreats, various themed retreats and offer courses and training in spiritual accompaniment. We are Roman Catholic and welcoming to all.
Contact Fr Roger Dawson SJ. ❏ *p 4*

January
7–11   Midweek IGR.

7–14   6-day IGR.
11–25 Spiritual direction course.
14–25 The Spiritual Exercises in 3 stages.
25–27 School of prayer.
25–27 Weekend IGR for people in their 20s and 30s.
January–February
6–11   The Full Spiritual Exercises.
28–1   Midweek IGR.
28–6   8-day IGR.
February
1–3   Weekend IGR.
4–8   Midweek IGR.
6–15   8-day IGR.
8–15   Prayer guides course.
11–15 MBTI. Prayer and the shadow. Sr Anne Morris DHS
15–17 Weekend IGR.
February–March
20–1   8-day IGR.
20–1   Course. Introduction to spiritual accompaniment.
27–10 The Spiritual Exercises in 3 stages.
March
1–3   Weekend IGR.
1–3   Weekend retreat for married couples. Growing together. Fr Roger Dawson SJ and Rose & Greg McCrave
4–11   6-day IGR.
4–20   The Spiritual Exercises in 2 stages.
11–15 Midweek IGR.
11–20 8-day IGR.
15–17 Weekend IGR.
18–21 Course. Living and working in an Ignatian way.
26–29 Workshop. Preparing the Holy Week liturgies.
29–31 Course. Psychology and spirituality. Dr Steve Noone & Fr Roger Dawson SJ
March–April
26–2   6-day IGR.
26–4   8-day IGR.
April
1–5   Midweek IGR.
4–11   Budget 6-day IGR.
4–11   6-day IGR.
6–17   The Spiritual Exercises in 3 stages.
11–17 5-day IGR.
12–17 Workshop for spiritual directors. Understanding the Exercises.
17–22 Easter IGR.
18–22 Easter at St Beuno's.
23–26 Art retreat. Tim McEvoy & Iona Reid-Dalglish
April–May
23–1   7-day IGR.
24–1   6-day IGR.
26–28 Weekend IGR for people in their 20s and 30s.
May
3–5   Weekend IGR.
3–10   6-day IGR.
3–12   8-day IGR.
6–10   Midweek IGR.
10–17 6-day IGR.
10–19 8-day IGR.
13–20 6-day IGR.
17–19 School of prayer.
20–27 6-day IGR.
20–29 8-day IGR.

27–31 Midweek IGR.
May–June
29–7 8-day IGR.
31–7 6-day IGR.
June
7–9 Weekend IGR.
7–9 Life before death. The psychology of flourishing.
Fr Roger Dawson SJ
10–14 Midweek IGR.
10–17 6-day IGR.
14–16 Weekend IGR for people in their 20s and 30s.
19–26 6-day IGR.
19–28 8-day IGR.
July
1–5 Midweek IGR.
1–12 The Spiritual Exercises in 3 stages.
5–7 Men for all seasons. Ignatian transformation for men. Greg McCrave, Stephen Hoyland, Tim McEvoy & Fr Roger Dawson SJ
5–12 6-day IGR.
8–12 Mindfulness, stress and Christian spiritual practice. Prof Mark Williams
12–21 8-day IGR.
22–31 8-day IGR.
August
2–4 Weekend IGR.
2–9 6-day IGR.
5–9 Midweek IGR.
9–18 8-day IGR.
19–23 Midweek IGR.
19–28 8-day IGR.
23–28 Discernment retreat. Changing direction. Vron Smith & Iona Reid-Dalglish
August–September
1–6 The Full Spiritual Exercises.
28–6 8-day IGR.
30–1 Weekend IGR.
September
2–6 Midweek IGR.
6–8 Weekend IGR.
6–8 Life before death. The psychology of flourishing. Fr Roger Dawson SJ
16–20 Midweek IGR.
18–22 Poetry and prayer. Fr Brian McClorry SJ
20–22 Weekend IGR.
20–29 8-day IGR.
23–30 6-day IGR.
September–October
23–4 The Spiritual Exercises in 3 stages.
30–4 Midweek IGR.
October–November
14–19 The Full Spiritual Exercises.
23–8 The Spiritual Exercises in 2 stages.
October–December
1–8 10-week course in retreat giving and spiritual guidance.

Please note that we programme our events on an academic year (October to September). A full programme of retreats and courses from September 2019 will be published on our website where you can also book a place on an event. These are published as a rolling programme approximately one year in advance.

FLINTSHIRE

169 Gladstone's Library

Church Lane, Hawarden, Flintshire CH5 3DF
01244 532350
email enquiries@gladlib.org
C, D, P, Q, S, Wf   *website* www.gladstoneslibrary.org

Rooms 26 boutique style bedrooms. 3 twin, 12 double, 11 single. Most rooms are *en suite*. There is no lift but there are 2 easy access ground-floor rooms. 4 meeting/conference rooms, the largest of which seats up to 40. Chapel. Library holding 250,000 items, with excellent theology and liberal arts collections.
Notes A relaxed and tranquil atmosphere ideal for contemplation and study for either individual or group retreat. For prices and more information visit the website.
Contact Reception.

GLAMORGAN

170 Nicholaston House Christian Retreat & Conference Centre

Penmaen, Gower, Swansea SA3 2HL
01792 371317
email retreats@nicholastonhouse.org
website www.nicholastonhouse.org
B, C, Ch, Co, D, E, I, P, Q, S, V, W, Wf

Rooms 11 bedrooms: 6 twin, 2 double + 1 single, 1 double + 2 singles, and 2 singles, all *en suite* with tea and coffee-making facilities. All are 1st-floor rooms with stairs or lift. 1 is partially adapted for people with disabilities. A self-catering studio apartment (double bed) for 1 or 2 people is also available for personal retreats and time out. The House sleeps up to 26 in total when all available bed spaces are utilised on a shared-occupancy basis.
Notes Nicholaston House is Swansea City Mission and Educational Trust's main charitable operation, having purchased the House in 1998 thereby establishing a Christian Retreat and Conference Centre overlooking Oxwich Bay. The focus of Nicholaston House is to be a centre for healing and restoration channelled through various retreats and courses, and to facilitate Christian groups for conferences and awaydays. There are resident staff at Nicholaston House forming a small intentional Christian community. This number is supported by full-time, part-time and casual staff. The work is also supported by a host of volunteers who undertake a variety of tasks, from maintenance and gardening to counselling and prayer ministry. Trustees, who are ultimately responsible for the work of Nicholaston House meet on a regular basis and continue to act with foresight, faith, wisdom and courage.
Nicholaston House, standing in its own grounds overlooking Oxwich Bay, is set in Britain's first designated AONB. Step outside and wander onto open moorland with its purple heather and golden gorse, and view the Gower

ponies grazing on the gently sloping hillside. A leisurely walk to the clifftop takes you to a beautiful view of Three Cliffs Bay – come and see for yourself.
Keep an eye on our website for availability, room-only tariffs, B&B rates and last-minute bookings. Facilities include a conservatory, conference room with audiovisual equipment, table tennis table, art and craft studio, prayer room, bookstall, lounge with TV and Wifi, garden and small 'Hermitage' for personal prayer and quiet times.
The Celtic Chapel endorses the vision of the House. Completed in March 2010, it is built in medieval style and is central to the daily rhythm of prayer and worship. Guests are welcome to join with staff for short devotional times in the Chapel during the week. At other times, guests may request the Chapel key for personal devotional times.
Contact Ian Ambrose, Operations Manager.

January
14–18 Low-cost retreat.
21–25 Low-cost retreat.
30 Quiet day.
January–February
28–1 Low-cost retreat.
February
4–8 Prayer and refreshing retreat/personal retreat break.
11–15 Personal retreat break.
15–17 Calling all Christian singles!
18–22 Overcoming eating disorders course (Foundations).
February–March
25–1 Personal retreat break.
March
1–3 Men's weekend.
4–8 Prayer and refreshing retreat/personal retreat break.
9 Times of revival seminar and prayer day.
11–15 Personal retreat break.
18–22 Personal retreat break.
22–25 Divorce recovery course.
April
1–5 Prayer and refreshing retreat/personal retreat break.
5–7 Time out weekend (group booking only).
8–12 Painting break.
14 Open garden and Easter egg hunt.
15–19 Low-cost Easter retreat.
17 Quiet day.
22–26 Overcoming eating disorders course (Transitions).
April–May
29–3 Personal retreat break.
May
20–24 Personal retreat break.
25–31 Prophetic art retreat.
June
3–7 Overcoming eating disorders course (Foundations).
10–14 Prayer and refreshing retreat/personal retreat break.
June–July
28–1 Breakfast on the beach.
July
6 Quiet day.

8–12 Prayer and refreshing retreat/personal retreat break.
12–14 Time out weekend (group booking only).
15–19 Painting break.
19–21 Christian singles' weekend.
26–29 Silent retreat.
July–August
29–4 Silent retreat.
August
5–9 Overcoming eating disorders course (Transitions).
10 Open garden and strawberry tea.
Planned closure for redevelopment works until spring 2020. Please see website for updates.

MONMOUTHSHIRE

171 Llansôr Mill

Llansôr Mill, Treherbert Road, Caerleon, Newport NP18 1LS   01633 450638
email llansor@btinternet.com
B, C, P, Pe, Q, V, W, Wf, Y   *website* www.llansor.org

Rooms Studio: 5 beds (shared space) Mill: 2 double rooms, plus sofa beds and options in large hall/gallery. We can accommodate groups of up to 14 residentially. A camping field is available, as is information about local hospitality.
Notes Llansôr Mill, situated in a beautiful, peaceful valley in SE Wales, offers a focus for an emerging community of people, some living locally, others scattered throughout Britain. Events held here offer the opportunity to explore and experience together what the contemplative 'spiritual journey' is about. The work of the Franciscan Richard Rohr and the tradition of the mystics such as Julian of Norwich are the wellspring for this non-dualistic approach. Many of us would identify ourselves as Christian, though from widely differing church backgrounds, and with differing levels of involvement in institutional Christianity. Others have different faith backgrounds; and others again don't have a faith background at all, and aren't sure if they want one! What unites our community is the spirit in which we approach the mystery of life rather than a shared set of beliefs. Central to this is a commitment to the challenge to be tolerant of difference and to celebrate diversity. The practice of silent contemplation, alone and together, serves us well and is always where we begin and end. The Mill welcomes groups who wish to organise their own events, and anyone needing to withdraw for a while to a place of quiet, just to be.
Catering can be offered by arrangement, and there are simple self-catering facilities available too.
Public footpaths all around and open sheep-grazing country to explore.
Contact Mary and Stephen Ashton, Hosts.
For events programme see the website, where you can register for regular newsletter. Programme includes regular men's and women's groups and weekends plus many interesting speakers and topics of interest, all experienced in a contemplative setting. For example, topics include regular Enneagram courses and groups, the work of dying, gratitude, spirituality and the arts, and much more.

172 The Society of the Sacred Cross

Tymawr Convent, Lydart, Monmouthshire
NP25 4RN   01600 860244
email tymawrconvent@btinternet.com
D, P, Q, V   *website* www.tymawrconvent.org

Rooms 5 guests in convent.
Michaelgarth Self-catering guest house. 5 single, 2 twin
with accommodation for day groups (up to 20 people).
The Old Print House For day groups.
Notes It is possible for women and men, with a serious
intention to deepen their life of prayer, to live alongside
the sisters for up to 3 months. For information about study
days please see our website or send SAE.
Contact The Guest Sister.

173 Tabernacle United Reformed Church

3 Rosecroft Drive, Langstone, Newport, Gwent
NP18 2LQ   07716 118791 / 01633 412760
email minister@urcllanvaches.org.uk
B, C, Co, D, I, P, Pe, Q, S, W   *website* urcllanvaches.org.uk

Rooms Non-residential.
Notes Tabernacle is only 20 mins from the city of
Newport, South Wales, and is located on Chepstow Road,
Llanvaches, Gwent NP26 3AY. Tabernacle is a space for
self-discovery, prayer and meditation, as well as providing
a tranquil and peaceful environment near the ancient
Wentwood Forest. Whatever the time of year, a visit to
Wentwood (Coed Gwent), which has a variety of trails that
are sure underfoot, is well worth your time.
When you spend time at Tabernacle you will be
experiencing history. Founded in November 1639,
Tabernacle was the first nonconformist and independent
church in Wales, and has been consistently open for
worship with a committed congregation. William Wroth,
who had a colourful life and an amazing conversion, was
the founder and first minister of Tabernacle.
We have a programme for individual or group retreat,
courses to help people on their spiritual journey. A visit to
Tabernacle is an opportunity to set aside time from the
stress and strain of daily life, to renew yourself, and to
deepen your search for, or relationship with, God. For
those who are not looking for a guided retreat, this can
also be a place to enjoy a quiet day. Rev Paula also offers
spiritual counsel or coaching for those who wish it.
Tabernacle is ecumenical and welcomes Christians of all
denominations and people of goodwill. Welcome, Croeso
and enjoy!
The events listed below include materials, tea/coffee and
lunch. Please email or phone for a complete programme.
We also offer private retreat days, with or without spiritual
direction and prayer, upon request.
Contact Rev Paula Parish-Foley.

March
30 Experience the presence of God among creation by
walking Wentwood Forest and ridge. A walk for all
abilities with fun, fellowship and reflective prayers.
Rev Paula

June
10 No matter your ability, find peace and purpose
through painting, prayer and reflection. For
personal prayer / counsel please indicate at
booking. Jenny Cooper, Newport artist & Rev Paula
October
12 You're worth it! Learn the art of Christian
contemplation, to help you lead a more peaceful,
productive and authentic life. Rev Paula

POWYS

174 Coleg Trefeca

College Lane, Trefeca, Talgarth, Brecon, Powys
LD3 0PP   01874 711423
                                fax 01874 712212
email colegtrefeca@ebcpcw.org.uk
B, C, D, P, Q, S, W, Wf, Y   *website* www.trefeca.org.uk

Rooms 14 twin-bedded *en suite* rooms, one adapted for
disabled use.
Notes A lay training and conference centre owned by the
Presbyterian Church of Wales set in 5 acres of grounds in
the Brecon Beacons National Park. An ideal place for
retreat and relaxation. Programme available on request.
Contact Mair Jones, Centre Manager.

175 Llangasty Retreat House

Llangasty, Nr Brecon, Powys LD3 7PX
                                     01874 658250
email enquiries@llangasty.com
B, C, D, I, P, Q, W, Wf   *website* www.llangasty.com

Rooms 10 single, 6 twin (includes 2 ground-floor rooms
with wheelchair access and *en suite* facilities).
Notes Llangasty Retreat House is an ideal location for
retreats and parish conferences. Whilst Anglican in
foundation we are ecumenical in outlook. The House is a
sympathetically extended Victorian rectory set in the
Brecon Beacons National Park, just off the A40, 6 miles east
of Brecon and overlooking Lake Llangors. With 2 main
rooms, a large chapel and smaller crypt chapel, Llangasty
can cater for individuals or groups of up to 22 people. The
ground floor and garden are wheelchair accessible. Larger
day groups can be accommodated.
Please see website for more details, events, quiet days and
drop-in days. The latter are an opportunity to pause for
prayer and personal reflection; come for all or part of the
day, bringing your own lunch (coffee and tea provided)
and no need to book for these.
Contact Booking Secretary. ❏ *inside back cover*

March
5–7 Pancakes and ashes. Exploring Lent in a Celtic way.
Ven Alan Jevons
19 Cader Idris: paradoxes in a mountain landscape 1.
Rev Canon Dr Mark Clavier
April
23–28 Rest, work and play. Time set aside for individuals
to come and read, walk and be refreshed. Stays
from a single night available.

139

30 Cader Idris: paradoxes in a mountain landscape 2.
Rev Canon Dr Mark Clavier
July
30 Cader Idris: paradoxes in a mountain landscape 3.
Rev Canon Dr Mark Clavier
August
3 Quiet day. Fellowship of the Transfiguration
6–13 CARM embroidery retreat. Ann Meek & Mildred Butterworth
September
6–8 Soul Spark. Rev Nick Helm
16–20 CARM painting retreat. Kay Andrews & Mildred Butterworth
November
18–21 Pre-Advent retreat. Fr Nicholas Stebbing CR
December
3 Advent quiet day. Fellowship of the Transfiguration

176 Llannerchwen (Society of the Sacred Heart)

Llandefaelog Fach, Brecon, Powys LD3 9PP
01874 622902
email retreats@llannerchwen.org.uk
C, I, P, Q, S, W   *website* www.llannerchwen.org.uk

Rooms 8 single, of which 3 are individual hermitages and 1 mobility-friendly semi-hermitage. The other 4 are self-contained units, each with its own private entrance. All accommodation is *en suite*. Facilities in each fully-equipped kitchen include a microwave and a fridge, and an electric cooker or a hob. Towels and sheets are provided, as well as tea, coffee, salt, pepper and oil. The accommodation and ethos are ideal for those seeking solitude, as well as stillness, contemplation and silence.
Notes Llannerchwen, 3 miles north of the small market town of Brecon, is in a secluded setting with panoramic views of the Brecon Beacons and Black Mountains. It is a place of great stillness and spirituality. There is a small chapel with the Blessed Sacrament and a newly-built cabin for creative arts. Most evenings there is an optional half-hour silent (evening) prayer. The centre schedules no other religious services or activities in common.
Individually Guided Retreats (IGRs) or Spiritual Exercises of St Ignatius of Loyola can be either fully self-catering, or have the main meal provided. This basket meal option is only available during scheduled retreats, not for solitude. Private self-catering retreats in solitude can be made between IGR times for a minimum of 2 nights and up to 6 months. The centre is closed in January and the first half of September.
For IGRs, choose a minimum of 5 and maximum of 8 days. Those wishing to make the Ignatian Spiritual Exercises in 3 parts (10 days each) can arrange this over the scheduled retreat times any year. The full 30-day Spiritual Exercises are available in February only. Familiarity with silence and Ignatian types of prayer are essential for the Exercises. 19th Annotation retreats are available by arrangement, and so is ongoing spiritual accompaniment. A pick-up from public transport in Brecon may be available. The suggested donations have not been changed for the last 4 years. Llannerchwen is run by lay women on behalf of the Society of the Sacred Heart, a Roman Catholic order. The resident

staff is assisted by visiting directors and helpers from several denominations.
Contact The Booking Secretary.
February–December Those wishing to make self-catering solitude retreats (minimum 2 nights, maximum 180 days) are welcome outside of the retreat dates below. Occasional spiritual accompaniment may be available. Familiarity with the Ignatian types of prayer is required only for the Spiritual Exercises (SE).
February–March
1–7 Full 30-day SE, by prior arrangement only.
March
11–20 IGR or SE (in parts).
April
1–10 IGR or SE (in parts).
May
9–18 IGR or SE (in parts).
June
15–24 IGR or SE (in parts).
July
13–22 IGR or SE (in parts).
August
1–10 IGR or SE (in parts).
19–28 IGR or SE (in parts).
September
21–30 IGR or SE (in parts).
October– November
31–9 IGR or SE (in parts).

TORFAEN

177 Ty Croeso Centre

Llantarnam Abbey, Cwmbran, Torfaen NP44 3YJ
01633 867317
email tycroeso@talktalk.net
D, I, P, Q, S, W, Wf   *website* www.tycroesocentre.co.uk

Rooms 7 single (including 3 *en suite*) and 1 twin *en suite* with access for disabled. All guests have use of the lounges, chapel, oratory, resource/art room, gardens and labyrinth.
A beautifully appointed 2-bedroomed self-catering hermitage in the grounds is available for retreats and for those looking for creative space. There is also a shop with a variety of religious objects such as books, CDs and cards for sale.
Notes Ty Croeso is beautifully situated in spacious grounds, bordered by woodlands, rivers and hills and is ideal for walking and rambling through all seasons of the year. We welcome people of all faiths and none and feel privileged to share our space. Ty Croeso is closed in January.
Days of reflection on dates listed below, 10am–3.30pm, please bring a packed lunch.
Contact Sr St Joseph Butler, Administrator.
March
11 Day of reflection. How can an 'ecological spirituality' motivate us to a more passionate concern for the protection of our world? (Pope Francis Laudato Si 216.) Sr Henrietta SSJA

21–30 8-day preached retreat. Jesus among women as seen in the gospels. Fr Mike Drennan SJ
April
5–7 Lenten journey. Ty Croeso Team
May
13–20 Preached retreat. God slipped in. 'Did not our hearts burn within us?' Derek Laverty SSCC
13–22 8-day retreat as above.
June
1–8 Directed retreat. David McLoughlin
1–10 8-day retreat as above.
July
29 Day of reflection. We are co-creators with God: we all have great inner power to enable us to do this, a power we have scarcely tapped into until now. Sr Bridget Pritchard SSJA
September
17 Day of reflection. What does 'ecological spirituality' mean for us today? Sr Henrietta SSJA
October
8 Day of reflection. The new Universe story invites us to expand our hearts to include all creation. Sr Bridget Pritchard SSJA
December
6–8 Advent journey. Ty Croeso Team

IRELAND

ANTRIM

🔢178 Corrymeela

5 Drumaroan Road, Ballycastle, Co Antrim, N Ireland BT54 6QU 028 2076 2626 / 028 9050 8080
email bookings@corrymeela.org
D, V, W, Wf, Y   *website* www.corrymeela.org

Rooms We are a residential centre that accommodates for groups (minimum group size 10). We have 2 units, The Main House: 60 beds (25 bedrooms) and The Davey Village (*en suite*): 38 beds (19 bedrooms). We have a range of meeting spaces with audiovisual capacities. All meals are provided during your stay.
Notes We're Ireland's oldest peace and reconciliation centre. We began before 'The Troubles' and continue on in Northern Ireland's changing post-conflict society. Corrymeela is people of all ages and Christian traditions who, individually and together, are committed to the healing of social, religious and political divisions that exist in Northern Ireland and throughout the world.
Contact Katherine Murphy.
January
18–20 Blessed are the brave. Retreat for Christian faith leaders who are inclusive of LGBT people. Pádraig Ó Tuama, leader of the Corrymeela community
March
22–24 Silent retreat with space for reflection, reading and rest. Pádraig Ó Tuama, leader of the Corrymeela community

July
26–28 Living well together with families. Fun weekend for families to take part in a 'Living well together' programme. Expressions of interest to be submitted by 24 May.

🔢179 Drumalis Retreat & Conference Centre

47 Glenarm Road, Larne, County Antrim, N Ireland BT40 1DT 028 2827 2196 / 028 2827 6455
email drumalis@btconnect.com
B, D, I, P, Q, S, Wf   *website* www.drumalis.co.uk

Rooms 3 single, 37 twin, 13 double, 3 group. Ground floor, *en suite* and disabled-friendly accommodation available.
Notes Drumalis is situated in spacious grounds overlooking the sea at the gateway to the scenic Antrim Coast. Although located close to the town centre of Larne, its elevated wooded position ensures a tranquil and secluded environment for all types of retreat, conference and workshop. Facilities include chapels, conference rooms, prayer rooms, group rooms, library and shop.
Contact The Administrator.
June
15–22 Preached retreat. Fr Mike Serrage MSC
15–22 Retreat. Nurturing inner stillness, compassion, unity and hope. Sr Joann Heinritz CSJ
24–28 Creation spirituality retreat.
June–July
29–8 IGR. Choice of 3-day, 4-day, 6-day or 8-day. Drumalis Team, Epiphany Group & Ignatian Spirituality Centre, Glasgow
August
13–22 8-day directed retreat.
15–22 6-day directed retreat.

DONEGAL

🔢180 Ards Friary Retreat and Conference Centre

Creeslough, Co Donegal, Ireland F92 Y23R
00 353 7491 38909
email info@ardsfriary.ie
B, I, P, Q, S, W, Wf   *website* www.ardsfriary.ie

Rooms 50 individual bedrooms, 4 *en suites*.
Notes The centre is a Capuchin Franciscan house, in the Roman Catholic faith. We have 2 lecture rooms (60 and 40 people capacity) and can cater for up to 120 people. It is set in 200 acres of grounds and the edge of the sea. Stunning walks and views.
Contact Retreat Centre Manager.

STOP! IN THE NAME OF GOD
12–14 July 2019 – see page 68

DUBLIN

181 Manresa Jesuit Centre of Spirituality

426 Clontarf Road, Dublin, Ireland D03 FP52

00 353 1 833 1352
email reception@manresa.ie

B, Ch, D, E, I, P, Q, S, W, Wf   *website* www.manresa.ie

Rooms 42 single *en suite* rooms, 1 accessible single *en suite* room.

Notes Manresa is Ireland's Jesuit retreat house, located on Dublin Bay, within easy reach of Dublin's city centre and airport. Our modern building in its pleasant environment enables us to offer a range of Ignatian retreats in silence in addition to a number of courses and events, including an accredited course in spiritual direction.
Contact Piaras Jackson SJ, Director. ❑ *p 82*

January
26   Oasis day.
January–February
28–6   8-day directed retreat (IGR).
February
16   Oasis day.
17–22   4-day preached retreat.
March
3–8   4-day preached retreat.
22–24   Weekend retreat.
23   Oasis day.
March–April
31–9   8-day directed retreat (IGR).
April
12–21   Holy Week guided retreat.
13   Oasis day.
May
14–23   8-day directed retreat (IGR).
18   Oasis day.
May–June
26–30   Full Spiritual Exercises (IGR).
28–6   8-day directed retreat (IGR).
June
8   Oasis day.
9–14   4-day directed retreat (IGR).
16–25   8-day directed retreat (IGR).
June–July
28–5   6-day directed retreat (IGR).
July
7–12   4-day directed retreat (IGR).
13   Oasis day.
14–23   8-day directed retreat (IGR).
25–28   Weekend retreat.
July–August
30–8   8-day directed retreat (IGR).
August
10   Oasis day.
11–18   6-day directed retreat (IGR).
20–29   8-day directed retreat (IGR).
September
10–19   8-day directed retreat (IGR).
21   Oasis day.

October
7–16   8-day directed retreat (IGR).
19   Oasis day.
27–31   Mid-term retreat.
November
2   Oasis day.
15–24   8-day directed retreat (IGR).
November–December
29–1   Weekend retreat.
December
2–6   Advent Triduum preached retreat.
6–8   Weekend retreat.
7   Oasis day.
9–13   Advent Triduum preached retreat.
14   Oasis day.
December–January 2020
29–1   New Year retreat.

GALWAY

182 The Hermitage

Sisters of La Retraite, 2 Distillery Road, Lower Newcastle, Galway, Ireland H91 WV8K

00 353 91524548
email hermitagegalway@laretraite.ws

I, P, S   *website* www.laretraite.ws

Rooms 1 single, 1 twin.
Notes Situated in the heart of Galway city, The Hermitage offers a welcome and space for those seeking inner stillness, meaning and God's presence in their lives, through individually guided or private retreats. Spiritual direction is also available throughout the year.
Contact Sr Moira McDowall.

183 Jesuit Centre of Spirituality & Culture

6 Ely Place, Sea Road, Galway, Ireland H91 F344

00 353 91 725363 / 00 353 86 8776537
email jesuitcentregalway@gmail.com

B, C, I, Q, S, Wf   *website* www.jesuitcentregalway.ie

Non-residential.
Notes We are a team of Jesuits and friends who draw our inspiration from St Ignatius of Loyola. Like Ignatius, we invite others to join us in our search for the presence of the Divine in the world around us and in all the ups and downs of our daily lives. We provide a variety of retreats and courses which offer space and opportunity to explore the deeper questions of life in the context of Christian faith and prayer. Spiritual direction available on request. For all further information please see our website.
Contact The Administrator.

WHERE THERE'S A WILL...

Have you thought about the Retreat Association in your will? Contact us for information and advice.

email: info@retreats.org.uk or phone: 01494 569056

KERRY

184 Ardfert Retreat Centre
Abbeylands, Ardfert, Co Kerry, Ireland V92 D438
00 353 6671 34276
email ardfertretreat@eircom.net
website www.ardfertretreatcentre.org
B, C, Co, I, P, Q, S, V, W, Wf, Y

Rooms 25 single bedrooms and 5 double bedrooms. 9 single rooms are on the ground floor with access to 2 bathrooms. Other rooms are located upstairs with shared bathrooms on each corridor. We have 1 double and 1 single room with *en suite* facilities. Within the centre we have a large conference room, chapel, dining room which can cater for 40 people, and several smaller rooms for one-to-one meetings. Outside we have a 7-circuit labyrinth, outdoor stations of the cross and lots of open space for walking and reflecting.
Notes Ardfert Retreat Centre is located on the outskirts of Ardfert village which is 5 miles from Tralee (on the Causeway road) and only 2 miles from the beautiful Banna Strand. Within view of the house are the ruins of Ardfert Cathedral 1256 and the Franciscan Abbey 1253. Ardfert Retreat Centre is a place of welcome which promotes prayer and provides opportunities for growth in Christian spirituality. The Centre is a place to 'come apart for a while' and find rest with God, returning to daily life refreshed and renewed. The Centre nurtures the development of Christian community, based on the Scriptures, reflections on life experience and the sacraments.
Contact Sr Elizabeth Gilmartin, Coordinator.

CHANNEL ISLANDS

185 Oasis of Peace, Jersey
The Presbytery, La Rue de la Ville au Bas, Le Coin Varin, St Peter, Jersey JE3 7EW
01534 861750
email Oasis@catholicchurch.org.je
D, P, Q, S, V, Wf,　　*website* www.oasisofpeacejersey.com

Rooms 7 bedrooms: single, twin, double, family and 2 *en suite*.
Notes A peaceful Centre in the heart of the Jersey countryside, established by the Catholic Church in Jersey for prayer, reflection, retreat and study. Comfortable accommodation, 2 large meeting rooms, a library, lounge, garden and chapel. It is open to all who wish to find some peace in their life.
Contact Deacon David Cahill, The Manager.

RETREAT ASSOCIATION SUMMER EVENT
3 July 2019 – see page 80
Guest speakers:
Father Anastasios Salapatas, Greek Orthodox & **Father Stephen Platt**, Russian Orthodox

CYPRUS

186 Katafiyio Retreat House
PO Box 22075, Nicosia 1517, Cyprus
mobile) 00 357 99 155092
(landline) 00 357 22 671220
fax 00 357 22 674533
email retreats@cypgulf.org
B, C, Ch, E, I, P, Pe, Q, S, W　*website* www.cypgulf.org/retreats

Rooms 1 double, 1 twin, studio area doubles as twin when necessary. Shared bathroom. Self-catering. Courtyard prayer room. Lounge/meeting room suitable for groups up to 20 with open fire. Snug room with open fire. Fully-equipped kitchen with dining area. Large veranda with dining table overlooking courtyard and garden. Small library. Craft materials and ideas.
Notes Katafiyio ('place of refuge') is the retreat house of the Anglican Diocese of Cyprus and the Gulf. Open every day of the year, Katafiyio is ideally situated for those living in the Middle East and Europe wanting time out to relax, reflect and pray. It is a traditional house situated in a small village which has a taverna and small supermarket. On the edge of the Machairas Forest, it offers excellent walking opportunities. Guided retreats for both individuals and groups. Team trained ecumenically.
Contact Retreats Facilitator.

DENMARK

187 Stella Matutina
Sisters of Saint Joseph Retreat Centre, Strandvejen 352, 2980 Kokkedal, Denmark
00 45 214 92855
email retraeter@csjdanmark.dk
E, I, P, Q, S, V, Wf　*website* www.sanktjosephsoestrene.dk

Rooms 15–20 single rooms, most with toilet and shower.
Notes The Retreat Centre is located 20kms north of Copenhagen facing Øresund and Sweden. It is easy to access by train from the airport. The Retreat Centre is ecumenical and run by Sisters of Saint Joseph of Chambery. There are good possibilities for walks or you may use one of the bikes from the house for free. The Centre has two chapels, dining rooms, living rooms, and a garden full of flowers and trees for you to enjoy.
Contact Sr Susanne Hoyos, Director.
Please see the website for more details of our programme of events.

January
18–20　Weekend retreat.
25–27　Weekend retreat.
February
3–8　5-day retreat.
22–24　Weekend retreat.
March
1–3　Weekend retreat.
15–17　Weekend retreat.
29–31　Weekend retreat.

April
15–21 Easter retreat.
May
3–5 Weekend retreat.
24–26 Weekend retreat.
June
14–23 10-day retreat. Bill Clark SJ from USA
June–July
28–7 10-day retreat (Danish Mass).
August–September
No retreats, while the sisters are reconstructing their communities.
October
25–27 Weekend retreat.
November
3–8 5-day retreat.
22–24 Weekend retreat.
December
6–8 Weekend retreat.

EGYPT

188 Wind Sand & Stars
Expertise House, 9 Cufaude Business Park, Cufaude Lane, Bramley, Hampshire RG26 5DL
                                          01256 886543 option 4
                      email office@windsandstars.co.uk
Q, S, W   *website* www.windsandstars.co.uk

Rooms Retreats may be based at St Catherine's Monastery or in a remote and beautiful desert location in South Sinai. Rooms at the Monastery Guest House are basic with *en suite* and food is simple but plentiful. Most rooms are shared but a few single rooms are available. In the desert it is a traditional Bedouin-style camp, with meals cooked on a camp fire and bottled water served, sleeping out under the stars each night. Facilities are simple and include a discreet latrine with tent enclosure.
Notes This area has many biblical associations and a long tradition of spiritual reflection offering a unique and enriching retreat experience. Forthcoming retreats are listed on our website. Some involve collective worship and prayer, while others are non-denominational. Guest speakers include members of the clergy, academics and specialists including Retreat Association Patron Sara Maitland who leads the annual Adventure into Silence. Days will normally involve periods of silence, with optional excursions on foot and camel. Many include a visit to the nearby St Catherine's Monastery and an ascent of Mount Sinai. Wind Sand & Stars has been operating here for over 25 years and all of our journeys are fully supported by our well-established and long-standing Egyptian partners and Bedouin guides. We are specialists in helping those who have never ventured into this type of environment before, as well as offering unusual opportunities for those seeking new retreat experiences. Tailor-made journeys can also be arranged for individuals and groups, from overnight excursions to 40 days in the desert.
Contact Fay Cox.

April
14–21 St Catherine's Monastery retreat. Based at the Monastery for retreat, exploration and ascent of Mount Sinai. Kim Nataraja
October
3–10 Adventure into Silence. A non-denominational retreat based in a beautiful desert camp in South Sinai. Sara Maitland

ITALY

189 Umbrian Retreats
184 Via Petricci, Montecastelli, Umbertide (PG), Umbria, Italy 06019 01733 552535 / 07702 341041
                      email florence.morton1@btinternet.com
B, D, S, Wf   *website* www.umbrianretreats.com

Rooms Casa Roberto has 3/4 twin *en suite* rooms (1 with disabled shower room) and adjacent apartments (Sopra and Terra) each have 1 double and 1 smaller twin bedroom, i.e. accommodation for up to 16 people.
Notes Casa Roberto has a spacious and well-equipped kitchen, dining room, living room and small chapel. Sopra and Terra each have a well-equipped kitchen, sitting room and bathroom. The house and apartments share lovely gardens, including a labyrinth, swimming pools, fig trees and vines. This ecumenical holiday–retreat centre is an ideal location for Franciscans or people interested in St Francis, as Assisi, Gubbio and La Verna are all within easy reach.
Contact Florence Morton. ❏ *p 72*
June
5–12 Enneagram holiday–retreat. Listen to your life. Qualified user of the Enneagram, Rev Dave Tomlinson
19–26 Art lovers' holiday–retreat. Ponder with Piero, exploring the Piero della Francesca Trail. Rev Nicholas Gandy
September
4–11 Life-balance and mindset-change holiday–retreat. Being human, being spiritual. Life coach and NLP practitioner, Rev David McCormick
18–25 Pilgrimage with St Francis of Assisi. Experienced pilgrimage and retreat leader, Rev Canon Andrew Hawes

NIGERIA

190 Christ Arsenal Retreat Centre
Sparklight Estate, Kilometer 2 Lagos/Ibadan Expressway, Ogun State, Nigeria
Or PO Box 75147 Victorial Island, Lagos, Nigeria   +234 809 111 2204 / 2205 / 2206 / 2207
                      email info@christarsenal.org
C, Ch, Co, E, I, P, Q, S, V, W, Wf, Y *website* www.christarsenal.org

Rooms Christ Arsenal has 17 single bedrooms, 3 twin bedrooms, 1 triple bedroom, all *en suite*, and a 2-rooms dormitory.

Notes Christ Arsenal has a domesticated, well-equipped self-catering kitchen, conducive indoor dining and outdoor restaurant, laundry, baptismal pool, duly equipped teaching/prayer rooms, Christian library, spacious halls, recreational facilities, digital audio recording studio and a Wifi-enabled environment.
Contact Adeleke Adeniyi, Retreat Manager.
3rd Saturday of the month monthly teaching of the ministry of Jesus.

NORWAY

191 Lia Gård

Postbox 106, 2481 Koppang, Norway
00 47 62 46 65 00
email retreat@liagard.no
D, I, P, S, W, Wf, Y   *website* www.liagard.no

Rooms 20 single/twin *en suite*, 14 other bedrooms, lecture room, library, lounge, dining room and sauna.
Notes A retreat and conference centre deep in the forest on a beautiful hillside above a lake. We offer private and group retreats, IGRs and individual accompaniment in English. Daily services in chapel. NEW labyrinth. Hermitage with individual guidance or just solitude. Lia Gård is 2½ hours from Oslo Gardermoen airport by train to Koppang. All retreats in English and Norwegian.
Contact Ingeborg Boe. ❑ *p 68*

January–February
28–3 6-day IGR.
April
8–11 3-day IGR.
May
5–8 Advanced Enneagram workshop. Andreas Ebert
9–12 Family issues, healing the family tree. Andreas Ebert
13–22 8-day IGR.
August
12–18 6-day IGR.
September
5–14 8-day IGR.
December
2–7 5-day IGR.

SPAIN

192 Cortijo Carranque

Partido Carranque 4, Coín 29100, Málaga, Spain
00 34 951 242865 / 0203 598 9699
(UK line rings in main house)
email info@cortijocarranque.com
B, C, Co, I, P, Pe, V, W, Wf *website* www.cortijocarranque.com

Rooms 7 *en suite* bedrooms, double or single. Chapel. Enclosed courtyard for quiet rest/reflection (can be used as a meeting space). Private garden with swimming pool. River and excellent countryside for walking etc.

Notes Cortijo Carranque was set up as a safe haven for people in need of a quiet space in which to step back from the front line and find rest, refreshment and a renewed vision for their lives. Most weeks there is no formal programme, just a quiet space in which to be alone with God and allow him to minister to your needs. We offer warm friendly hospitality, a daily time of prayer and reflection, and a 'listening ear' prayer ministry for any who want it.
For details of guided retreats and events please see our website. Please contact us for more detailed information.
Contact Angela Tomlins.

February–June
1–30 Rest and refreshment breaks.
July–August
1–31 Family holiday time. Self-catering only.
September–November
1–30 Rest and refreshment breaks.
December–January
1–31 Closed.

193 Los Olivos Retreats

Calle Sierra Nevada 19, Torremeulle, Benalmádena, Spain 29630   01865 685024
email losolivosretreats@outlook.com
C   *website* www.losolivosretreats.co.uk

Rooms Rooms and facilities vary by retreat venue. Please see website for details.
Notes Los Olivos Retreats is an inclusive Christian ministry, offering guided retreats in Spain. The retreats build on the ministry of the Hacienda Los Olivos retreat centre, which began in 2010 in the Sierra Nevada mountains, and which in 2019 moves from its original spiritual home to other equally stunning locations and venues in Andalucia. These retreats will be led by guest speakers and retreat leaders, and will follow a rhythm based around morning and night prayer, shared meals, teaching and conversation, and personal space for rest, reflection and relaxation. In addition, they will include guided visits to relevant sites in each of these historic cities, connected with the theme of each retreat.
Contact Guy Wynter.

June
3–9 (in Cordoba). An introduction to the dynamics between the three Abrahamic faith communities in medieval Al-Andalus. Includes visits to Cordoba cathedral-mosque and synagogue.
September
9–14 (in Malaga). Exploring the Roots of Wonder in Christian Spirituality, through the work of poets, theologians, mystics and activists, whose vision shaped the heart of the Christian tradition.

**PLEASE SUPPORT THE WORK OF
THE RETREAT ASSOCIATION**
See our website: **www.retreats.org.uk/donate.php**
for ways in which you can support us.

145

SWEDEN

[194] Te Deum

Christian's Acre, Landsvägen 1022, 23195
Trelleborg, Sweden (landline) 00 46 40 487059
(mobile; use for SMS) 00 46 708 743994
email tedeum@telia.com
B, D, I, P, Q, S, W, Wf, Y *website* www.tedeum.se

Rooms 1 single, 5 twin (3 ground-floor access), 1 quad, separate accommodation for leader, full board or self-catering available.
Notes A small guest house in southern Sweden set in lovely rolling countryside, close to Malmo, Lund and Copenhagen. 15-min walk to railway station. It is linked with the parish of All Saints Notting Hill in the Diocese of London. The Chapel of the Holy Cross and the Oratory of Our Lady and All Saints can be used for private prayer or for small groups. A small library of theological and spiritual literature with the emphasis on the Church of England and the Church of Sweden is being developed. We want to develop contacts between the Church of England and Christians in Sweden and we want to offer a place 'just to be'; a place for prayer and reflection; a place for study, rest and recreation.
Groups, families and individuals welcome. Divine office said daily. Special programme, including visits and contacts with local churches, can be arranged for each group as required. For details of quiet days and retreats, please check our website.
Contact Rev Sr Gerd Swensson, preferably by email.

INDEX TO ADVERTS & RETREAT HOUSES